Speaking the Unspeakable

Marital Violence among South Asian Immigrants in the United States

MARGARET ABRAHAM

RUTGERS UNIVERSITY PRESS
New Brunswick, New Jersey, and London

Library of Congress Cataloging-in-Publication Data

Abraham, Margaret, 1960–
    Speaking the unspeakable : marital violence among South Asian
immigrants in the United States / Margaret Abraham.
        p. cm.
    Includes bibliographical references and index.
    ISBN 0–8135–2792–9 (cl. : alk. paper) — ISBN 0–8135–2793–7 (pa. :
alk. paper)
    1. Conjugal violence—United States.   2. Family violence—United
States.   3. South Asians—United States—Social conditions.   I. Title.

HV6626 .2.A27 2000
362.84'914073—dc21   99–045632

Manufactured in the United States of America

To

*My parents, Mary Attokaran Abraham and
Thachil Porinchu Abraham, for teaching me
the value of life, love, and learning*

Pradeep Singh for a wonderful partnership

*The women who participated in this project
for sharing their lives with me*

Contents

Preface

In the fall of 1984, I left my family in India to pursue graduate study in the United States. Like many South Asians, I carried with me a personal limited vision of the "normative family" based on my own family experience. I was the youngest in a middle-class family of four children, and my father had died the year before. For the first time in my twenty-four years of sheltered life, I was going to live alone and in another country. I remember sitting in the plane, peering through the window, overcome by a sense of loneliness at the thought of no longer having my family near me. Although intellectually aware of the diversity of families, at that time I believed that most South Asian families were like mine—a place of love, nurturance, support, and safety. From the outside, most of my friends' families appeared no different and those that deviated from the norm could be explained away as exceptions to the rule. In fact, I was to understand later that some of these families were the antithesis of what they outwardly presented. Some of my friends' mothers had been abused and even some of my friends had been abused by their own parents. At the time, however, we dared not tell one another. We kept up pretenses and rarely revealed the darker side of our family relations.

In her book *Family Violence*, published in 1984, Mildred Daley Pagelow states that "living in the privacy of our homes tends to restrict our vision of others' lives." On the basis of my own family experience, I was inclined to believe that the "normative order" and the "factual order" were one and the same when it came to the South Asian family.

There lay the common problem of false universalization which for me was to be systematically undone in the next few years through the nexus of scholarship, teaching, and interactions with friends who had experienced domestic violence or had actively addressed the problem. I came to recognize the limitations of my original view of the world.

Prior to my work on marital violence, my research interest lay in the areas of ethnicity and migration. I explored how minority groups become marginalized and the impact of migration on these groups. Underlying all my work was an interest in power relations, at both the micro and the macro levels. I believed that an approach grounded in sociology, but drawing upon anthropology, women's studies, and history, offered me an avenue for understanding the sociopolitical construction of categories such as ethnicity and gender. My research on marital violence among South Asians started about 1989 when I began teaching courses on family issues from a cross-cultural perspective and discussing issues of domestic violence with friends who were volunteers at a women's shelter. The sheer enormity of the problem led me to begin a serious review of the literature on domestic violence. What became increasingly clear was that while there was considerable scholarship on the issue of domestic violence, there was little research on its prevalence among ethnic minority communities. Around the same time, through the electronic media and several talks I attended, I learned of the emergence of South Asian organizations that were addressing the problem of domestic violence within the South Asian community in the United States. At the forefront was Manavi, a South Asian organization in New Jersey. Soon other organizations, such as Apna Ghar in Chicago, Maitri and Narika in California, Sakhi for South Asian Women in New York, SEWAA (Service and Education for Women Against Abuse) in Philadelphia, and Sneha in Connecticut, emerged. All these organizations contributed in important ways to the common struggle to end domestic violence among South Asians. Having just finished a project on ethnic identity and the marginality of an ethnic group in an immigrant context (the Indian Jews in India and Israel), and given my research interest in power relations and my growing interests in issues of gender and violence, I was increasingly drawn to the issue of domestic violence among South Asian immigrants in the United States.

This work does not contain the type of statistics typical of quantitative mainstream research on domestic violence. Rather this study seeks to effectively capture the subtleties of culture, the varying situational contexts, and the in-depth insights that elude large-scale data collection.

Women's voices are at the core of this book. Their narratives demonstrate the relevance of culture and social structures for analyzing marital violence. Audre Lorde notes that "the Master's Tools will never dismantle the Master's House" (Lorde 1984). So too, when we assume there is one overarching problem and one way to address it, we limit both our vision and our ability to individually and collectively contribute to the struggle to end domestic violence. Just as the myth of the undifferentiated family experience leads to false assumptions about the family, addressing marital violence without examining the experiences of different categories of women similarly leads to the false assumption that there is homogeneity in women's experiences of violence. While marital violence cuts across race, ethnicity, and class with devastating effect, the complex ways in which ethnicity, citizenship, and class intersect with gender must be examined if we are to make substantive progress in addressing the problem.

I believe that an understanding of violence would be incomplete without an account of the experiences of those who are often deemed "invisible others" because of their ethnicity, race, class, and legal status. I hope that this book will give the reader some sense of what it is like to be an abused immigrant woman and the nature of the cultural and structural processes that shape the immigrant experience.

Traditionally in the United States, race relations have been primarily contextualized in terms of black versus white with little attention paid to how other minority groups fit into this framework. Similarly, gender relations, to a large degree, have been understood primarily using white women's experiences and ideas with little attention devoted to how race/ethnicity and class fit into the analysis.

Because each ethnic group has its own sociohistory in the United States, and because notions of cultural heritage and ethnic identity shape social relations, it is important to understand the term "South Asian." South Asian is a label that has been used in different ways, including cultural identification, regional identification, and as the basis for collective action. Today the term South Asian is used in popular parlance, though large segments of the South Asian population still identify themselves primarily in terms of their specific nation-states. Although the term has conceptual and representational limitations in its usage, it is still a useful label and as such it is important to briefly review its sociohistorical framework.

The term "South Asian" is a social construct that refers to people whose ethnic origins are from countries known today as India, Pakistan,

Bangladesh, Sri Lanka, Bhutan, and Nepal within the situational context of these peoples' immigration to North America in the twentieth century. The term's evolution and usage, especially by South Asian activists in the 1980s in the United States, was indirectly an outcome of the interaction between these immigrant groups and the dominant American culture. Peoples of these geographically, politically, and culturally distinct groups, with histories of conflict between their native countries, were often lumped together by Americans and treated as a homogeneous entity under the extremely narrow category of "Indian" or the broad-based racialist construction of "Orientals" or "Asians."

However, what was essentially a process of the dominant group's construction of "Asians" as one of the categories of "other" was gradually translated by Asian Americans into a sociopolitical movement to build political unity based on the commonality of experience that different Asian groups endured in the United States. Essential to this mobilization process was the sensitivity to the heterogeneity of the ethnic, cultural, religious, and political differences of the groups that came together under this pan-Asian rubric for political empowerment. What was essentially an externally imposed negative label became a symbol of pride and a source for coalition building and political unity. Much of the political impetus for this shift originated in the Asian American movement of the late 1960s (Wei 1993). This movement contributed to the creation of various Asian American studies programs at universities whose central goal was to address the Asian American experience and develop theoretical and pedagogical tools to address the dynamic changes of Asian America (Omi 1988, 1992; Mazumdar 1991; Okihiro 1991).

The sociopolitical conditions of the 1980s, the pan-Asian movement, the resurgence of ethnic pride, the various controversies surrounding the concept of multiculturalism, and the unprecedented growth of the South Asian population in the United States increasingly influenced the vast number of South Asian students, both immigrant and native born, entering American universities in the 1980s. An important political outcome was the increasing development of a "South Asian consciousness" among these groups. Historical differentiation and group formation within the South Asian community continued to exist on several axes, including language, religion, region, class, and nativity, for the maintenance of subgroup identification and intra-ethnic pride (Khandelwal 1996). The term "South Asian," however, was increasingly used among politically conscious members of the South Asian community to signify the need to blur historical antagonisms between their mother countries. The goal was to consolidate and enlarge the political potential of substantive gains for South Asians, both immigrant and native born, in the context of their social, economic, and political position in the social structure of the United States. Yet the usage of the term South Asia/South Asian is problematic at times, as it often becomes synonymous with the term India/ Indian, thereby making invisible or marginalizing other population groups that come under the rubric of South Asia (Dhaliwal 1994, 18–19; Grewal and Kaplan 1994; Islam 1994, 244; Das Dasgupta 1998).

Today there are many levels of identification used by members of the South Asian population. The use of the term "South Asian community" by many activists, scholars, and some members of the South Asian community (including myself), is in no way meant to assume a monolithic South Asian community. Rather, I and others see the community as different segments coming together, cooperating, negotiating, intervening, and often transcending the tyranny of previously assumed barriers to exert greater influence in the shifting situational contexts of national and transnational structures. As South Asian activists and scholars we realize that as diverse as we may be, we are all part of the collaborative effort to transform the interactional processes and institutional structures that oppress us and to thereby bring about substantive social change. I am acutely aware of the limitations of the label "South Asian" in terms of its conceptual and representational practices by those of us who use it. I am also acutely aware of the ethnic, class, region, religion, and gender divides within the South Asian community and the need to avoid universalizing all South Asian women's experiences. Yet I believe there are times when one must not allow such fragmentation and particularism to cloud important commonalities of the South Asian immigrant women's experience. Because this book incorporates the narratives of women of Indian, Pakistani, and Bangladeshi origin as well as organizations that define themselves as South Asian, I find it useful and more representative to use the term South Asian despite its limitations.

In most cases the approach of the "united we" is important especially when addressing the commonalties of oppression based on ethnicity, race, class, or gender. To use "we" or "I" when writing about the abuse of the women I interviewed, however, would be to let the reader assume that I had had similar experiences that allowed me to appropriate such a voice. Although in most cases I could identify with the broader cultural experiences that have shaped our lives as immigrant women and as women from South Asia, the differences in our experiences must be acknowledged to remain honest to the multiple aspects that shape identity—both my own identity and that of the women included in this book. Toward this end, I have tried to weave the multiplicity of our voices into the text while being careful to balance the specificities and commonalities of our experiences as South Asian immigrant women in the United States.

Acknowledgments

Many people have helped make this book happen. I am grateful to all the women who believed and participated in this project. Their generosity of time and spirit is immeasurable. I am indebted to Shamita Das Dasgupta, Susan Wadley, Cynthia Bogard, and Pradeep Singh for carefully reading through the entire manuscript and offering incisive criticism. They raised important questions and helped clarify my ideas. Thanks also to Madhulika Khandelwal, Patricia Mann, and my sister, Taisha Abraham, for their valuable comments on parts of the manuscript.

This project could not have been accomplished without the support of the following South Asian women's organizations: Sakhi for South Asian Women, SEWAA (Service and Education for Women Against Abuse), Apna Ghar, Maitri, Manavi, and Sneha. I am grateful to Kanta Khipple and Usha Ari for sharing their homes with me on my trips to Chicago and Philadelphia. I also thank my sister-in-law, Kirti Singh, for research assistance and support in India. These groups and individuals, together with Cecilia Castellino, Geeta Misra, Hemalee Patel, Kala Menon, Lalita Krishnan, Mallika Dutt, Meena Seth, Megha Bhouraskar, Mona Sehgal, Monica Bose, Purvi Shah, Prema Vohra, Ranjana Bhargava, Robina Niaz, Romita Shetty, Sunita Mehta, Tula Goenka, Vatsala Vivek, and Lajwanti Waghray, have greatly aided my understanding of the complexity of domestic violence and organizational struggles in the South Asian community. Some of them also helped me connect with the participants for this project. Eileen Moran, Esther Ngan Ling Chow, Huma Ahmed Ghosh, Jack Tchen, Jyotsna Vaid, Louisa Gilbert, Malahat Baig

Amin, Margo Machida, Nabila El Bassel, Sucheta Mazumdar, and Sujata Warrier have also provided important insights. Mallika Dutt and Prema Vora played an important role in helping me bridge the gap between activism and scholarship.

I want to express my gratitude to Martha Heller, the original acquiring editor for this manuscript for Rutgers University Press, for her faith in this project. Her support in the early stages of writing was invaluable. Thanks also to David Myers who replaced Martha, and his assistants, Sarah Blackwood and Suzanne Kellam, for their continued support, and to Elizabeth Gilbert, for great copy editing. A special thanks to Brigitte Goldstein, production editor, who is a pleasure to work with, and also to Tricia Politi, production manager, Amy Rashap, marketing director, and Lisa Gillard, publicity manager, at RUP. I owe a big thanks you to Mary Delave at marydelave.com for use of her artwork on the book's cover. This project was supported by a Rockefeller Fellowship from the Asian American Center, by CUNY Queens, and, at Hofstra University, by a Faculty and Research Development Grant, a Presidential Grant, the Office of the Provost and the Dean of Hofstra College of Liberal Arts and Sciences.

Chapter 5 is an updated version of my article "Sexual Abuse in South Asian Immigrant Marriages," *Violence against Women* 5, no. 6 (1999): 587–590. Chapter 8 appeared in an earlier form in "Ethnicity, Gender, and Marital Violence: South Asian Women's Organizations in the United States," *Gender and Society* 9, no. 4 (1995): 450–468. An earlier version of chapter 4 is forthcoming as "Isolation as a Form of Martital Violence: The South Asian Immigrant Experience," *Journal of Social Distress and Homelessness*.

Over the years, many of my teachers have influenced my worldview, especially Aghenanda Bharati, André Béteille, Barry Glassner, Ephraim H. Mizruchi, Gary Spencer, J.P.S. Uberoi, Kathleen Newman, Malvika Karlekar, Nina Misal, P. D. Khera, Patricia Uberoi, Susan Borker, Susan Wadley, T. N. Madan, Veena Das, and Vinay Srivastav. My peers at the departments of sociology at Delhi University and Syracuse University, particularly Brenda Uekert, Cheryl Carpenter, Chris Ingram, Doug Challenger, Emelda Driscoll, Julie Thomas, Margo Clark, Nancy Rosen, and Omita Goyal, have also influenced me as a sociologist. My colleagues in the department of sociology and anthropology at Hofstra University, expecially Cheryl Mwaria, Cynthia Bogard, Edward Albert, and Marc Silver, have not only contributed to my sociological imagination but have also been a great source of support. Special thanks to Carol Jimmenez, Jennifer Pusateri, Jennifer Stern, Melissa Hartman, and Tara Bess for their research assistance, Anuradha Palit for great transcription and friendship, and Phyllis Droessler, department secretary, for her patience in handling some of the correspondence. Credit must also be given to my students at Hofstra University who have shown a great interest in my work, asked important questions, and challenged me to think of ways to explain the relationship of gender to the social construction of knowledge.

Much of this could not have been done without the support of my immediate family, Mary Abraham, Taisha, Annie, Francis, Mathew, and Amrita, who have always been there for me. I have also been fortunate in having a large community of extended family and friends. While the list is too long to name all, I am particularly grateful to my in-laws, M. P. Singh, and Vir Bala Singh, and my friends Bhaskaran Balakrishnan, Chandra Sunkara, George Mathen, Kislaya Prasad, Loretana Lombardi, Madhu Goyal, Manohar Prasad, Nikhil Roy, Omita Goyal, Ponnamma Mathen, Raj Singh, Ritu Agarwal, Ruthe Kassel, and Sunanda Ghosh for making the transnational experience a positive one. Last but not least, I am grateful to my husband and partner, Pradeep Singh, who made it all possible, and, to my six-year-old son, Arun Abraham Singh, who has grown along with this project and gives me hope for the future.

Speaking the Unspeakable

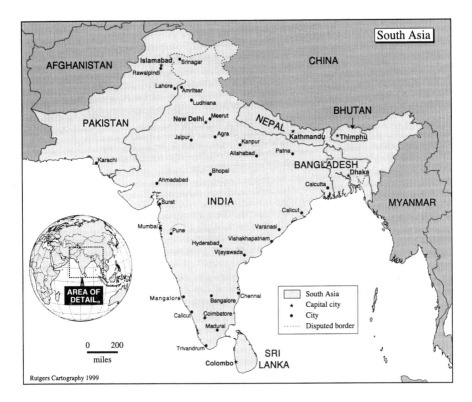

A Map of South Asia. *Commissioned by author from Michael Siegel of Rutgers Cartography.*

1 Introduction: Framing the Issues

On September 13, 1995, Syeda Sufian, a young Bangladeshi woman residing in Jamaica, New York, was doused with gasoline and set on fire by her husband, Mohammed Mohsin. Hearing her screams, neighbors called an ambulance. Four days later Syeda woke up in a hospital with severe burns covering her body. Having miraculously survived, Syeda Sufian took the courageous step of fighting back against her batterer and his family, who had been abusing her since her marriage in 1992. With the help of the organization Sakhi for South Asian Women, members of various groups were brought together to participate in a demonstration outside the Mohsins' home to publicly condemn this atrocity, shame the batterer and his family, and show that violence against South Asian women in the United States would not be tolerated and kept private for the sake of family and community harmony.[1]

Syeda Sufian is only one of thousands of South Asian women in the United States who are abused daily by their husbands and other family members. She is also one among the increasing number of immigrant women who are seeking the support of South Asian organizations such as Sakhi for South Asian Women, Manavi, SEWAA, Narika, Sneha, ASHA, Raksha, Saheli, and Maitri.[2] This book is about the lives of these abused South Asian immigrant women and the emergence of South Asian help organizations that address the problem of violence against them.

Since the 1980s, increasing attention has been devoted in the United

States by social scientists, policymakers, and social workers to domestic violence as a social problem. Yet little attention has been paid to the causes, manifestations, and resolutions of marital violence among ethnic minorities, especially recent immigrants. Although there is a vast amount of literature on domestic violence, with most works addressing a particular type of domestic violence such as incest, wife beating, child abuse, marital rape, or elderly abuse, examinations of its prevalence among ethnic minority groups are few. This deficit has enormous consequences for abused ethnic minority women. Their problems remain invisible, and the common myths and stereotypes that oppress them persist. Inattention to their situation precludes the effective identification, intervention, and prevention of the forms of abuse perpetrated against them. It also prevents an understanding of the systemic ways by which American cultural, economic, and political institutions contribute to the violence against ethnic minority women, especially immigrant women, both legal and illegal. Most important, it leads to inadequate policy formulation in efforts to mitigate the problem.

In the 1990s domestic violence is increasingly being viewed as a social problem of national concern by legislators. Yet the complex causes, manifestations, long-range consequences, and resolution of the problem of domestic violence remain partially unaddressed due to the narrow approach taken by state and federal policymakers. Today domestic violence is increasingly criminalized, yet the problem and its resolution are still juxtaposed by policymakers within the framework of "family preservation." It is the lack of a comprehensive understanding of domestic violence that leads to narrowly defined policy formulation and implementation with undue overemphasis on the criminal justice system. Recent issues such as immigration and welfare laws that negatively target certain categories of immigrants, are often excluded from consideration though they frequently affect abused immigrant women in complex ways and force them to stay in abusive relationships at great risk to their lives.

The United States is a country built on immigration. Much of its recent immigration is the outcome of laws closely connected to concepts of citizenship, family unity, and the economic value of labor.[3] At the same time, the nation's people of color have traditionally experienced institutionalized cultural and economic racism. Immigrant women of color thus experience particularly great difficulty as they face issues of gender, ethnicity, race, and lack of citizenship. It becomes imperative, therefore, to include these issues as categories of analysis in seeking to understand power relations within the discourse on domestic violence. Both the rising anti-immigrant climate in the United States and increasing fundamentalist politics in South Asia contribute to cultural and struc-tural violence against South Asian women as well.

This book focuses on South Asian immigrant women's experiences of marital violence in the United States.[4] Here, I use the term "marital violence" to mean any form of coercion, power, and control—physical, sexual, verbal, mental, or economic—perpetrated on a woman by her spouse or extended kin, arising from the social relations that are created within the context of marriage. I include extended kin in my definition of marital violence because marriage for South Asians is normatively defined not as a relationship between two individuals but as an alliance between two families. Often the extended kin are partners in the husband's crime, whether through their silence or their active involve-ment in the perpetration of the abuse. It is within the institution of mar-riage that patriarchal control over a woman is most manifest, through her multiple subordinate statuses as wife, daughter-in-law, sister-in-law, and mother.

In this book, I draw attention to those immigrant minority women, specifically South Asian immigrant women, whose voices have been si-lenced by the lack of inclusion of their narratives in our study of do-mestic violence in the United States. By focusing on South Asian women's experiences of marital violence, I seek to explain how immigration is-sues, cultural factors, the relative unfamiliarity of the American social, legal, economic, and other institutional systems coupled with the ste-reotyping of immigrants exacerbate vulnerabilities associated with gen-der, class, and ethnicity for immigrant women in the context of domestic violence.

The narratives of the twenty-five abused South Asian women whom I interviewed tell of the cultural constraints and structural impediments that they have encountered as immigrant women (see appendix A).[5] We see their vulnerabilities and their strengths. These narratives make clear that the subjective and objective realities of these abused women's experiences of domestic violence must be situated within the larger cul-tural, social, economic, and political context. By exploring the com-monalities and differences in the sources, manifestations, and outcomes of power for abused South Asian women at the interpersonal, commu-nity, and macro-institutional levels, we see how each individual woman's oppression is closely interlocked with cultural and structural oppres-sion. We see both the individual strategies of resistance against their abus-ers that these women pursue as well as the pivotal role played by some of the South Asian organizations in helping these women get out of abu-sive relationships. By shifting the problem of marital violence from a "private matter" to a "social issue," this study points to some of the ways in which South Asian immigrant women are vulnerable both within the South Asian community and within society at large. In addition, this study examines the way in which activism in South Asian women's organizations simultaneously challenges the oppressive elements of South Asian culture as well as those structures of power in the United States that create and maintain the "oppressive differences" that exacerbate domestic violence.

By combining an analysis of abused South Asian women's narratives with a study of South Asian women's organizations (see appendix B), this book sheds light on the rarely recognized phenomenon of marital violence within a community frequently viewed as a model minority. It also demonstrates the central role played by South Asian activism as it emerged in the 1980s in the United States, in challenging not only the ideas and practices within the South Asian community that stereotype, discriminate, and oppress but also those structural impediments that South Asians confront in the social construction of their everyday lives.

Often the discourse on racial issues in the United States tends to be framed in dichotomous terms, such as black/white relations. In the process Asians become invisible or marginalized in ways that exclude their experiences of racism. Most important, these women's narratives and South Asian activism point to the need to reconceptualize the problem of domestic violence. Differences in power, privilege, and control that have been a part of early analyses of domestic violence must be viewed as additionally constructed around the multiple axes of citizenship, ethnicity, language, religion, race, class, and gender at the individual, interpersonal, and institutional level.

By making women's narratives central, I have moved away from the dominant assumption in mainstream academia that only through "scientific" interpretation can social phenomena be explained. Instead, in the feminist tradition, our methodologies demand that we believe women's accounts of their lives and lived experiences (Smith 1987). The complexities of beliefs, values, and actions that shape marital relations and contribute to marital violence are often most succinctly put by women who are abused. This allows for an understanding of marital violence not just for that particular individual but for the many others who are in a similar position. I aim to intersect the individual and the collective, the personal and political, the cultural and the structural through the experiences of these abused women. We may thus move beyond common stereotypes, assumptions, and ethnocentrism toward some insight into the complex issues around the social problem of marital abuse against immigrant women.

An Ethno-Gender Perspective

Although I have been influenced by the major theoretical approaches to domestic violence and draw upon them, I see my own approach as not just reconciling these approaches, which are often seen as diametrically opposed, but as being part of a group of scholars that increasingly see the intersection of ethnicity, class, race, gender, and citizenship in power relations as vital to conceptualizing a framework for the analysis of domestic violence (Klein et al. 1997; Richie and Kanuha 1993; Sorenson 1996).

The two major sociological theoretical perspectives on domestic violence are the "family violence perspective" and the "feminist perspective." In the former, the family is considered to be the basic unit of analysis; in the latter, the abused woman is taken as the unit of analysis (Straus, Gelles, and Steinmetz 1980; Kurz 1989).

The family violence approach views marital violence as stemming from the personal characteristics of the wife or husband or from the internal and external stress factors that affect the family. Family theorists see violence as arising from character flaws in the individuals forming family units. The causal factors of violence are thought to range from violent socialization during childhood or learned behavior in the male's family of origin to alcoholism, drug addiction, mental illnesses, or lack of self-control (Stacey and Shupe 1983). Variations in this approach regard violence within the family as a product of frustration stemming from factors such as an individual's lack of goal fulfillment, unemployment, poverty, or cultural deprivation. Some early psychological perspectives pointed to the wife's psyche as the causal factor for marital violence and as such seem to adopt a "blame the victim" approach (Snell, Rosenwald, and Robey 1964). Understanding violence as learned and cyclical in nature is a popular view among adherents of the family violence perspective (Walker 1979, 1983; Launius and Lindquist 1988).

The second theoretical framework, one frequently termed feminist, does not limit the causes of domestic violence to psychological and micro-sociological factors, but considers the global pervasiveness of violence and its acceptability. Rather than focusing on the family as the unit of analysis, feminist theorists emphasize the position of the wife as the victim and see wife abuse as a reflection of the social structure (Pagelow 1984). According to this view, wife abuse is not an act of deviance or a breakdown in the social order, but arises out of the very same normative structure that defines women as inferior, reaffirms dominance and aggression as positive attributes in men, and underrepresents women in all spheres of social, economic, and political life (Dobash and Dobash 1979, 1981). The dominance by men in heterosexual intimate relationships is seen as having its roots in the patriarchal values of society at large. This dominance is further mirrored in the legal structure.

It is ironic that while feminist scholarship in the United States has addressed the issue of marital violence and criticized mainstream work for excluding gender concerns, it has overlooked or excluded the experiences of ethnic minority women, especially immigrant women (Ngan-Ling Chow 1993). There is a conspicuous gap in the literature concerning the structural and cultural factors that legitimate domestic violence among ethnic groups, especially recent immigrant groups. Focusing on gender alone, as Jane Gaines (1990, 198) points out, keeps women from looking at other structures of oppression and as such works to the advantage of the dominant groups. In the context of addressing domestic violence in a stratified society such as the United States, a contextualized feminism must explicitly acknowledge both the commonality and the differences of experiences based on the intersection of ethnicity, gender, class, and citizenship. Neither the family perspective nor the feminist perspective has adequately addressed the linkages between these multiple dimensions in addressing the problem of domestic violence, its resolution, or sources of change. The relevance of ethnic-based women's organizations in addressing violence against women has received almost no attention in the organizational or social movement literature despite the fact that these groups are playing an increasingly important role in providing more comprehensive ways of addressing the problem of violence against women.

While drawing upon both the family violence and the feminist perspectives, I intend my approach to extend the existing framework of analysis by specifically focusing on the intersections of culture and structure in addressing violence against women. Earlier I termed this an ethno-gender approach, based on the intersection of ethnicity and gender as significant analytical categories in the discourse on domestic violence (Abraham 1995). However, this can lead to an assumption that issues such as class and legal status in the immigrant context are unimportant. I have therefore redefined the ethno-gender approach here as one that examines the multiple intersection of ethnicity, gender, class, and legal status as significant categories in the analysis of domestic violence with a special emphasis on the relationship between ethnicity and gender. Here gender is a social construction that defines and evaluates the roles and expected behavior patterns based on one's biological sex. Gender thus means to be male or female in terms of appropriate role performances, personality structures, attitudes, and behaviors accomplished in concrete settings (West and Zimmerman 1987; Richardson 1988). Ethnicity has two dimensions: one, as cultural differentiation based on some element of primordiality, such as race, origin, history, and language, combined with cultural specificity, such as distinct religious practices, nomenclature, particularized customs, and beliefs and values (Geertz 1963); two, as a social construct that is dynamic, manipulated, mediated, and symbolically manifested in social interaction in situational contexts (Hecter 1975; Ben Rafael 1982; Shokied and Deshen 1982; Abraham 1989).

Although ethnic minority women who experience marital violence confront problems on multiple fronts, this approach emphasizes the intersection of ethnicity and gender because cultural differences form an important basis for the social construction of a national culture in a foreign land. Ethnicity is frequently the first explicit marker of differentiation that the dominant group and other groups use, especially women's physical appearance, and can be used as an easy source of distinction in the construction of the ethnicized other. Specific physical features and cultural habits remind the dominant group and the immigrant group of their foreign background—regardless of their previous socioeconomic class—thereby stereotyping, boundary marking, and restricting total acceptance of the immigrant by the mainstream (Ngan-Ling Chow 1993). Sonia Shah defines "cultural discrimination" as "a peculiar blend of cultural and sexist oppression based on our clothes, our foods, our values and our commitments" (1994, 182). The dominant group (in this case, mainstream white American society) forms the core and the subordinate group (in this case, recent immigrants) is allocated a peripheral position in the social, economic, and political structure of the setting. At the same time, for minority groups, ethnicity becomes the basis for group identification and solidarity in an alien country. Consciousness of being distinct from others in the same setting can thereby lead to boundary formation, efforts to maintain the created boundary, and some degree of latent or manifest conflict for both groups. However, this differentiation arises because of discrimination based on a dominant-subordinate structure in the social, economic, and political context.

Although studies have shown that class identities are of declining significance and that identities and solidarity are created by more manifest markers and politicized issues such as race, ethnicity, and gender (Graetz 1986, 1992; Emmison and Western 1990; Waters 1994), this framework does not preclude or minimize the role of class, but rather emphasizes the increasing importance of the inclusion of ethnicity with gender in addressing marital violence. Ethnicity and gender may gain or recede in salience in reaction to specific contextual changes. Similar is the case of class. It can be said, however, that while class differences do exist within the community, for most immigrants, previous class distinctions become decontextualized. Frequently ethnicity cuts across class in the immigrant's identification with the dominant group as well as in defining the relationship between the dominant group and the immigrant community. As already noted, ethnicity is frequently the most visible marker of differentiation. Often members of the dominant group define immigrant groups in terms of ethnicity and attribute a homogeneous class position to the immigrant community within the American class structure. Thus although clearly fragmented from within along gender, class, religion, and subethnic lines, the immigrant community is seen as a whole from the outside and relegated an externally defined position within American society—one that constructs ethnic minorities as the ethnicized marginalized other.

As women, immigrant women (unlike immigrant men) have to cope with gender boundaries that define them as subordinate on the basis of the patriarchal norms and values of both the immigrant and the mainstream cultures. As an ethnic minority, regardless of their class affiliation in their home country, immigrant women (unlike women from the dominant culture) have to cope with semi-permeable boundaries that allow them, as subordinate group members, to partially internalize the norms and values of the dominant culture while being simultaneously excluded by the dominant group from total membership in that culture. Ethnicity becomes the most manifest marker that is intricately woven with gender and class in the fabric of an immigrant woman's social identity. As Hossfeld (1994) states, often immigrant women are worst situated among women generally owing to their gender, race, class, and lack of citizenship. They are frequently perceived as desperate for work at any wage, particularly if they are known to be undocumented workers, have language barriers, or need an income to sustain themselves or their family.

This ethno-gender perspective posits an interaction between ethnicity and gender. Focusing on gender alone excludes cultural distinctions in gender relations and ignores the impact of majority/minority ethnic group distinctions in the causes, manifestations, and resolutions of the social problem of marital violence. Looking at oppression solely in terms of male domination and female subordination is to deny the importance of other forms of inequality in the United States such as class and race (Stacey and Thorne 1985, 311). As Harding (1991, 179) aptly points out, within the United States, a racially ordered society, there are no gendered relations that stand alone but only those that are constructed by and between races. Here, I would add ethnicity and class. Although gender-role stereotypes oppress all women under patriarchy, ethnic minority women, especially recent immigrant women, experience multiple subordination on the basis of their gender, ethnicity, and class.

The ethno-gender approach asks how gender relations are constructed and how cultural concerns are articulated at the individual, organizational, community, and societal level. Attitudes, perceptions, belief systems, abuser aggression, response of victims, forms of resistance, social networks, and organizational strategies can be best explained by analyzing the complex pattern of gender relations within a cultural milieu chosen or imposed on marital relations. Measures of success appropriate for the mainstream movement against domestic violence cannot be arbitrarily defined as the criteria to evaluate ethnic minority women's concerns. Courses of action, strategies, distinctiveness of culture, and structural arrangements have to be understood and addressed by seeing ethnic minority women not only through their gender but also through their position in terms of class and as an ethnic minority in the United States. Women of color have to deal with not only sexism in their day-to-day lives but also systems of racial and ethnic stratification that label and control the minority group as a whole (Healey 1995, 26).

The Myth of the "Model Minority"

In the epilogue of his book *The Ethnic Myth: Race, Ethnicity, and Class in America,* Stephen Steinberg states: "Myths are socially constructed. They arise in specific times and places, in response to identifiable circumstances and needs, they are passed on through processes that can be readily observed. . . . To explain why some myths persist, we have to explore the relationship that these myths have to larger social institutions that promote and sustain them, and that in turn are served by them" (1991, 263).

The social construction of the myth of the model minority lumps together people with very different histories, nationalities, and cultures and implies that Asian Americans, especially some ethnic groups among them such as Japanese, Koreans, and Indians fare better in mainstream American society than other ethnic and racial minorities (Wei 1993, 49). The implication is that such groups have achieved a measure of success that approximates the American ideal as defined by mainstream Anglo-America. These groups have made it by upholding two traditionally cherished and central American values—family unity and individual economic success through hard work. This success has occurred at a time when mainstream Anglo-Americans are increasingly perceiving African Americans as violating these so-called cherished values and making illegitimate demands for changes in status quo (Kinder 1986, 189–194).

It is important to note, however, that, despite their being dubbed models of success, these minorities are still considered the "other" or "inassimilable alien" (Wong 1993) by the dominant group on the basis of their physical features, accents, food, clothing, and values. Most important, labeling people as model minorities allows a redefinition of the socioeconomic situation of certain other minority groups in the United States, such as African Americans and Native Americans, as rooted in their own "cultural inadequacy" rather than in historically structured inequality. The "model minority" image, to some degree, also involves the gendering of ethnicity whereby certain gender characteristics, in this case a passive femininity, are applied to the ethnic other (Kim 1990; Espiritu 1997). As Patricia Hill Collins (1990) points out, those in power frequently construct "controlling images" that label subordinate groups in specific ways that legitimize sexism, racism, and exploitation. Controlling images also serve the dominant group's interests by manipulating oppressed groups against one another, thereby deflecting these groups from examining the reality of their structured inequality. This manipulation was well demonstrated in the Los Angeles riots after the Rodney King verdict (Kwong 1992). The model minority is a controlling image that has serious consequences for race, ethnic, class, and gender relations in the United States. The label "model minority" has been used to deny governmental assistance to these groups. The controlling image of the model minority is one that portrays an ethnic group as compliant, docile, politically apathetic, or with questionable political allegiances, one clearly subservient to those in power—unlike African Americans, who are constructed as the demanding demonized minority.

The construction and maintenance of a model minority image is problematic in several ways. First, it denies the diversity of individuals and the diversity of groups within an immigrant community. It forces the community to be treated as a monolithic entity. Internally and externally, the more successful members of the community dismiss or shun those who don't fit the model. The segments that don't fit the "success mold" experience a sense of shame, deficiency, and failure. To avoid this shame, individuals and the community often play the cover-up game. Fun-filled cultural activities and stylized social functions are held by the community to reinforce its collective identity as one that is predominantly successful.

Second, the maintenance of a model minority image places South Asians in a position where they disassociate themselves from other minorities and are sometimes resented by other racial and/or ethnic minorities and by certain groups of whites as well. For mainstream American society and its leadership, the use of an operative label such as "model minority" has served the vital function of "divide and rule" by creating ethnic contrasts that have kept minorities hierarchically apart. Emphasizing the cultural component as a source for South Asian success allows the dominant groups to condemn other minorities as culturally deprived, culturally deficient, and to blame for a gamut of problems such as poverty, illegitimacy, crime, and decaying neighborhoods, rather than looking at the structured inequalities based on ethnicity, class, race, and gender in the United States. Such categorization and perceptions deny South Asians the opportunity to form productive coalitions with other groups to address the commonality of their oppression as minorities. Other minority groups come to perceive South Asians as materialistic and colluding with the oppressor. Those who identify with the model minority image in the South Asian communities live with the false consciousness that self and community interest is best served through association with the dominant group and disassociation with other minorities. This attitude is validated for many model minorities because many carry their own forms of racist beliefs from the countries from which they emigrate: these beliefs are then further exacerbated in a racially ordered society such as the United States (Mazumdar, 1989b). Often it is not only the elite among the South Asian community that holds on to the model minority image but also economically exploited classes who feel that it is this model minority status, especially in terms of family values, that differentiates the South Asian community from economically exploited classes in other ethnic communities. Thus while acknowledging the importance of defining community identity in positive ways in an immigrant-based society, it is also important to recognize the problems within the community as well as the negative outcomes of externally imposed and internally accepted labels.

Third, such terms place a constant pressure on the community to manipulate the group's collective identity so as to portray its model minority status (Bhattacharjee 1992). This model minority status frequently means denying or making invisible any issue that is perceived as eroding that image, such as poverty, AIDS, homosexuality, substance abuse, and domestic violence; none of these fits into the concept of the "model minority." It is assumed that addressing such issues may pull a minority down rather than helping it to move up in the socioeconomic hierarchy of ethnicized, economically and socially divided America. The success stories of segments of those groups labeled a model minority easily hide the fact that other segments of these groups, some of whom are not even included in census data, are not prosperous and experience poverty and exploitation both within and outside of their community. It is easier to talk about success, especially if it allows a minority to dismiss all that is problematic as untrue, with no bearing on its community. Then there is no need to acknowledge these "imaginary problems" as real—problems such as domestic violence. In general, this has been the case in the mainstream South Asian community in the United States.

Until the mid-1990s, acknowledging the problem of domestic violence within the South Asian family was extremely problematic. It challenged the very concept of "good family values and strong family ties" or what Linda Gordon (1989) calls "the myths of harmony of the normative family." The public image of the South Asian community in the United States has been primarily male-defined, with women as the cultural transmitters. Although South Asian immigrant women deal with the multiple forces of international migration, the different economic demands of American economy, and various familial and cultural obligations, their gender identity is primarily culturally defined in terms of the home.

Domestic patriarchy has been assumed by the mainstream immigrant community and has not been an issue for public discussion. While women were responsible for the home, men still assumed greater power and control within it. To talk of marital violence within the community was to shatter the social construction of the community's image, challenge domestic patriarchy, and threaten the moral solidarity of community—a moral solidarity frequently reflected in the rhetoric of the collective and religious practices of the community (Rayaprol 1992; Khandelwal 1995). In the immigrant context, although South Asian women were to be economic contributors, they were increasingly constructed in cultural terms with the immigrant home as the site for defining gender relations and ensuring traditional patriarchy. At the same time, immigrant women and men were struggling against the ethnic/gender image that frequently placed them as targets for ethnic, class, and racial discrimination in American society.

The profile of the South Asian community up to the 1990s was that of a "model minority," one whose members adhered to the valued principles of economic success in the public sphere while retaining strong cultural values in the private sphere. This tendency to portray South Asian success, especially among Indians who arrived prior to 1980s, can be seen in the works of writers such as Nathan Glazer and Parmatama Saran (Saran 1983). Glazer characterized the Indian population in the United States as being "marked off by a high level of education, by concentration in the professions, by a strong commitment to maintaining family connection, both here in the United States and between the United States and India" (Glazer 1976, vi). For the South Asian community, whose community identity had been constructed around a professional and business community, interested in demonstrating its ability for economic success without forgoing cultural authenticity, the label of model minority was to be promoted and sustained.

As members of a small community, with a history of colonization in their native countries, many South Asians carried their own notions of racial and ethnic boundaries. Many South Asians necessarily sought identification with the dominant group by drawing the color divide between themselves and African Americans. Hence, under racist constructions by South Asians, African Americans and other dark-skinned minorities were given the lower status "other." Many South Asians accepted the distorted imagery of blacks set by the dominant white society. Investing in the image of successful, hard-working South Asians, in an attempt at upward group mobility, these South Asians effectively used avoidance and disassociation strategies toward other minorities whom they perceived as unsuccessful.

Unlike South Asians who immigrated to the United States as professionals in the 1960s, the demographic composition of the South Asians in the 1990s changed owing to "chain migration," whereby immigrants who become citizens sponsor their relatives who in turn sponsor other relatives to migrate to the United States. The 1980s immigration of many sponsored relatives of previous South Asian immigrants brought about considerable variation within the community along dimensions such as education, occupation, class, and gender experiences.

Although South Asians had an ethnic identity and a broad-based common cultural heritage, differentiation and group formation also existed within the community on axes such as language, religion, region, and class and fostered subgroup identification within the community. In terms of community representation, however, it appeared that a small number of business and wealthy professionals were defining the image, shared activities, and interests of the community. Often their politics and the articulation of community interests, especially in New York and New Jersey, lay in those areas that protected the vested interests of businesses (Khandelwal 1996, 1997b). Common cultural heritage, shared values, customs, and ties to the "homeland" were the basis for ethnic identity, communal consciousness, and solidarity within the United States.

The 1980s also witnessed the more visible phenomenon of the predomination of South Asians (especially in New York and New Jersey) in the newsstand business, as taxi drivers, and as motel owners. In part this can be attributed to two South Asian investors who offered the Metropolitan Transit Authority a large amount of money for fifteen-year leases to create a near South Asian monopoly of subway newsstands. This became known as the "Kapur coup" and became a source of inspiration to other ethnic investors, who tried to own their own stores in strategic places as an investment and to use the cheap ethnic labor provided by chain immigration. The complex stratification system involves a process of leasing and subleasing within the larger American economic system whereby extremely wealthy immigrant owners hire cheap immigrant labor. It is the small-time owners and employees, putting in many fourteen-hour days working at kiosks, gas stations, and motels, who became the more visible "image" of the South Asian (Khandelwal 1995, 1996). Many of these employees, including South Asian women, confronted with language barriers and limited economic opportunities, are often compelled to work long exploitative hours to support themselves or their families in these low-paying jobs.

In the 1990s ethnic homogeneity was internally, at least, replaced with a class- and region-based heterogeneity. In general there is at least a three-tier class system, with an upper class comprising specific categories of professionals (doctors and lawyers) and wealthy businessmen; a middle class comprising college students and mid-range professionals; and a lower class of low wage earners, blue-collar workers, and, in some cases, undocumented workers. Despite this class and income heterogeneity, the South Asian population continues to be represented generally as an economically successful community. Extrapolating generalities from economic variables alone does not truly reflect the community's recent socioeconomic heterogeneity.

Mainstream and community leaders continue to portray the community as a monolithic whole—that is, a model minority that believes in strong family ties and is well educated, economically successful, and has achieved a fine balance between upholding the cherished values of South Asian culture while simultaneously adopting the principles of modern American capitalism. Women become the main symbol of cultural continuity and are faced with both external and internal pressures to uphold the culture in specific ways, including adhering to culturally prescribed gender roles. South Asian women in the United States become responsible not only for family honor but also for the honor of the "model minority community" (Abraham 1998; Dasgupta 1998).

Members of the community worry about their community image. Often as a reaction to the dominant American society's racism and cultural imperialism, they avoid looking at their own community self-critically. They become so invested in portraying the community in positive ways that they oppress some segments, including women, by, for example, denying the violence perpetrated against them. Since the family is viewed as part of the private realm and social control of marital violence entails an intrusion of the community into normative domestic patriarchy, problems such as marital violence lie unaddressed. Any incident that comes to light regarding members of the community is ignored, denied, or explained away as merely a case of particular violent individuals or relationships rather than as a social problem.

Marginalized both by the male-dominated leadership of the South Asian community vested in the model minority image and by a white, middle-class women's movement that has not seriously included the experiences of ethnic minority women, South Asian women in the 1980s and 1990s organized and challenged the model minority image by addressing the problems faced by the women in their community while also fighting structured inequality such as discriminatory immigration laws that indirectly contribute to violence against women.

Organization of This Book

Immigrant women's voices are at the center of this book. Although many women's experiences will be addressed, the major focus of each chapter will be drawn primarily from one or two women's narratives. I have done this intentionally to avoid extensive fragmentation of the narratives. While all the women experienced multiple manifestations of marital abuse, in each case, one or two of these forms were more prevalent or had a greater impact.

Chapter 2 describes South Asian forms of marriage and family and their significant contributions to the ways in which South Asian women are defined, especially in terms of their relationships to men, to their families, and to their social group. Women feel pressured to marry owing to the high cultural value placed on marriage in defining a woman's social status. Additional complexities occur in transnational marriages, in which social relations become reconfigured with significant implications for immigrant women in the United States. Chapter 3 provides an historical overview of United States immigration and discusses the role of racist, sexist, and capitalist-oriented immigration policy and regulations in exacerbating violence against immigrant women.

Chapter 4 examines the different ways South Asian immigrant women are isolated. I focus on the social, psychological, and economic isolation abused women experience at the interpersonal, community, and institutional level. We also see some of the different ways by which abusers intimidate and threaten women into staying in abusive relationships. Chapter 5 addresses forms of physical and sexual abuse. Here I show the range of physical abuse and argue that sexual abuse takes on primarily three forms: forced sex, the manipulation of women's reproductive rights, and the manipulation of sex through the abuser's use of the concept of the "other woman."

Chapter 6 looks at the internal and external barriers that abused immigrant women face. Internal cultural barriers take the form of parents, in-laws, friends, family, and other members of the South Asian community. External structural barriers take the form of institutional entities such as the police, the courts, and service providers. Immigrant women experience multiple barriers that include language, culture, religion, health care, and law. I also argue that "important others" contribute to the violence perpetrated against these women through their indifference, strategic silence, or active participation. As such, they are partners in crime.

Chapter 7 focuses on the different strategies of resistance that my respondents saw themselves as having used within their relationship. Their stories contradict the traditional image of South Asian women as docile and submissive, willing to accept the abuse perpetrated against them. We see the way in which the women play an active role in challenging their abusive husbands and ending their own oppression. I also detail some of the cultural and structural barriers they encounter in the process and the reasons behind their actions and inactions in specific situations.

Chapter 8 examines the emergence of South Asian organizations in the United States that address domestic violence. Some of the women in this book sought help from these organizations in getting out of abusive relationships. A number of these organizations have become an integral part of the empowerment of South Asian women in the United States. South Asian women's organizations confront the issue of domestic violence and shift it from a "private problem" to a "public issue." We also see the complex ways in which ethnicity, gender, class, and citizenship play out within the United States social, economic, and political structure.

Finally, chapter 9 concludes by linking all the previous chapters in a discussion of the politics of empowerment and, particularly, the type of empowerment essential for a progressive politic that will lead to substantive cultural and structural change in the struggle to end violence against women. Toward that end, scholars, activists, and policymakers need to work together to systematically integrate their work in ways that will form the basis for a modified paradigm to achieve a more holistic approach in addressing domestic violence.

2 Marriage and Family

. . . and my initial rebelliousness would kind of surface and I would say "no I am not going to do it. I won't do it" And then there would be fights and I would, in spite of it stick to my thing. But after a couple of years, I think your resistance kind of wears down and you come to a stage when not just your immediate family, your relatives but everybody sees you as being unmarried, even the place I was working. I was working in a school. You see your friends get married. They too go through the same thing. I mean their marriages are arranged. And they are fine people like me, who have my kind of sensibility, but they went through all that and they got married as they were supposed to.

—Yamuna

This chapter focuses on the institutions of marriage and family, specifically the cultural context for the transnational marriages of South Asian immigrants in the United States as it affects spousal relations and can contribute to marital violence. According to Jean Bacon (1996, 17), "when immigrants arrive in America, they carry with them a worldview grounded in their culture of origin. Likewise, people born and raised as Americans share an understanding of an American worldview." Often these two worldviews may be radically different, compelling immigrants to adjust and reconfigure parts of them. For South Asian immigrants, a part of this worldview involves notions of marriage and family as they exist in South Asia in contrast to the United States.

Marriage and family are important both in the United States and in South Asia, and the relationship among class, race, ethnicity, sexuality, and patriarchy is complex and diverse in both contexts. In both countries, there is cultural pressure to get married at what is normatively defined as an appropriate age and to be part of a normative family. Both

societies attribute a high value to marital status and have various explicit and implicit criteria that influence societal notions of what entails
an ideal family (Zin and Eitzen 1990). Similarly, in both societies, various myths and images of the family are constructed that support the interests of those in power, two of them being the notions of family unity
and family harmony.

Researchers have adequately demonstrated that whatever the patterns of domestic activity in which members of a family are involved,
most cultures seem committed to presenting and upholding a unified
and harmonious picture of *the family*. Historically, the material conditions, the structure of the economy, and the nature of its political state
have played a critical role in shaping the institution of marriage and the
family in the United States. The privatization of the family there resulted
in the strong belief that the sanctity of the family as a core institution
could only be maintained if its right to privacy was protected. Any form
of external intrusion was a serious violation of the fundamental principle of domestic patriarchy, traditionally legitimated by the state (Anderson 1993). The importance of the sanctity and privacy of the family is
reflected in the major institutions of American society. Underlying public
sentiment is the belief that the family needs to be protected from public and institutional encroachment on its autonomy and its members'
rights to privacy. This privacy is mostly male-defined however upheld
by both men and women.

The privatization of the family has allowed for the proliferation of
myths such as the myth of the harmonious home, the myth of family
consensus, the myth of an undifferentiated family experience, and the
myth of the patriarch as the protector of family members and their interests (Zin and Eitzen 1990). It has allowed for the maintenance of a
monolithic image, which in reality contradicts the diversity of family
form and experience based on class, race, ethnicity, and sexual orientation (Collins 1990; Anderson 1993). Problems such as domestic violence
have been made invisible or viewed as a private matter and frequently
justified as a prerogative of the male as patriarch and protector of the
family (Pleck 1983; Davis 1987). To address domestic violence has been
to challenge cherished American values such as family unity and family as the bastion of morality, and to violate the heavily safeguarded concept of family privacy. Since the concepts of family unity, domestic
patriarchy, and privacy are at the core of American values, it has taken
years of women's grassroots struggle and mobilization, especially by the
battered women's movement in the 1970s, to systematically demystify
the family and shift the problem of domestic violence from a "private
problem" to a "public issue" (Kurz 1989).

The Construction of the Family:
Collective versus Individual Orientation

Unlike the United States, where there is an emphasis on the notion of romantic love and independence in choice of marriage partners, among South Asians marriage is an alliance between two families. The assumption is that such an alliance allows for greater long-term security and stability for families, because part of the choice of a spouse involves various rational criteria evaluated by families, such as economic worth, social status, education, appearance, and family background, rather than the emotional criterion of love between two individuals. As opposed to the West, the assumption in South Asian culture is that as long as the larger familial issues are covered, love will develop after marriage as the couple negotiates their relationship.

Unlike the dominant U.S. culture, since South Asians perceive themselves as family oriented rather than individual oriented, divorces are frowned upon, especially for women.[1] The family- and group-oriented structure views the individual as a representative of the family. In this context, shame and guilt attain a different meaning whereby the failures of the individual result in the "loss of face" or loss of honor for the entire family. Therefore among South Asians, as is true for many other Asians, there is considerable pressure to maintain harmony and minimize any actions that would potentially jeopardize the family and community.

Status of Women within the Institution of
Marriage and Family

For women, leaving a marriage is extremely difficult, as remarriage is much more difficult for women than it is for men. Further, the notion of family orientation is really one that is structured to benefit men more than women. Family orientation is in reality synonymous with the interests of men. South Asian women who leave their husbands can experience extreme hardship in multiple ways. They are frequently labeled "loose," "immoral," "unlucky," "a burden on the parents," "selfish," and "uncaring," and are socially ostracized. This labeling and the accompanying exclusionary practices cause divorced women to experience social and psychological isolation. The social ostracism is usually extended to the woman's family. For example, if a divorced woman has unmarried female siblings, the stigma associated with divorce will have negative ramifications on the marriage eligibility of the unmarried sisters. The probability of such social ostracism of the entire family can thus inflict mental trauma and increase the vulnerability of a woman's position in her affinal home. Often the strongest determinants of values, attitudes, and behaviors toward women are morally legitimized by religious prescriptions and proscriptions. Therefore women in many cases feel compelled to stay within an abusive marriage, wary of the social and economic consequences.

Traditionally, in most parts of South Asia, the extended family was the ideal norm and women were relegated to the home in rhetoric if not in reality. Urbanization and industrialization led to the breakdown of the extended family, particularly for the middle and upper classes, and a shift to a nuclear family structure. Class played a key role in the gendered relations and structure of the family (Sangari and Vaid 1989).[2] Women of lower socioeconomic class were always compelled to work, but the growing need for dual incomes to sustain the urban family led to larger numbers of middle-class women entering the work force while still bearing the major burden in the domestic realm. That is, larger numbers of women were part of what Arlie Hochschild (1989) calls the "second shift." Despite major economic changes and a gradual reconfiguration of gender relations, the institution of the family and the notion of women both as the upholders of culture and as responsible to men continues to dominate gender relations among South Asians.

In the South Asian context, under the rubric of culture, the relation among gender, status, and speech is socially constructed to portray South Asian women through mythology and popular culture in specific ways that make her the main symbol of the culture. Although the concept of "women" in South Asia does not exist in exactly the same form within each and every region, class, religion, or ethnicity, the dominant image of the role of women in the cultural milieu is a relatively monolithic one. It is an image in which she is defined primarily in terms of her reproductivity and her subordinate status to men. Although her labor may be essential to the economic viability of her family, her image is rarely defined in terms of her economic value, as it is for men (Sangari and Vaid 1989). While a woman's cultural and economic roles are constantly being shaped and shifted by economic and structural forces such as colonialism, urbanization, capitalism, and globalization, the monolithic image is one that cuts across class, religion, and material specificity to define women in cultural terms and in relation to men. South Asian women are expected to sacrifice their individual identity to the priorities of their fathers, husbands, in-laws, children, and community. Many of the representations of women in this monolithic form can be seen in mainstream films in South Asia. In her analysis of Hindi films produced in India between 1975 and 1990, Dasgupta writes that "women are presented in these films as helpless prey in the hands of powerful men and an even more powerful social system. Women's existence as individual beings is shown to have negligible value in society. In many cases, even women's survival is threatened without the support of men" (1994, 58–59).

Rather than a self-defined image, a woman is subject to patriarchal perceptions of woman as defined in religious and cultural rhetoric. To this is added the complexity of her class and caste position, it being most important to protect upper-class and upper-caste women from men of low socioeconomic means and lower-caste status. By no means, of course, do all South Asian men and women subscribe to this view. But it is one image that is central in the dominant religious and cultural rhetoric and shapes gender-role expectations. Women who do not fit this image or challenge it are often seen by the conservative segments of the population as deviant, without shame, not caring for the honor of the family, too westernized, or feminist. Such labeling often involves social ostracism.

One of the most common forms of marriage in South Asia is the arranged marriage. Various criteria such as wealth, education, appearance, age, and family background are used to evaluate the relative worth of the woman and the man and by extension their respective families. Although it is a process by which two families mutually evaluate each other, it is inherently unequal since the position of dominance lies primarily with the prospective groom's family. The very process of negotiation and its outcome are expressive of the power and control exercised by the man's family (Van Willigen and Channa 1991). This long-standing double standard favors men's interests.

It is important to note, however, that marriage ceremonies and customs do not exist in exactly the same form in every country in South Asia, or among every class or religious group. For example, there are monogamous and polygamous marriages. Among Muslims in India, Pakistan, and Bangladesh, the tradition is usually to marry a cousin, while among many Hindus, Christians, and Sikhs, the general practice is not to marry within one's own kin network, especially from the patrilineal side.[3] Although the dowry is generally a North Indian high-caste Hindu custom, many communities in North and South India have adopted the practice, in which the bride's family gives gifts and money to the groom's family.

Among Muslims, however, there is another tradition. A specific sum of money, fixed prior to the marriage, is to be given to the wife by the husband. This is called a *mehr*. This prenuptial contract is supposed to economically protect the woman and as such is a relatively progressive concept. The mehr is supposed to be given during the wedding ceremony. More often in recent times, however, the mehr is treated more as a symbolic gesture and only a minimal amount is set aside. The bride's parents want to show that the alliance is one that they are confident about, and there is pressure from the groom's side for them to do so. In practice, the token mehr serves to deprive women of this economic safety net in a situation where it is relatively easy for a Muslim man to divorce his wife and leave her with little economic support.

Whatever the variation in terms of class, religion, or region, South Asians see marriage as an essential institution and one that defines the social status of a woman irrespective of the economic worth of her labor. Despite variations in marital form, the position and roles of South Asian women in the context of marriage remain very similar. It is within the institution of marriage that patriarchal control is exercised over a woman on the basis of her multiple subordinate statuses as wife, daughter-in-law, sister-in-law, and mother. It is also within the institution of marriage that men dominate, exploit, and demand various rights and privileges in their position as husband and son-in-law.

To remain unmarried, especially for women, is a stigma, and hence there is considerable pressure to marry. The average age at first marriage is relatively lower than it is for women in the United States. In Sri Lanka it is 19.2, Pakistan 16.0, Nepal 15.6, and in Bangladesh, 12.3 years (Lauer and Lauer 1997).[4] A woman's fertility is central in defining her status and identity, as the birth of sons is essential in continuing the patrilineage. Lack of children, especially male children, is defined as a failure on the part of the woman to fulfill her primary role as reproducer. Whether it is as daughter, wife, or mother, a woman's status in her consanguine or affinal family is defined by her relationship to other males—her father, her husband, and her son. Even when she is a mother-in-law and traditionally holds power over her daughter-in law, this power stems from her position as the "husband's mother." Until relatively recently in South Asia, images of the home and the family as a private haven, combined with gender-role conditioning, have allowed problems such as marital abuse to be kept hidden and unaddressed as a social issue. Abusing a wife is one of the common ways in which the man asserts his dominance. He and society see it as a manifestation of his power and control over the woman in a traditionally unequal relationship. Both the dominance of the male and the view of women as ignorant justify the abuse (Wadley 1994). In addition, traditionally there was an underlying assumption that beating those of lower status was acceptable, including teachers beating students, parents beating children, men beating wives, and high caste beating low caste. Frequently the husband's parents, through their status as in-laws, also abuse their daughter-in-law (Fernandez 1997).

Changing patterns in South Asia and in the global economy, coupled with shifts in the social and political fabric of South Asian societies, have brought new conflictual relations between men and women in the private sphere. Segments of the South Asian male population expect their wives to "modernize" in some areas that are external to the home and which increase the household income while retaining their "traditional" subservient, gendered roles within the context of the family. Simultaneously, guided by the doctrine of obedience, segments of the South Asian female population experience external and internal pressures to stay within the parameters that define them as obedient, self-effacing, and content in the private realm while simultaneously struggling for self-expression, individualism, socioeconomic equality, and an end to violence perpetrated against them. Although struggling with changing patterns within the family, many South Asian immigrant women and men, brought up to think of the family as sacred, feel compelled to stay within the cultural parameters and assume this is part of cultural authenticity. Often this socialization then becomes the initial condition that shapes subsequent relationships South Asian women and men have within the family and community and gets extended to the immigrant worldview.

Marrying One's Own: Immigrant Responses to Marriage and Family

Gradual changes are occurring in marriage practices in South Asia as well as among South Asian immigrants in the United States today. More South Asian women, particularly of the second generation, are marrying outside their community. Most marriages still tend to be within the broader South Asian community, however, and often involve a spouse from South Asia itself. In general, some form of arranged or "introduced" marriage remains the pattern for first-generation South Asian immigrants. This was the case for many of the women I interviewed. Either the prospective spouse went to South Asia to find a marriage partner or they themselves went back to marry a South Asian. This practice was seen as important for upholding and maintaining their South Asian roots.

South Asian immigrants see the family as the focal point of one's experience of cultural identity and one's maintenance of the ties between "back home" and the United States. The family is also seen as an arena whose structure and form express the divergence between mainstream American society and South Asian society. As such, marriage to "our own" is perceived both by South Asians and by the larger South Asian community as an important mechanism in maintaining "our values, beliefs, and practices" and the cultural element that defines us as a model minority. A part of this need to marry from "one's own community" is also linked to the notions of the difference in values and attitudes of "American people" toward marriage, family responsibilities, and divorce. The underlying assumption is that although we may adopt the economic values of individual worth, retention of South Asian cultural values of family provides needed stability in achieving economic success while protecting "us" from the immorality of the West. Needless to say, an important part of these cultural values, beliefs, and practices revolves around religion and gender relations and is explicitly articulated in the selection of marriage partners.

For South Asians immigrants, racial and class divides in the United States also make it hard to marry outside their ethnic group. This difficulty is compounded by the need to maintain their own cultural identity and ensure cultural continuity. Most immigrants find that they are caught between the cultural values of their home country and the country to which they have relocated. For South Asians this conflict is particularly visible in the context of marriage. Caught in the bind between different values, they often respond in specific ways. Some go back to South Asia to get married. Others place matrimonial advertisements in ethnic newspapers or make contacts through personal networks and at various ethnic cultural functions of the immigrant community (Luthra 1989).

In general, South Asian immigrant women in the United States are the main symbol of cultural continuity. There are both external and internal pressures to uphold the culture in specific ways, including adhering to culturally prescribed gender roles. Through marriage and the maintenance of the family unity, the South Asian woman then becomes responsible not only for her family's honor but also for the honor of the "model minority community" in a foreign society where immigrants perceive that there is an erosion of family values and a low sense of morality. For example, South Asians pride themselves in having lower rates of divorce as an indicator of their strong family values and high morality as compared with Americans.

South Asian men in the United States often return home to marry a South Asian woman with the help of family members and friends. Underlying the assumption is often the premise that women raised in South Asia will be more culturally bound and socialized with strong South Asian values, especially regarding gender relations. It is assumed that they will be better at promoting family stability and unity than their Western or Americanized counterparts. Issues of sexuality, linked to morality, are another reason that many men in the United States prefer to marry women from their home country. Underlying this preference is the assumption that "Americanized" South Asian women tend to be sexually promiscuous, unlike their counterparts raised and living in

South Asia. Often a groom's concept of a marriage is based on his parents' marriage and does not take into account the changing socioeconomic environment. Moreover, interracial relationships, especially between South Asians and African Americans, are denigrated within the community, which reflects mainstream South Asian's racial prejudice and colonial legacy. Similarly, marrying below one's class is also frowned upon and a source of family shame. This is particularly true for first-generation immigrants. Their own racial and class prejudices often place considerable pressure on second-generation South Asians to avoid marrying blacks or individuals who are not considered professionally "successful" as defined by the community. In terms of gender relations, there are cultural prerequisites based on concepts of the ideal man and woman. Although the general tendency is to marry within the community, more recently in the immigrant context there appears to be less rigidity in defining the specifics of South Asian identity within some segments of the population for marriage purposes.

Talking about Indian men in *India Today* (Jan. 12, 1998, 24e), Shamita Das Dasgupta says, "Indian men want their women to be more docile, more passive." In the same issue Sital Kalantry says of men who return to India to seek a more accommodating wife, "Many Indian men who grew up here were raised by Indian mothers who gave them certain ideas about how things are supposed to be." Often the images that immigrant men have of women living in South Asia are similar to those Western men have in choosing "picture brides" from Asia (Narayan 1995).

As stated earlier, the marriage is set in motion through proposals, often mediated by a third party such as a relative or a friend. Sometimes a marriage is arranged through a "marriage broker" or through matrimonial advertisements in newspapers. While a large number of such arrangements do result in successful marriages, the practices related to such marriages, the assumptions of compulsory heterosexuality, and the controlling dimension of the male's family often make them extremely oppressive to women. Such marriages objectify them and perpetuate their subordinate position as a group in South Asian society. The very process of selecting a mate, especially in arranged marriages, often exhibits women's lower status and role in society.

This is well illustrated in Yamuna's story, whose experience of the marriage process itself was similar to that of many of the women I interviewed. The marriages were arranged; the women had little choice in the matter and did not know their spouse very well prior to the marriage (although in some cases the families knew each other or were related). Like Yamuna, some of the other women I interviewed married men who came to South Asia to get married and arrived as immigrants in a new country to live with their husbands with almost no support structure for themselves.

Transnational Arranged Marriage Type A: Groom Seeks South Asian Bride (Yamuna's Story)

Yamuna was the second woman I interviewed. Approximately 5 feet 3 inches tall, slim, dark-complexioned, with dark eyes, an expressive face, and a beautiful smile, Yamuna was thirty when I spoke with her. At the time she was living alone, and had recently received her green card and divorce with the help of a South Asian women's organization. Among the women I interviewed, Yamuna was the only one who stated that her family of origin had also been abusive. Yet her story about the arranged marriage process and the power dynamics of the different parties involved is not an uncommon experience for South Asian women. Her account also makes clear the various components involved in an arranged marriage in India.

Raised in an orthodox South Indian, middle-class Hindu family, Yamuna was the eldest of five children. Her father was an engineer and her mother a homemaker. Yamuna told me that her mother was ambitious and had wanted to go to school, but owing to the early demise of her parents she was forced by her brother to end her education and get married to Yamuna's father, who was totally opposed to his wife's working outside the home. Yamuna's father was an alcoholic for a long period, and many of Yamuna's memories of her childhood are of her father's getting drunk and becoming violent with her mother and sometimes with the children. After high school Yamuna went on to higher studies, but much to her parents' disappointment completed a B.A. and M.A. in English rather than in the natural sciences. She was seen as a rebel, and Yamuna's mother often chided her for having a "sharp tongue." This rebellious streak was demonstrated when Yamuna converted to Christianity both as a way to resist her father's oppression and as a way to give some meaning to what was happening in her life. Her college years punctuated by crises at home, were not easy. Around this time, however, her father stopped drinking. During this period she also met a male professor, a surrogate father who was to encourage her to be less of a rebel. With his influence and with increasing familial responsibilities, Yamuna was to gradually shape her identity as a young woman into one closer to the cultural prescriptions for women.

Matrimonial Advertisements

By the time Yamuna was about twenty-three, the usual pressures for her to get married started. Interestingly, around the same time she also fell in love with her sister's friend's husband, both of whom regularly visited Yamuna's home. However, nothing really became of this relationship. In the meantime, her parents initiated the process of seeking a potential groom for Yamuna, although personally she wanted to "marry for love." As in many arranged marriages, a variety of strategies were used for selecting the marriage partner, including matrimonial advertisements. Yamuna describes the process:

> Yeah, there were lots of ads. I mean, there was a lot of correspondence that used to go on between my parents and I mean, you know, the other side. There were lots of letters. They maintained almost like a file about the guys that showed up—I think they [Yamuna's parents] put up an ad. This whole thing, process went on for many years—about four or five I years I think. I remember some of the men. . . . There was one ad that my parents put, and I found it very humiliating. I mean it was like your own parents seeing flaws in you, and um, it was very humiliating. Like say, like lying, they had to, um hide the fact that I was not very fair. I wasn't fair, so they would not really mention my complexion you know or put it as you know [fair]. Oh, it was terrible. There was this man, a relative who suggested to my parents that he had a son who got married. He put an ad . . . he put very fair when in reality he was dark and he suggested to my parents to do that. He said that's all right. And my parents put an ad like that. And it humiliated me no end you know that they did such a thing. . . . I don't know I just couldn't put up with this sort of thing. I saw it as my own parents seeing something about me as a flaw. It humiliated me no end that they did such a thing. And there was a whole lot of correspondence, I mean a whole!

In South Asia, the racial component—expressed in terms of the color of the woman's skin—plays a major role in mate selection. Because a potential groom has not seen her, the way she is marketed in the advertisement plays an important role in the probability of an initial contact. Like Yamuna, women who are dark-complexioned often face the humiliation of a society that is color conscious and uses color as a marker of class, beauty, prestige, and femininity. This image of fairness equated with beauty is constantly reflected and reinforced through popular culture and female icons in religious mythology such as Sita. The notion of fair as beautiful and dark as unattractive or evil takes on importance not only in judging physical appearance but also in terms of economic value related to the dowry.

The wording of the advertisement is seen as vital to marketability. In the immigrant context, many of the South Asians who are looking for marriage partners use matrimonial advertisements as a source. Examples include:

> Alliance invited for Hindu/Sindhi girl, physical therapist, 23/5'4" fair, slim, beautiful, Indian values; from well-educated Sindhi Professional.

> CORRESPONDENCE INVITED from professionals for 34 yr old physician, practicing in San Francisco area. Never married. Good blend of eastern and western values.

> UK EDUCATED CHRISTIAN PROFESSIONAL, 42, seeks correspondence with Christian female with a view to marriage.

> LOOKING FOR A HINDU Lingayat, Kannada speaking match for a Hindu, Kannada girl of 26, 5'5", MSC (Agr), Bangalore. Call Brother.

> SOUTH INDIAN PADMASHALI male, costume designing and tailoring business. Looking for Padmashali girl who is interested in fashion design and business. Write with photo. LA, CA

> Parents of Sunni Muslim girl, beautiful, 23/5'6", born, raised in America, Medical student; seek handsome medical student from respectable family. Biodata, Photograph. (*India Abroad*, Jan. 30, 1998)

These advertisements are often the starting point in matchmaking. Photographs, religion, ethnic group within South Asia, education, color, and family values are all important variables in determining the basis for the initial contact between prospective brides and grooms.

Dressing Up to Fit the Image

The very process of meeting the groom is not simple. Dressing up is an important aspect of the process of mate selection and an important aspect of gender relations and role expectations. Traditionally, a woman has to get dressed up regardless of her own feelings on the issue so as to look her best when the prospective groom's family arrives. This is essential to add to her marketability. The clothes she wears are based on the way her family wishes to portray her to the groom's family—usually the image is of someone who is modest, beautiful, and can fulfill the multiple roles that may be required of her. She is usually portrayed as the preserver of the culture. Yamuna says:

> Having to dress up and so—it just bothered me. I mean wearing a silk sari for the occasion. Just sitting there talking to these people. It bothered me a great deal, just somebody coming like that—in all probability he is going to reject you or I am going to reject him . . . to be dressed and to be looked at by them. Like there was a whole part of me that just didn't matter to anybody at all. There was a whole inner life to me that perhaps they were just not interested in at all. Having to wear all those clothes and jewelry. It made me feel [bad] when my father would say dress up like this, dress up like that. This looks good on you, that doesn't. And my initial rebelliousness would surface. . . .
>
> I was working in a school. . . . Most of the teachers were married with children. For them this was not so much of a career, maybe to supplement the income. So naturally for them, every woman had to be married. There was this one woman who was like thirty-eight and she was unmarried, and it was terrible to hear people talk of her and you kind of see yourself in her. She was not a very pleasant person and they would all put it down to her not being married. Like I saw that they were wrong, this had nothing to do with you're being married or not being married. I mean what you are. Despite all, you know you see things and yet something in you begins to feel unmarried too. My God! Will I turn out like her? Her whole life was such a terribly lonely life. There is something pathetic about that life you know. Eventually she did get married at the age of forty. Again it was an arranged marriage by some of her friends. She got married. I think even she could not take the pressure. The fact that it was difficult to fight my parents, difficult to fight the pressure from people at work, from relatives and everybody—I mean you go anywhere and they know that you are old and not married. You see all your friends married and things like that. Despite everything, I mean, you know, just some part of you feels that need to be married and um, you'll marry the next person that comes along.

Yamuna's narrative points to the fact that in South Asia, single women not only are encouraged to marry but are stigmatized if they remain single for a long time. Underlying her single status is the belief that "there is something wrong with her" or that "she is undesirable."

Therefore there are societal pressures to "get married" at an appropriate age or face the "shame" of remaining a burden on one's family. This
pressure to get married was confirmed in my interviews with other
women and also in my informal conversations with South Asian women
and men. Here, youth is relative, but for a woman marriage usually occurs between the age of sixteen and twenty-four years. Today, with many
women working outside the home, the age level has increased slightly.
The older a woman gets, however, the lower her eligibility. Even professional men, who want to marry professional women, look for younger
women who may be on their way to becoming professionals. Among this
group, women older than twenty-six are usually seen as less eligible.
What makes the process extremely humiliating is the concept of rejection.

The Shame of Rejection

In the early stages of her marriage proposals, Yamuna
did reject some of the prospective marriage partners. Although women
do reject partners, in most cases the power structure gives men much
more of a prerogative to object. Since South Asian culture tends to place
men in a dominant position over women, it is women who are frequently
rejected and experience a loss of self-esteem, shame, and a sense of failure. This was the case for Yamuna, who was rejected by a number of
prospective grooms.

> At that point the men that my parents had arranged to meet me
> were rejecting me. There was this man in ———. We were sup-
> posed to go and meet this guy. We went all the way to ———
> and this was arranged with the parents and everything. I was
> supposed to meet him that afternoon and then comes this call
> that this guy does not want to see me because he does not want
> a girl with an arts degree. He wanted somebody with a science
> degree. The rejects aren't really a personal one but it hurts. I
> remember crying and I remember I cried my heart out and it's
> like a personal thing.
>
> Then another proposal came along. It was like an interview
> I had. My father, my mother, and some relatives were there. The
> boy [prospective groom], his father, and his relatives were there,
> and one of his uncles was asking me questions. He asked me
> questions like, "Do you know how much the gas cylinder weighs
> exactly? Do you know something about a refrigerator, how it
> works?" I did fumble on a few of those. I mean, why should I
> answer those questions really. I mean it was absurd. But it
> seemed as if the whole thing rested on my knowing those things.

It seemed like it was all out to find some flaw somewhere, where I wouldn't be able to answer some question. At that point my father did get up, a little upset, and leave. There was a fight or something. I didn't want an unpleasant situation. I sort of quieted them down. After this, this boy liked me or some such thing, and it seemed like there was going to be a wedding. At that stage the father came up and said he wanted more dowry and um my father said he couldn't raise that much money like that. So the marriage fell through. There was a lot of unpleasantness in the house after that. My mother thought that my father was not as enthusiastic as he should be about his daughter's wedding. She felt when it comes to marriage, you should not think of money.

Then again there was somebody else. This family was supposed to be a terrible family, very orthodox, where women had absolutely no hope to work. I mean if I married into that family I wouldn't be able to work and I would also have to follow some of these terrible rituals. There's no flexibility to your life. This man was about twenty-five but he looked like thirty-six, and to me he looked very retarded. I tried to make conversation, tried to speak. I just got the impression that he was perhaps retarded. The worst thing was I was resigned to marrying him. I said O.K. if he would—the only thing that matters is that he says yes. But it turned out he didn't. I think the mother didn't agree. So that was that . . . it lowered your confidence. I mean whatever little confidence that you had. By that time some of my friends were beginning to feel sorry for me, that I was being put through so much. It took away every bit of self-confidence. I had reached a point where I was just willing to marry anybody at all. As long as I could just get married and didn't have to think of anything else. My parents were continuing to look and feeling unhappy—my younger sister had met someone at work . . . I had no opportunities of meeting men [on my own]. I don't know what would have happened if I had had more opportunities to meet men. I was beginning to feel like you're being a burden. Like it was time for me to get married [because Yamuna was blocking the chances for her younger sibling]. And I said I must get married. It's just important, very important, that I get married.

Through Yamuna's narrative, we see how the context in which a woman must make decisions leaves little space for her autonomy. Her needs and desires are seen in terms of others' needs, such as those of her parents, sisters, friends, her social group. She is often viewed as property, and the economic conditions of her household are factored into her marriage chances and the subsequent quality of her marriage. Individual worth is linked to a family's economic worth. Although the acceptance of a dowry in a marriage is legally prohibited, normally the groom's parents continue to make immense material demands on the bride's family and a system of socially expected dowry continues.

Dowry

In many cases the fulfillment of a dowry, be it in the form of gifts or cash, becomes a necessary condition of marriage, as in Yamuna's case.[5] The amount of a dowry varies depending on factors which include the bride's physical appearance, education, and family background as well as the eligibility of the groom, especially his occupation. With increasing urbanization, consumerism, and the expectation of a lifestyle that cannot be met by an individual's sole earning power, there has been increasing pressure to use the dowry as a means to achieve nonwage purchasing power. In many cases, after a marriage the groom and his parents begin to harass the bride, urging her to extract more dowry from her family. In India, especially North India, the inability to meet these continuous demands sometimes results in the murder of the bride, in what are known as dowry deaths.[6]

Despite the male-dominant sex ratio, especially in North India, there seems to be no dirth of marriageable women, because hypergamy (women being married into higher-status groups) is increasingly practiced. This is achieved by compensating men at the top of the hierarchy with a larger dowry (Sharma 1984). Thus the ability of the bride's family to supply the increasing demands for immovable and movable assets by the groom's family becomes an important factor in determining the alliance. In addition, with women's increasing potential or real ability to work in an economy where a two-income family is becoming essential, a women's education and occupation skills become another important variable in determining eligibility. Although the dowry has been illegal in India since the Dowry Prohibition Act of 1961, it has been redefined as voluntary gifts to the bride from her family at marriage. Thus a large segment of grooms or their families still search for a dowry or "voluntary" gifts in their attempt to enhance their own status. The dowry is used as a symbol of the groom's prestige, for ostentatious display to other families of his family's patriarchal ability to command such wealth from the bride's family, or as a mechanism for the embourgeoisment of the groom's family. The bride's parents continue to give a dowry for fear that otherwise their daughter will remain unmarried, with the hope that she will be treated well by the groom and his family, and out of a belief that it is part of the normative order, especially among Hindus. Often this becomes a vicious circle in that those who have daughters and sons may take a dowry for their son in order to be able to give a dowry for their daughter. The whole transaction is one that disinherits women and compels them to depend on men. Women in the Indian dowry system are not the inheritors of property but the vehicles of property transmission. In transnational marriages, however, one of the most important factors determining one's "worth" is U.S. citizenship or possession of a "green card."[7]

Overseas South Asian Groom Seeks Bride from "Back Home"

It was around the time when Yamuna was feeling the pressures of rejection and the need to get married as quickly as possible that her parents answered an advertisement from the man who was to become her husband, Raghu. By the time Yamuna met Raghu, she was desperate to get married owing to immense social and familial pressures and hence was most vulnerable: she was twenty-seven years old, had been rejected a number of times, and felt that she had no more choices left in terms of a marriage partner.

Yamuna's marriage, like that of many of the women I interviewed, took place shortly after she first met her future husband. Many South Asian men from the United States who come to South Asia to marry perceive themselves as very eligible. They come to marry women from their own community who they think will fit the image of the traditional South Asian woman. Often phrases such as "a good blend of eastern and western values" are used in advertisements to signify such a choice. Because these men come for an extremely short visit with the intention of getting married, the whole matchmaking process is accomplished quickly with help of parents, relatives, or friends. There is little or no time for the man or woman to get to know each other before deciding to marry. Often time and other constraints result in minimal information being transmitted about the prospective bride or groom. Most of the background work, if any, is done by family and friends and in many cases is extremely limited. Such inadequate information later contributes to marital abuse. This was the case with Raghu. Telling me about it, Yamuna described her first meeting with Raghu this way:

> There was this man from [a city in the United States] this was through an advertisement . . . he was coming down [to] India, he was looking for a wife, what kind of wife I have no idea. Some of his friends in [a city in South India] were doing all the

correspondence from his side. . . . One day when I was at work
at school, my sister came up to me and said get ready to go, there
this man coming from ———, and he would be coming this
evening. He is in a bit of a hurry. He's coming at a sudden notice. You have to come and so forth. I went and was dressed up
for the thing. It was the usual thing. His sister and, I think,
brother were there. His brother was a much older man—about
fifty-eight, as old as my father, and his sister looked like my
mother's age. I just had lost all critical faculties, anything would
have done. There was food and some light conversation. You
know what the tradition is. Usually when a man comes to see
you, then the next day or something your parents go to their
house and ask what he thinks. So the next day my parents went,
they said yes, he liked the girl and would like to have the wedding in a week's time because he had to go back [to the United
States]. So before I knew it, the next day or couple of days there-
after was my engagement. I hardly ever had anything to do.
Things are such a family affair. I don't even remember exchang-
ing words with this man at all. It gets like there are so many
relatives, it's just so hectic, all of a sudden it's there. I mean that
you are married, going to get married, you just get caught up in
this kind of activity. I realized that he didn't speak [English] too
fluently, didn't speak that much, and wasn't terribly good looking. The marriage was fixed for that week

[After the wedding and reception Yamuna and her husband
went to a hotel for their wedding night.] My first contact with
him came after the wedding. That's when I realized what a horror the whole thing was. You know that it's not the easiest thing
being in a hotel, I mean being with someone you don't even know
and you are starting off a new thing. I think I must have been
nervous actually. He started off very aggressively. . . . He knew
that there was no response from me but he continued obviously.
He said, "you should not be shy." He just took it to be shyness. . . .

We went to ——— to file for my green card. We stayed at a
hotel out there. We had sex and he continued the way he was.
He was very harsh with my breasts. . . . If I went to the bathroom
and locked it, he would get angry. He would say, I am your husband and there should be nothing between us. You can't close
the door, so I could not latch the bathroom door. I tried to explain to him about my father and that the slightest aggression
would frighten me, hoping that he would understand, but he

didn't listen. He didn't pay any attention to what I said. He would wake me up at four or five in morning, usually the time I really go to sleep and would say that men like to have sex at that time. That's when they feel their best. That used to bother me and I couldn't sleep after that. It was almost time to leave —— and go back to the U.S. and he got angry that I got my periods and he was angry with me.

I was just disgusted and thought of him as a bad man. I thought of him as an ugly, dirty person . . . some such thing. I mean, it would save me in some way I guess. . . . But the worse thing was I saw myself as a part of all this. I mean, I saw myself, just like it was a further degradation uh, like it was a completion of the degradation of what had started with my parents looking for somebody. Ultimately this is what I was [an object]—that was really the worst. . . . When you feel you're wronged, then you fight against it or something—but then when you kind of accept it, when you think it's what you deserve, it takes a lot. It just makes you hate yourself.

Many South Asian women have little sexual experience prior to marriage. Yamuna was no different. Within South Asian culture issues of sexuality are rarely discussed with unmarried women, and the culture ascribes a high value to women's purity. Purity is especially understood in terms of premarital virginity, as will be discussed in chapter 5.

Frequently sex also becomes the basis for the husband's appropriation of power in the future.

Waiting for a Green Card

Typical of transnational marriages, after three weeks in India, Yamuna's husband left for the States and she returned to her parents to await her green card.[8] Staying at home gave Yamuna time to ponder the whole marriage and the surrounding issues—the kind of marriage she had entered into and the type of man she had married. A month after Yamuna's wedding, her younger sister got married. Yamuna, meanwhile, lost her job as a teacher at school because the principal knew she would leave for the United States. Not wanting her to leave in the middle of an academic year, he asked for her resignation. During the time she waited for clearance of her immigration status to join her husband, they corresponded through letters and telephone calls. The telephone calls frequently resulted in misunderstandings, with her husband getting upset, and were a great source of pressure for Yamuna. For example, her husband insisted that she pretend that they had a "love marriage" when she came to the States so as to portray a particular image of himself to his western colleagues. In another instance Yamuna explains:

> I remember I once mentioned the word "bored" and he just put down the phone . . . he thought I had called him a bore and he wouldn't write and my parents got upset. There was this constant pressure to please him, to make him happy . . . and there was this double pressure not to make my parents unhappy as it was upsetting my parents that that something had come up between us. . . . So I wrote a letter saying, "I didn't mean it, how can you be a bore . . . and you are everything, and you are, uh, you mean the world to me and I am sorry, I made a mistake." You know I really had to grovel and apologize.

The long period that dependents of green card holders have to wait prior to coming to the United States often exacerbates the tension in transnational marriages and as such is conducive to marital abuse. This abuse takes two forms: (1) the citizen or green card holder may abandon his spouse, never filing for her green card and leaving her behind in the home country, thereby causing her loss of face and considerable tension during the waiting period, and (2) he uses the waiting period as a source of power once the dependent is in the United States waiting for her permanent green card, as is discussed in chapter 3.

Finally Yamuna's conditional green card came through and once again, as a way of demonstrating his power and control over his wife even from a long distance, her husband made all the decisions for her departure without consulting her. He ordered Yamuna's ticket within two weeks of her receipt of her green card. Although she wanted to fly out of City A so that she could visit her friends and relatives before departing, he objected and routed her ticket so that she flew via City B, where she had to stay a couple of days with his sister. Yamuna's mother and brother came to City B to see her off. Prior to her marriage to Raghu, Yamuna had never traveled abroad. At six in the morning on a March day, Yamuna boarded a flight to the United States with two suitcases holding all that was precious to her and with all the anxiety of an immigrant making her first trip to a foreign country. Thirty-six hours later, Yamuna arrived, only to find her luggage lost in transit and herself totally dependent on her husband, with no family or friends to support her in settling into what would become some of the most difficult and challenging years of her life.

Transnational Marriage Type B: U.S. Bride's Family Seeks Groom from South Asia (Mandeep's Story)

Another pattern of marriage that contributes to marital abuse arises when the woman is the green card holder and returns to her home country to marry a South Asian man. Both structural and cultural factors contribute to the marital abuse that these women face. In particular, the husband may perceive his traditional notions of male superiority undermined because the wife is the green card sponsor. Some of these men, feeling that their status is being reduced, use violence against their wives as a means by which to assert or regain a sense of dominance. This violence may occur before the husband receives his green card or once he gets the green card and feels that abusing his wife can no longer jeopardize his legal status. Many of the abused women I interviewed who sponsored their partners' green cards mentioned that their spouses felt that this dependency had somehow taken away from their masculinity. Other scholars have also shown that among Asian immigrants there is considerable pressure on both women's and men's sense of independence and well-being from the shifting gender roles and expectations within the immigrant marriage, thereby leading to a higher incidence of abuse (Espiritu 1997, 75; Chin, 1994, 53–69; Luu 1989, 68). This loss of power is exacerbated for immigrant minority men because they are already publicly relegated to a subordinate position in relation to white middle- and upper-class men in the United States. The institutional class and ethnic structure of the United States does not provide much opportunity for ethnic minority men to exercise power in the public realm in comparison with white middle-class men. Given the South Asian cultural milieu and the structural isolation that immigrants experience in the United States, some dependent husbands abuse their wives and may justify their violence as stemming from frustration at their ethnic or class disempowerment. In my interviews, however, the abuse by husbands seemed to be used as a mechanism to reassert loss of status and power in a situation where the woman as the sponsor was perceived as having power over her dependent husband.

Why do immigrant women residing in the States "go back to South Asia" to marry? While the answer is in many ways similar to that of the men who return, there are some important differences. For men, a key factor in returning to their countries of origin to marry is the desire to find a South Asian woman who fits the "traditional mold." For women, the situation is more complicated. Women face parental pressure to get married to someone from their own community, and they often have led relatively sheltered lives in the United States and have not had many opportunities for dating or developing serious relationships either within or outside the community. Given the primacy of the family in South Asian values, the pressure to marry within the community is often felt by women as they are socialized to be the upholders of culture. Further, many immigrant women who return to South Asia to get married have usually migrated to the United States as a result of chain migration or have come as students at a later stage in their life. As such they have already spent some time in their countries of origin and have internalized some of the South Asian values of marriage. In other cases the socialization process within the family, cultural factors, and structural constraints make immigrant women believe that marrying within their own community is the best for a long-term commitment, for fulfilling their duty to their parents, and for the future of their own potential children. Most of the women I interviewed did not really think of marrying outside the community as an option, either due to their own notions of compatibility or due to their parents' expectations. In fact, they assumed marriage within their community was a given, especially as most had spent a considerable number of years in South Asia or were raised in relatively conservative households in the United States where arranged marriages were the norm. This was the case with Mandeep. One day upon returning home, Mandeep found her husband had left, taking with him all their worldly possessions, primarily bought with Mandeep's money. I met Mandeep at her home in 1991. At the time she was living alone and was in the process of obtaining a divorce from her abusive husband. She had sought the help of a SAWO in obtaining her divorce and in denying a petition for her husband's permanent green card.

Born in 1960, Mandeep completed her education in a city in North India. Her father was an accountant for an export-import company and her mother was a housewife. In 1984 Mandeep and her brother came to the United States, sponsored by their mother who had been sponsored by her oldest daughter. Because Mandeep was sponsored by her mother, a green card holder, Mandeep came as a dependent and as such could enter the country as a single woman. Talking of her initial stay, Mandeep explains some of the difficulties she encountered as an immigrant:

> The first month I liked it because you know it was entirely different. I liked the stores, the elevators, I mean everything. Because in my [hometown] they don't have all these facilities. After a month I got bored and started looking for a job and I had a real hard time because you know they ask for experience and stuff like that. Well I didn't have any experience up here. So anyway, finally [six months after arrival] I got an offer from one

of the Indian banks and also ——— Savings Bank. I decided to join a South Asian bank since I was missing India, but they wanted me to resign my bank job back home which I was not sure whether or not I should do. Who knows? I probably might go back or lose this job and it's hard to get a job in India. So I went to ——— Savings Bank. In the beginning I really didn't like it there, you know whenever they had parties and stuff like that, I never used to enjoy because I don't drink and I am a vegetarian. They used to tease me a lot like where is your boyfriend and I did not have one. I was close to my manager she told me how to answer back like "it is none of your business." After a while they stopped. Anyway after a year I changed to an Indian bank and I felt I got back my respect.

In 1986, I went back to India to get married. I took a month and a half of leave. Actually my parents wanted me to get married, although I was not ready at the time. At the time they thought that something was wrong with me. Why am I not ready for marriage? So I thought to please my parents let me go and see. I went to India along with sister. My father and other sister were there already. They had advertised in a newspaper and selected three or four guys. On the very second day [after] I landed we went to see Baljeet [Mandeep's future husband]. Unfortunately, due to some emergency he was not there. They insisted we wait for him. Well he came at four in the evening. We were there from morning. When I first saw I did not like him. There was no physical attraction but that did not matter much to me. Basically I looked at the family. I wanted to marry into a small family, educated and religious. That was the main thing. He had only one sister. His parents seemed nice at that time. We were told that he had an MBA from Canada. Later, we found out that it was a lie. Anyway, at the time everybody was there so I could not really talk to my husband. So they wanted us to go out for a few minutes. We went to a restaurant. Maybe I was shy at the time, but I just couldn't ask him anything. We came back saying that we needed more time.

So the next day we went to see somebody else and somehow I liked this guy better. He was friendlier but I didn't like that he was a heavy drinker. He told me himself. He was very open. He told me how his father was very rich and would invest $50,000 in a gas station in the U.S. if he were to come here. He also said that he was going to cut his hair when he comes here. We are Sikhs and our Sikh religion does not allow this.

> My father and sister were against him because of his drinking.
> They said, at least [the other guy] does not drink nor smoke.

Pressured by her father, sister, and brother-in-law and the persuasive tactics used by her future in-laws, Mandeep married Baljeet despite her own ambivalence. Once the wedding was over, her husband showed little interest in her and returned to his business. Upon the completion of her leave and having filed for her husband's green card, Mandeep returned to the United States. It was one year before she saw him again and almost two years before he came to the States. Mandeep experienced the pressures of a long-distance marriage. Her frustrations included her telephone calls to her husband, which involved more talking to his parents than to Baljeet.

Upon his arrival, Baljeet began asking for money, asking her to buy him a ticket to visit India, and not searching for work in the United States. Mandeep felt that he should contribute to the household and helped him find two jobs. However, Baljeet rejected them, saying that they were not appropriate for him and that within six months he would find himself a managerial job. Although Mandeep continued to financially support him, Baljeet complained to his parents that Mandeep did not give him enough money and did not look after him well. His parents began placing pressure through his relatives [in the United States], and there were constant arguments at home. Baljeet began abusing her not only verbally but physically. Mandeep was slapped and on at least two occasions almost choked to death. The second time this occurred was during a fight when she refused to sign a petition for his permanent green card. By then she had realized that he had married her only to get a green card. Given his abusive treatment of her, she was reluctant to file his petition for permanent status. Ultimately he threatened to kill her. She in turn threatened to call the police, but he disconnected the phone.

The next day, Mandeep's husband called her at the office and told her that he was leaving and taking his things. She went home immediately, only to find that he had taken everything that Mandeep owned. Still desperate to get his green card and despite the fact that Mandeep had changed her number, Baljeet would call her, threatening her again about the status of the petition. Fearing for herself, in March 1990, Mandeep took her husband to court to get an order of protection. At the second hearing, she arrived late and the case was dismissed. In May of 1991, she had found herself an attorney to help her and was in the midst of obtaining a divorce when I interviewed her. Ultimately Mandeep did not file a petition for permanent status on Baljeet's behalf.

Nontransnational Marriage Type C: Love Marriage (Zarina's story)

"I could not tell my parents that he abused me because I had a 'love marriage.'" While arranged marriages are the norm, "love marriages" are becoming more common among South Asians, although only three women of the twenty-five I interviewed said that they had love marriages. In South Asia, love marriages are those marriages in which the woman and man date each other and make their own decision to marry rather than having it determined by their respective families. Yet these marriages are also problematic for women in several ways and often lead to their being even more oppressed and silenced in the context of domestic violence, given the larger culture of arranged marriages. If she is abused, the woman often feels that she is solely to blame for the choice of her partner. Having gone against the cultural norms, she feels that she is at least partially responsible for her situation or that significant others will view it as such. Zarina's case is an example of the pressures a South Asian woman can face when she marries for "love" and goes against her parents' wishes. Zarina and some of the other women I interviewed married their spouses when both lived in South Asia and migrated to the United States at a later point in their married life. In two of these three cases the abuse started in South Asia and continued in the United States, with the major difference being that there they were more isolated, especially in the early years of immigration.

Zarina is from Bangladesh and was forty-eight years old when I interviewed her in her flat in a predominantly South Asian immigrant neighborhood. The interview was conducted in Bengali, with the help of an interpreter. Zarina lived there with her husband and an adult daughter who was mentally handicapped from birth. According to Zarina, this handicap was most likely an outcome of the battering she received while pregnant with her daughter. She arrived in the United States in 1990, three years after her husband came from Bangladesh to work there. Zarina has been abused for more than thirty years. At the time I interviewed her, she was in the process of looking at the options available to her financially and in terms of support systems prior to leaving an abusive marriage.

Born in 1943, Zarina married her college mate in a "love marriage" when she was seventeen, much to the dismay of her father. According to Zarina, for the first six months of their marriage, there was no violence. Then her husband began to kick and push her. Although shocked at his abuse, Zarina did nothing about it. At the time she felt it was totally out of the question to go back to her parents as they had initially objected to this marriage. Nor could she leave her husband and live on her own, as that was not considered an option for women in those days. To make matters worse, her sister had married her husband's brother in an arranged marriage and therefore there was no way of completely severing contact with her husband and his family.

In the first four years of their marriage, Zarina was forced to have four children, as her husband did not believe in contraception. During this period he also had affairs with various women. According to Zarina, his infidelity was so flagrant that she could not keep a female domestic help, because he would abuse the worker. Anytime that Zarina challenged his power by confronting him or did something that displeased him, he would beat her up and sexually force himself on her.

> My reaction to most of the abuse was to cry by myself. I couldn't think of telling my parents because they would point a finger at me saying that I had got myself into this situation and I was nervous about telling them because if they didn't offer me shelter and I left my husband and they turned their back, there would be nothing I could do about it.

Although Zarina lived in an extended family and her in-laws saw the abuse, they were usually unwilling to get involved. When they did try and help, they were ineffective. When her parents got to know about the abuse, they told her to leave the children with her husband and come back home. They felt they did not have the financial means to support the children and that it would also be an appropriate punishment for the husband if he had responsibility for them. Zarina did not want to leave her four children behind, however, and since neither the in-laws nor her parents were willing to look after them, she continued to live with her husband. He in turn used her lack of options to torment her by telling Zarina that she could leave anytime as he knew he could have other women.

Zarina tried to get legal help in Bangladesh, only to be told by a lawyer that because she had lived so long with her husband there was really no the point in leaving him now. In 1987 Zarina's husband migrated to the United States, and he first sponsored his children and then his wife. When Zarina got her visa, however, her husband refused to bring her to the United States and it was one of her daughters who financially sponsored her. Upon arriving, Zarina continued to be abused by her husband. Around the time of my interview, she had just started the process of getting help from a SAWO to understand what options were available to her as an immigrant.

Zarina's story demonstrates how abuse in a love marriage, especially in South Asia, can be extremely oppressive. The woman is seen to have brought her troubles on herself by deviating from the norm. The family and the community take a stand that usually increases the power of the abuser and reduces perceived viable options. Nondisclosure of the abuse is often reinforced by the societal attitude toward women's status and women's anticipation of a lack of familial and community support, especially given gender relations in South Asia. In general, we see how men appropriate power and oppress their wives through marriage. The man, and by extension his family, exercises more power than the woman and her family in the marital relationship. One way of expressing this is through marital violence.

———

Through Yamuna's, Mandeep's, and Zarina's stories we see broad, culturally approved ways of thinking, speaking, and behaving as they pertain to the institution of marriage and family for South Asians. The culture often persuades both men and women to see social reality in terms of a received collective representation that defines gender relations in a preferred way, usually one that oppresses women. These cultural representations are not limited to defining gender relations within South Asia, but extend to South Asian immigrants in the United States. The complexity of transnational arranged marriages and the perceived cultural dissonance in the United States in terms of both marriage and the structural factors surrounding immigration all contribute to the complexity of marital violence as experienced by South Asian immigrants. In addition, the divisive ethnic, race, and class relations that shape marriage and family in the United States lend themselves not only to the process of immigrants marrying among their own but also to the reconfiguration of marital relations in the immigrant context.

3 | Immigrant Status and Marital Violence

According to the 1990 U.S. Census, approximately one million South Asians reside in the United States. Of these, 815,371 are Indians, 81,371 are Pakistanis, 11,838 are Bangladeshis, and 10,970 are Sri Lankans. Indians alone form the fourth-largest Asian group with approximately 35 percent residing in the Northeast, 17.9% in the Midwest, 24 percent in the South, and 23.1 percent in the West. Among Pakistanis the percentages are 34.3 percent, 18.9 percent, 26.5 percent, and 20.4 percent. For Bangladeshis, they are 57.9 percent, 9.6 percent, 20.3 percent and 12.1 percent, and for Sri Lankans, 25.2 percent, 14.9 percent, 21.6 percent, and 38.3 percent (Barringer, Gardener, and Levin 1993). One of the most important factors affecting the size, growth, composition, and distribution of the South Asian population in the United States is immigration.[1]

To truly understand the cultural and structural factors that affect abused South Asian women, we must look at the way in which gender, class, race, and legal status play out in U.S. immigration policies. Historically, especially in the context of the twentieth century, U.S. immigration policies and practices have been framed around overt and covert racial discrimination, the shifting demands of a labor market for the accumulation of American capital, and the principle of family unity. For immigrants, gender, class, and ethnic relations frequently get reshaped as women and men adapt to life in a foreign country. Yen Lee Espiritu, in her study of Asian American women and men (1997), points out that through the immigration and settlement process, "patriarchal relations undergo continual renegotiating as women and men build their lives in a new country."

The Green Card Factor: Seema's Story

Although some South Asian women emigrate on an independent status, many come into the United States as spouses of U.S. citizens or lawful permanent residents (LPR). Prior to 1995, this legal dependency often placed the husband in a position of dominance and control over his wife. It placed the legally dependent wife in the dangerous position of needing to remain with her abuser. If she left an abusive marriage prior to obtaining a green card, she typically faced the loss of her legal immigration status and risked possible deportation. Some of the women I interviewed were subjected to the "immigration status factor" as a mechanism of abuse within the marriage and as a structural impediment to leaving a marriage. Although this chapter focuses on providing a historical overview of the racialized and gendered nature of immigration policies, I start with Seema's narrative because her immigration status was an important source of power in the hands of her citizen husband.

I interviewed Seema in August 1992. Seema, then twenty-six years old, was an extremely petite woman, about 4 feet 10 inches tall. When I first met her, she was wearing a red dress, had her hair tied in a ponytail, and looked much younger than her twenty-six years. Although I did not notice it from a distance, as I came closer I saw that one of her eyes was glass. We spoke to each other in Hindi. Initially she seemed a little reserved. She started by telling me that although she had agreed to the interview, now that she had come for it, she was not sure whether she wanted to do it. She said, "After all I have moved on and want to put it behind me." I told her that I understood and that she should feel no compunction to talk to me. I said it was nice of her to have met me anyway and was ready to see her leave, when she asked me if she could sit there for a while. I said sure. A while later, she came up to me and said that she had decided that she wanted to do the interview. I asked her if she was sure; she could always come back at another time. She was adamant that we do it then, however, and suddenly it seemed important for her to tell me her story.

> I was married in October 1990. He had come over for a month. The marriage was through a newspaper advertisement. For fifteen days he saw girls. Then he chose me. He had seen my photograph. Then we got married. He said he doesn't want anything

[like a dowry], only a good girl. His parents wanted something. We had to spend five thousand rupees and invite people for a party. The marriage got fixed in one day. I couldn't make him out. After the marriage I stayed with his family. He used to behave well. He is an U.S. citizen, so he filed papers for me and got me here. He came back [to the States in fifteen days].

[During the fifteen days in India] he used to speak nicely, but he used to get angry quite often. But I didn't say that to anybody. He would get angry about small matters. Once he got angry about a purse. I had borrowed my sister's purse, which wasn't very big, and couldn't carry everything. He got very angry and said that he will straighten me out, once I come to America. I used to just listen, as I can't answer back to somebody who is so angry. I just started crying. Then we went back to the house, and he started behaving properly, but still used to get very angry. All his family knew that he is very short tempered. His mother used to tell him not get so angry with me. He always said that he had to straighten me up. I don't think I was doing anything wrong.

He started hitting me from the first day I was here [in the United States]. I wanted to call my father, as he was very anxious to know whether I had reached safely. I told him I wanted to call my father. He was already upset with me because I had called [a U.S. city where her husband lived as a manager of a motel] from Europe. He wanted me to wait till I reached the U.S. before I called him but I had already called him from Europe. He was very angry and said I was out to waste his money. I told him to forget about it as the money was already spent. He got very angry and started hitting me. I got so upset that I began to cry.

He put me to work [at the motel] from the very first day, even when I was tired. I had to clean the rooms. He didn't let me rest even for a day. He wanted to check my two suitcases that I brought from India. He asked me not to get spices but as I was the one who was going to cook I got some. He wanted to see what I got. He was married earlier and had a daughter. He didn't tell me but told my father. He was angry because I didn't get something for his daughter. He had asked me to get something but I didn't have the size. I had got things for everybody in the motel, got clothes for his friend's family. All these were bought with my father's money. He did not give me a dollar.

When I asked where the child and mother lived he would beat me—it was only the second day.

He would beat me on my head and face with his hands. He would hit me everywhere. I tried to forget it. I was angry with him for hitting me. Things would settle down, but again after a few days it would start. He was always picking fights over little things. He used to tell me not to tell lies, and straighten up. He didn't want me to ask him anything. If I ever asked him anything he would get angry with me because I had asked him and shouted instead of explaining to me. I started hating him as he never answered my questions and was always angry. He used to get very angry. He used to drink beer and not let me sleep the whole night. I didn't want to have his child. As I didn't have any birth control pills, I would refuse him. He would get very angry and thought that I had spoiled his life. He accused me of that every day. He said I had gone there for the green card. I stayed with him for three months. I didn't want to stay with him just for the green card.

He would be drinking beer and verbally abuse me. I couldn't sleep as I was scared of him. There was no guarantee that he wouldn't beat me even in the middle of the night. Sometimes he wouldn't even say anything, just hit without explaining anything. So I couldn't sleep.

I used to work the whole day, but he would take away all the money. He had told me about that arrangement earlier in India. Later when I started getting scared, I thought I should have money. Even if I asked him, he wouldn't give me a dollar. And he would bother me the whole night, after a whole day of working. I would clean the rooms in the motel. Dust and clean the mirrors. Then cook at night and make tea for him in the morning. Every couple of days he would hit me. He would leave marks on me. Once I wanted to drink water, he tried to choke me to death. He did that three times. There was nobody nearby to tell. I didn't know anybody. I didn't think of calling the police. Then he hurt my fingers and I was in a lot of pain for a week, then it healed.

The motel owner was a friend of his for over twenty years. He is a fool. He knew that my husband beat me as he could hear everything downstairs. The motel owner knew everything but didn't help me. I had told him a few times when my husband had gone out. My husband rarely took me out. Most of the time

I was inside the four walls. Even when I went out to the gallery to see outside, he would call me inside. If I ever drew the curtains to get some fresh air, he would ask me to close them. This continued for three months. I had one month left to get my green card. He used to be so abusive that I had decided that once I got my green card, I would run away. I was just waiting for my green card to run away. I didn't have any support, as I didn't know any Gujarati people to ask advice. I couldn't tell the motel owner anything as he repeated it to my husband, so I couldn't rely on him.

As he is a citizen, the green card came within three months [of her arrival] but he never let me collect the mail. I knew the green card had come but he kept it with him. I hadn't even seen it. He would challenge me to get my green card from him. I never replied to anything. Then he started saying that one day he would murder me. I didn't let his words bother me, as he was abusive all the time. I didn't say anything back to him, as he was so short tempered that he would hit me.

One day he had given me a used and torn blanket to cover me when I sleep. First I refused, but later took it. Then later I went and got another clean blanket from the motel's linen closet. He was not in the room. He was downstairs as customers come at all times of the night. In the morning he came to the room and was very angry to see that I had taken a blanket. So he threw the blanket. It was six o'clock in the morning and I was still in bed. I didn't react to his anger. That made him angrier. He said I had only come for the green card. He knew I had asked his friend about the green card. His friend had repeated everything to him. He kept on saying that I had married him for his green card and was going to ruin his life. He went to the kitchen and picked up a fork—a pitchfork. The big one, made of iron. He went to the kitchen and picked it up and brought it. He aimed it to poke me in the eyes. I hadn't fully woken up so I couldn't run away. He hit with the fork on the left side. I became unconscious briefly. When I regained consciousness, I realized that I was all alone. There were no Gujaratis in the motel that I could talk to. Just his friend and the American customers. I saw myself bleeding profusely. He was just standing there, watching what he had done. I asked him if he had seen what he had done. One eye was damaged, he just went off to work. I rushed to a store in front. I wasn't dressed properly, didn't have my shoes on, just ran away. When I went to the store he ran away with all the money. I went to a medical store in front and told them that my husband had hurt me. I knew a little bit of English. They called the police and ambulance. They put a bandage on my eye and took me to the hospital. At the time I was conscious, could hear and understand everything. That night they operated on me.

I told the police what my husband had done to me. They called the motel owner. He came promptly, but my husband had run away. The motel owner was an idiot. The police took down my statement. I think if the police had gone there quickly, they could have arrested him. But by the time they went there, he had run away. Anyway he had his car. That night I had my operation.

My sister was in [a city in the United States] but she had just come to this country ten days back, so she couldn't tell anything to her husband. At the hospital, there were all Americans around me. I wanted to meet some Gujarati people, as I wanted to tell my story. I told the doctors that I wanted to meet some Gujaratis and they arranged that. The Gujarati people from the community would come and visit me and brought me food. I hadn't eaten properly for the past three months. They collected some money and gave it to me. Then from ———— with the help of some social workers who had been contacted by the police I came to ————. The social workers told the police about [a South Asian women's organization, or SAWO] and they sent me here. [A SAWO] gave me some money and found my social security number. A lawyer, who comes to [the SAWO] helped me to apply for my green card. I was their client. . . . I stayed [in a shelter] for three months. I used to get a lot of bills. I couldn't get any job, even though I tried my best. But after the lawyer finalized the divorce, the bills stopped coming.

Earlier I used to get very scared. But L [a SAWO member] told me that everything would be O.K. and searched for some job for me for a month. First I got a job in a doctor's house, a housekeeping job. I saved some money there but they were not good people and bothered me. Didn't let me go out. Made me do a lot of work. Taking care of the children, cleaning the house, and cook. I did all three types of job there. I told L that they were not good people. Then I came back to the shelter and stayed for three or four months. Then I was able to get a job. [All this happened a year and a half ago.] Now I work in a company as a packer and get $5 an hour. Now I like it. It has been quite some

time and I am forgetting all those horrible experiences. So I feel
better now.

Although the problem of marital violence is universal, Seema's story
demonstrates that immigration status frequently becomes an important
basis of power and control in the hands of an abusive spouse. Not only
do victims of marital abuse have to face the different manifestations of
abuse that all such victims experience. Additionally, some immigrant
women have to face structural obstacles erected by an immigration system that has not totally addressed the legacy of coverture. Inherent in
the early immigration laws, strengthened in the 1986 Immigration Marriage Fraud Amendment Act, and partially rectified in the acts of 1990
and 1994, coverture is a legal concept that situates a wife as inferior to
her husband and vests all legal power in him.[2]

Three fundamental ideas have played a pivotal role in shaping U.S.
immigration policies and practices. These have been individual economic
worth to American businesses, family unity, and racial/ethnic selectiv-
ity. Although all three concepts are interrelated in immigration law, the
main focus of this chapter is on the assumptions of patriarchal power
relations within the family that historically underlie the concept of "family unity" in U.S. immigration policies and their impact on abused immigrant women. Some of these policies have specifically targeted Asians.
Through male-centric immigration policies, the state indirectly ensured
that minority women were subject to a racist patriarchal order and thus
were made more vulnerable to the power exercised by an abusive spouse.
The chapter also addresses how more recent attempts by the state to provide better legal protection for abused alien spouses have not been entirely successful due to restrictive regulations and deficiencies in
legislation. This problem is compounded by a legislative and regulatory
framework increasingly based on the notion that the United States must
prevent aliens from using fraudulent means to gain legal immigration
status and citizen benefits.

Coverture, Chastisement, and the
American Family: Historical Background

The concept of family has been and continues to be
fundamental to the normative order of American society. Families are
seen as the crucible for upholding American values and morality. Historically, however, the family has been one of the major mechanisms for
the perpetuation of gender-based inequality and male control. On the
basis of the doctrine of coverture, the two members of a married couple
were not perceived as equals in the eyes of law. Instead, the husband

was legally granted all power over his wife and children. A secondary notion in the form of the "the right of chastisement" was added to ensure that the totalitarian power of the husband over his wife and children could be enforced.[3]

By the mid-nineteenth century, some state legislatures began to address the lack of legal rights held by women by providing them with a larger role in decision making regarding child raising and disbursal of family wealth through the Married Women's Property Act (H. Clark 1987, 503). By the 1960s, the women's movement had brought considerable attention to the issue of sex discrimination in existing family and property laws and had compelled Congress to remove much of it.

While the legacy of coverture was recognized by the state and rectified to a large degree through laws addressing the rights of married women who were American citizens, no equivalent measures were taken within the framework of immigration laws to fully eliminate the assumptions of coverture and the potential for spouse abuse underlying those policies and practices.

Race and Gender Discrimination in Immigration Policy, 1875–1950

During the United States' first hundred years there were minimal restrictions on immigration. Between 1875 and 1882, various laws were passed that denied the entry of certain aliens on the basis of criteria such as prostitution, illiteracy, contagious disease, and so on. These laws were frequently targeted at Asians, specifically Chinese, with the first group being Chinese women. In 1875, the Page Law prohibited Chinese and other "Mongolian" prostitutes and contract laborers. The assumption was that most of the Chinese women were prostitutes and as such should be denied entry, while those already living in the United States should be deported if suspected of prostitution. As Espiritu puts it, "The Page Law, with its focus on defining the *morality* of Asian women as the basis for entry in the United States, illustrates the (hetero)-sexism and racism underlying U.S. immigration laws" (1997, 18). Similarly, other exclusionary laws passed in 1882, 1917, 1924 and 1934 were to have a major impact on the lives of Asian Americans. In 1882 Congress passed the first major racially constructed discriminatory immigration law, the Chinese Exclusion Act. This was done to appease the white labor force, which felt that its jobs were threatened by immigrants who worked hard—in mining, agriculture, and railroads—at extremely low wages.[4] On the basis of this law, Chinese were not only ineligible for citizenship but Chinese immigration was suspended. (This law was in place for almost sixty-one years before it was repealed by the

Immigration Act of 1943.) In 1917 the Immigration Act went further by prohibiting the immigration of laborers from what was termed the Asiatic Barred Zone. This geographical area included China, India, Indochina, Burma, Thailand (then Siam), Asiatic Russia, the Malay States, sections of Afghanistan and Arabia, Polynesia, and the East Indian Islands. In accordance with U.S. labor interests and notions of the family, excepted from this exclusion were professionals (teachers, students), tourists, government officials, missionaries, and their accompanying wives. Accompanying husbands were not included, however, an exclusion that underlines the importance of the patriarchal concept of the family.

On May 29, 1921, temporary restrictions were put forth that limited the number of aliens who could immigrate to the United States with the goal of moving from a resident alien to a citizen. Furthermore, the Immigration Act of 1921 persisted in the assumptions of coverture. First, it required the husband to file a petition on behalf of his wife, or she had to accompany him, before she could obtain immigrant status. This law thus gave a husband complete power and control over his wife's status. Second, the act stipulated that preference be given to wives, but not husbands, of U.S. citizens and some categories of resident aliens.[5] It reaffirmed the dominant position of the husband by not allowing the equivalent process for the immigration of husbands of women who were citizens or lawful permanent residents (Calvo 1991).

In 1924 Congress made numerical "quotas" on immigration permanent. It designated a "nonquota" category, however, whereby some immigrants would be exempt from these quota restrictions. An important nonquota category was the wives of U.S. citizens, demonstrating how entrenched the notion of coverture was in immigration law. The immigration status of the alien wife was totally controlled by her citizen husband. An "alien" wife could not designate herself as a nonquota immigrant but was beholden to her citizen husband to file a petition on her behalf.[6] As Mohanty aptly puts it, female immigrants were treated as "legal appendages of men" rather than being accorded independent legal status (1991, 26).

The 1924 law also mandated preferences within the quota system. One of its categories sought to meet the labor demands of specific sectors of the U.S. economy, giving preference to "a quota immigrant skilled in agriculture, his accompanying wife and children."[7] The intention was to obtain cheap, exploitable labor. In the 1930s and 1940s, some of the existing discriminatory policies and practices in the treatment of female U.S. citizens and LPRs with "alien" husbands were partially rectified through the institution of equal legal rights for citizen wives and citizen husbands in the eligibility of their alien spouses. But the concept of one spouse being able to dominate and control the other spouse's immigration status lay unaddressed, leaving room for potential spousal abuse.

Immigration and Nationality Act of 1952: The Persistence of Racism against Asians

The Immigration and Nationality Act of 1952 (McCarren-Walter Act) was an important juncture in immigration law. It both strengthened and altered prior immigration laws and is the foundation of most contemporary immigration law. Prior to 1952, the United States government set up various barriers to Asian immigration and citizenship (Barringer, Gardener, and Levin 1993, 28). In 1952, however, Congress passed the McCarren-Walter Act, which abolished the exclusion of the previous category of "aliens ineligible for citizenship." This law attempted to rectify existing racism by shifting to quotas based on nationality rather than race and as such was extremely significant in principle, for it meant that any immigrant, including those who had resided in the country for many years, could apply for citizenship. In practice, however, it failed to totally address racism toward Asians. The 1952 act perpetuated racial discrimination against Asians by stipulating minuscule quotas based on race rather than country of origin as the criterion for immigration and citizenship eligibility. That is, an Indian born in another country would still be counted under the Indian quota rather than the quota for his or her birthplace. This was not the case for European countries, where birth was the criterion (Barringer, Gardener, and Levin 1993, 30). In keeping with American economic interests and family values, preference categories were created within these quotas, with high priority given both to highly educated, skilled immigrants and to family reunification. In addition, a nonquota "exempt" category without restriction was created to allow immediate kin of citizens to immigrate.

The 1952 law also supported the concept of "family unity" and partially rectified existing gender biases in immigration by changing the word *wife* to *spouse* in immigration law. Yet it did not truly address the power and control factor in marriages, since one spouse still controlled all aspects of the other spouse's life in the context of immigration. For example, the act allowed for either a wife or a husband to be included in the spouse's national quota, a change from prior law.[8] However, an alien spouse was still dependent on the willingness of the citizen or lawful permanent resident spouse to petition that the alien spouse be given legal immigrant status. She could not petition on her own behalf, despite the fact that she had in good faith married a U.S. citizen or LPR. Thus, through a mere change in wording, the 1952 immigration law superficially appeared to be gender neutral when in reality, through the petitioning process, spousal domination persisted. Contrary to Congress's belief that through the 1952 act it had eliminated the sexism and racism prevalent in prior immigration laws, in reality it had only partially addressed the problem. It never systematically confronted the legacy of coverture, which could potentially play an important role in the power an abusive citizen or LPR husband had over his alien wife (Calvo 1991, 604).

The Hart-Cellar Act of 1965: The Entry of South Asian Professionals

In 1965, Congress passed the Hart-Cellar Act to further rectify the remaining elements of racism and ethnic discrimination in the 1952 act. There was also a marked shift in the Hart-Cellar Act from the earlier racial and ethnic focus to a greater emphasis on the notion of family unity and meeting the growing and shifting demands of the U.S. economy. This act abolished the previous quota system that had discriminated on the criteria of race and substituted a limit of 290,000 immigrants per year, with each country in the Eastern Hemisphere limited to 20,000 immigrants. Children, spouses, and parents of citizens were excluded from these restrictions. Family reunification was given an even greater priority than it had received in the 1952 act (Barringer, Gardener, and Levin 1993, 31). But no similar limits or preference system was set up for the Western Hemisphere. Rather immigration was based on a first come–first served basis.

Preference was given to spouses of citizens or LPRs. In both cases, however, the citizen or LPR continued to control the immigration status of the alien spouse. The citizen or LPR had to initiate the process by filing a petition for the alien spouse's legal immigration status, could withdraw it at any point in the process, and was the individual who could appeal the denial of a petition by the Immigration and Naturalization Services (INS). Thus an alien spouse was completely at the mercy of the citizen or LPR and had no avenue to self-petition even if she had married the husband in good faith, was currently living with him, or had children with him. This structure had major ramifications for immigrant women in abusive situations. As such, the immigration policies still had a racial component.

In addition, the 1965 act stipulated occupational preferences to address the demands of the American economy. This change had a major impact on Asians, including South Asians. The act was an important landmark for South Asians, since many who immigrated soon after 1965 entered under the third category of occupational preferences, namely professionals and scientists. As a result, America was able to draw cheap labor in the form of highly educated, highly skilled professionals without incurring the costs of educating or training these individuals. Thus the South Asian population profile prior to the mid-1970s was composed primarily of highly qualified individuals, culturally bound to their homeland but seeking the opportunities for professional growth and economic success that they felt were lacking in their own countries at the time. A numerically small ethnic minority, professionally oriented with little interest in participating politically in American society, these immigrants established themselves and raised their families. They felt, as part of their larger familial obligations, the need to assist other family members still living in their native countries to gain the greater economic opportunities and quality of life America had to offer. This was achieved by sponsoring the immigration of their immediate kin to America under the family reunification criteria established in the Hart-Cellar Act. The result was chain migration. Since family unity was an important feature underlying this immigration law, spouses of citizens and LPRs enjoyed certain benefits such as exemption from numerical restriction, quicker visa processing, and the ability to apply for naturalization sooner than those not married to an American citizen. Many potential immigrants who fit this category availed themselves of this opportunity. It is important to note, however, that spouse-based immigration still had to be initiated by the American citizen or LPR spouse. By 1980 the U.S. South Asian population was 409,808; by 1990 it had more than doubled to 925,803 (U.S. Census figures).

Immigration Marriage Fraud Amendments of 1986: Questioning the Legitimacy of Immigrant Marriages

In 1986, concern by legislators regarding the misuse of spouse-based immigration to gain immigration benefits through falsified marriages led to the passage of the Immigration Marriage Fraud Amendments (IMFA). In an attempt to guarantee that a marriage to an alien was "bona fide," the criteria for proving the legitimacy of the union was that it had lasted a duration of at least two years. Until these two years were completed, the INS would provide the alien spouse with only a conditional resident status. Prior to IMFA, though a citizen or LPR had to file the initial petition requesting permanent residency for the alien spouse, INS had granted this unconditionally, regardless of the duration of the marriage.

Based on the INS interpretation of IMFA, the conditional status did not start on the date the couple married but only upon the conferring of this conditional status by INS. Therefore neither the actual date of the marriage nor the waiting period by an alien for her visa were included within the two-year conditional residency period. This provided an abusive spouse an opportunity to make the waiting period even longer. In addition, once the INS conferred conditional status based on marriage, the alien spouse could not change her status to LPR within the two-year period. This implied that to avoid loss of legal status and possible deportation, an alien was compelled to remain married for those two years regardless of other issues. Further, loss of immigration status meant the inability to obtain employment legally as well as the loss of legal status for daughters and sons whose resident status had been based on their mother's marriage to a citizen or LPR.

Within ninety days of the completion of two years of conditional residency, the alien spouse and the sponsoring citizen or LPR spouse had to jointly petition to remove the conditional status and be interviewed by an INS official if this was deemed necessary. Under IMFA, the citizen or LPR spouse controlled the initiation and withdrawal of a petition as well as the appeal of the denial of a petition. All of these conditions set forth under IMFA were to have an extremely detrimental impact on an alien spouse in an abusive relation with her citizen or LPR spouse. In an attempt to control so-called fraudulent marriages, IMFA gave immense power and control to a citizen or LPR over his alien wife through his control over her immigration status, as we saw in Seema's case. IMFA had in reality allowed a citizen or LPR spouse to control all aspects of an alien spouse's life—her legal status, her children's fate, her ability to work or to seek any form of financial independence. At a time when gender inequality and the problems of domestic violence were being addressed by the women's movement in America, the double jeopardy that immigrant women faced owing to the complex intersection of gender and immigration status still lay unaddressed.

To help offset some of the powerlessness that IMFA had bestowed on the alien spouse, this legislation had two extremely limited discretionary waivers. An alien spouse could request the discretionary power of the U.S. attorney general for a change from conditional to permanent status even though she could not meet the joint petition requirements by proving that: (1) she had entered into a good faith marriage, that the marriage had been ended due to good cause and that she was not at fault for not meeting the joint petition requirements; and (2) deportation would lead to extreme hardship for her and her children. Yet even proof of these conditions did not necessarily imply the automatic approval of a waiver. This was entirely in the hands of the attorney general, whose designee for the interpretation and implementation of the statute was the INS. Hence decisions were in the hands of a large bureaucratic institution whose officials were, in some cases, insensitive or unaware of cultural differences in the institution of marriage as well as the diverse cultural, social, and economic ways that an alien spouse can face "extreme hardship." Because the alien spouse was already experiencing extreme hardship as the result of domestic abuse in the United States, to avoid deportation she had to show that the deportation would cause "extreme hardship." To do so was particularly problematic given that the interpretation of extreme hardship was at the discretion of an INS official.

Calvo (1991) cites the insensitivity of an INS official in whose opinion the extreme hardship waiver seemed improbable in domestic violence cases, since "the hardship has already been suffered while in the US and it would be unlikely to be aggravated by departure from this country."[9] INS also took the position that unless the alien spouse initiated the divorce or annulment proceedings, she was ineligible to apply for the waiver even in the event that the citizen or LPR spouse was found at fault. This meant that an abused woman, whatever the cultural and structural obstacles, must somehow be the first to file for divorce. Such a position assumes that abused women have access to lawyers and support systems, have funds at their disposal, and have no language barriers in communicating their situation. The good faith/good cause waiver was still problematic for abused alien spouses and contributed to the legacy of coverture. This is demonstrated in the obstacles that Yamuna encountered with her immigration status.

According to Yamuna:

> In August I went for a couple of appointments at legal aid and met the lawyer. He told me about this conditional status thing and what one has to do to make your status permanent. If I could prove that the marriage [was abusive], I could get a waiver. I didn't know that there was anything like a waiver at all. I knew that the visa was a conditional status thing. That at the end of two years I would have to apply jointly with my husband to file for my green card. I knew that but I didn't know of this waiver. He told me that there is a waiver and you have to show that the fault was not yours and therefore the marriage broke up. That's when there seemed like some opening, that I could do something about it. It was around September before I started working. I was still looking for a job and I was desperate for a job. I was also looking for an apartment.
>
> They [a member of a South Asian women's organization that was helping her in dealing with a lawyer and looking for a job and an apartment] also helped me with a lawyer. I needed legal advice. I had an appointment with the American Legal Defense

Fund. They have free legal advice. So they [the SAWO] put me in touch with them. So I met a matrimony lawyer and I met an immigration attorney so that I could get a picture of what my situation was. I mean get an idea of what I should do, how I should proceed and things like that. I knew now that it was important for me to get a divorce—that I should get a divorce on my grounds. So I had to go about filing a divorce before he did. [The SAWO] helped me find a lawyer. I had to file an out-of-state divorce because he was in ——— and I had been in ——— for less than a year, so I couldn't file from [here] as I didn't meet the residency requirement. These are things, information I got from meeting these lawyers.

[The SAWO] knew that I did not have financial resources, so after a lot of looking around for pro bono lawyers, but nobody would do it free, they put me in touch with this firm in . . . that would do it on an extended payment plan. But what happened at the time I had moved from living with those people and I moved to live by myself by December 1989. [The people Yamuna lived with were upset at her moving out, because they wanted her to continue living with them and contribute to the household.] Up to this point I let my husband believe that I was in India. In the first week of January [1990] I had this call at work and my husband calls and says "what the hell do you think of yourself" the moment I recognized his voice I put the phone down. I mean I just panicked. . . . He also called my home and spoke to my roommate. He said, "I am going to tell her, what I am going to tell the police, I am going to tell the immigration that she's a cheat, she's a liar and everything." I tried to figure out how he got my home and work number. There was only one family that knew both these numbers and they also knew his number.

Again that put me into a big panic and I thought that he may just turn up somewhere, someday and do something to me. I mean I was constantly living in fear. So my lawyer felt that we should start the proceedings as soon as possible, before he started it. They tried serving him papers but it so happened he served me before my lawyers did. This was served in September of [1990]. So I had to counter claim. I mean I had to file a counter claim to his divorce or whatever . . . OK we filed a counter claim, and then we weren't sure when the date would be. Like my visa was expiring in April 1991 and I wasn't sure when the trial date would be. So now I had to also decide if I wanted to contest the divorce. You know, I mean I could have just not contested the divorce because I knew it involved a lot of expense. And then just say, "because of lack of expense." In filing for this waiver it was important to get the divorce on my grounds. Although I could perhaps even take the chance and say that I did not have the financial resources to fight a divorce and so maybe show some kind of other documentary evidence toward [the waiver]. I mean I didn't have substantial documentary evidence of his abuse. I mean I didn't have like say bruises and things like that but maybe I could substitute through affidavits from friends and you know people like that. The people from [SAWO] did my filing for me. We got affidavits from my friends who knew me before the marriage and attended my wedding. I had photographs of the wedding. Anyway I decided to go ahead with the divorce and the trial was for May of 1991. I had been given a six-month extension from immigration— . . . before they decide on the status.

Then this new thing had come that had not been put into practice yet [the 1990 act, described below]. It may no longer be necessary to prove to get the divorce as long as you can prove the wedding itself was a real one. It was a good faith wedding. Somewhere in November 1990, came this law, uh waiver—you have to show a good faith marriage. Before this 1990 law in order to get the waiver you had to show a good faith marriage and also show that the breakup of the marriage was not your fault— which means you have to get a divorce on your grounds. Now then in 1990 came a law that it was not important to show that the marriage breakup was [initiated by you]. But just show that the wedding was a good faith one. In which case I would not have to get the divorce [as stipulated in the 1986 IMFA]. It would have saved me expense, saved me the trouble of a trial and so forth, but it was not put into practice yet. Here I had to fight a divorce and get it on my grounds.

So we had the trial. He, of course, was keeping track of when my visa expired. So what he did was call the city hospital I worked at. He called the director of that place. There was an anonymous call saying that there is such and such person working in the hospital who is not qualified for the job and who is working there illegally. So what happened was that those people got in touch with our personnel department and they started looking into my files. And they found that I was perfectly eligible for the job and my status had not yet expired. I wasn't illegal. My status was expiring in a month's time. So they called me and said, "you have to show us an extension. We need to see an extension of your visa." I said that I had filed for it and I should be getting it soon and I got the extension.

At the trial we had an expert witness. The trial just went on. I had a judge who must have made a difference. She was a woman. It was not because she was a woman as if she was biased toward me. I could sense that because I sat through other trials too and I could sense that she was listening. It was a family court, and naturally it had all to do with divorces and fighting for custody, and this right and that right. She listened carefully to everything and there was no bias toward man or woman. She was a very fair person. So that also gave me confidence. There were many things that she could not understand because many of my reactions were all very cultural too, I mean you know. You should see in a certain cultural [context]. And so she tried to. She was very sympathetic. She tried to understand what made me react the way I did to certain things. Asked me questions herself and it all went off perfectly and I got my divorce on my grounds—that it was not my fault. That if I broke up it was because he was responsible for that. In order to maintain my self-respect and maintain my health I had to break up. And so even if I counterclaimed I got it on my grounds and that was very fortunate [for the immigration waiver].

Although Yamuna finally received her permanent resident status, it was her tenacity and organizational support that helped her through the ordeal. In general, however, the INS interpretation left few options for alien spouses trapped in abusive situations. The IMFA and INS's interpretation of the statute left battered immigrant spouses with the option of continuing within an abusive marriage until becoming an LPR, or leaving the abusive relationship and risking deportation if the sponsoring spouse withdrew his petition, or taking the chance of going through the elaborate procedures set forth by INS to obtain a waiver, knowing it might be denied and thus once again risking deportation. It is not just legislation but the regulations and the interpretation of them that affect alien spouses, especially those in abusive relationships. IMFA, and its interpretation by the INS, strengthened the notion of coverture and indirectly exacerbated the conditions under which an immigrant woman could be trapped in an abusive relationship by creating various barriers in the form of conditional resident status.

The Immigration Act of 1990:
The First Small Break for Abused
Immigrant Women

The Immigration Act of 1990, passed in November of that year, brought about major revisions. Family unity, however, was still a central principle in the new law.[10] Spouse-based immigration was given preference, but an alien spouse was still dependent on the citizen or LPR to file a petition for resident status on her behalf. But in an important step that removed some of the obstacles that abused alien spouses faced due to IMFA, the 1990 act changed the good faith/good cause waiver and also added a battered spouse/child waiver.

Three waivers to the joint petition to avoid the removal of conditional resident's legal status were added by this legislation. First, a conditional resident can show that she entered a good faith marriage but the marriage has been ended. However, she no longer has to be the first to file for divorce or show that there was good cause for terminating the marriage. Second, a conditional resident can prove that she entered the marriage in good faith, but that she or her child was subject to extreme cruelty and battering by the citizen or LPR spouse. Third, a conditional resident can demonstrate that deportation would result in "extreme hardship." To counterbalance some of the attorney general's discretionary powers in decisions on waiver applications, Congress stipulated that in the case of battered spouse waivers, denial of the waiver by the attorney general could only be made under the "rare and exceptional circumstances" when the applicant posed a threat to national interest. This law partially helped women like Seema and Shahida when they applied for their green card.

It was under the battered spouse waiver of the 1990 Immigration Act that Shahida, a Pakistani immigrant spouse, was able to file for permanent resident status. Shahida married a U.S. citizen of Pakistani origin in 1989 and came to the United States in 1990. She left her abusive husband within seven months, and thus had not completed the stipulated two-year conditional status mandated in the joint petition necessary for changing from conditional resident status to permanent resident status. Fortunately for Shahida, with the help of a SAWO she was able to file for a waiver to the joint petition requirement as stipulated under the 1990 act. She requested that the office of the attorney general prevent the termination of her conditional resident legal status and change her status into that of a permanent resident. She sought this under the "good faith" waiver. That is, she entered into the marriage in good faith, but was subject to extreme cruelty by her citizen spouse.

I have a green card now. Earlier I had an alien registered card [conditional resident status]. I got it after my marriage, under the condition that I will have my interview after two years, and then they will make it permanent. But I separated within seven months of my coming here. So the interview that needed both the husband and wife could not be held. Therefore, I applied to the Immigration Department. I had to file for my green card separately. There is a different form, for the people who for any reason cannot be together for two years, say somebody dies or something. One has to fill it up and give it in for their consideration. They decide whether to give it to you or not. I had filed it and I won the case. So now I have permanent status.

[A SAWO] helped me a lot with filling it [the waiver application] out. They helped me in whatever way they could. They wrote letters for me. During my first interview they [the INS] had letters from my cousin, my uncle, a family friend and [the SAWO] explaining the whole situation. When they [the INS] saw the [SAWO] letter, they wanted to know whether it [the SAWO] was registered or not. They needed more information and gave me a date a month later for another interview. Then [three members of the SAWO] helped me a lot. U came over as a social worker and took a long interview and gave a four- to five-page-long report about everything from the beginning. When I went again they [the INS] asked me if there were any Pakistanis in the organization. I said, "No, it was only Indians." They didn't ask many questions and gave me permanent status.

Shahida was fortunate that she had an organization to help her get her green card. Many abused women may not be so fortunate and may be daunted at having to deal with the legal bureaucracy.

Despite attempts at reducing some of the restrictive components of IMFA, the 1990 Immigration Act was still problematic for victims of marital violence. Under the rules for a modified "good faith" marriage waiver, the alien spouse or conditional resident had to prove the legitimacy of the marriage in terms of both when it occurred and when it was terminated.[11] For many South Asian immigrant women who get married in their native countries and have gone through marriage ceremonies that don't involve a formal registration, it becomes harder to prove the legitimacy of the marriage in terms of when it occurred. While they may have photographs, gaining access to these photographs can be time-consuming. Verification of the legitimacy of the marriage in the absence of documented evidence becomes another structural impediment that immigrant women have to face owing to the cultural practices in their native countries.

Unlike the good faith waiver, the battered spouse/child waiver did not necessitate that an alien be divorced or separated, but she had to prove that she or her child was battered or subject to extreme cruelty by the citizen or LPR. The process was problematic, however, because neither "battery" nor "extreme cruelty" is clearly defined in the 1990 act. While it can be assumed that this was done to minimize the restrictiveness of the law's applicability, in reality it caused a hiatus between the legislation and the final regulation, making it harder for alien spouses to leave abusive relationships.

The wording in the regulation emphasizes the impact of the abuser's behavior on the victim rather than the abuser's behavior itself when it defines battery and extreme cruelty as including, but not "limited to, being the victim of any act or threatened act of violence, including any forceful detention, which results or threatens to result in physical or mental injury. Psychological or sexual abuse or exploitation, including rape, molestation, incest (if the victim is a minor) or forced prostitution shall be considered acts of violence."[12]

In addition, although the legislation used the term "extreme cruelty" for broader applicability, the ultimate regulation used the phrase "extreme mental cruelty," a restrictive and erroneous interpretation.[13] This disparity between the legislation and the regulation was to be extremely important because of the different evidence required for physical and mental abuse as set in the INS final regulations. Thus, while Congress did not intend to differentiate between the evidentiary requirements for mental or physical abuse, the INS regulations did. Since the regulation provides only a single definition of abuse but differentiates between the evidentiary requirements for mental and for physical abuse, the type of abuse becomes a crucial determining factor in defining the nature of the process.

The evidentiary requirements for physical abuse in the regulations seemed to be consistent with Congress's intent and, as such, included a broad range of evidence of abuse as acceptable. The regulation stipulated, "Evidence of physical abuse may include, but is not limited to, expert testimony in the form of reports and affidavits from police, judges, medical personnel, school officials and social service agency personnel."[14] But this was not the case for the claim of mental abuse. Here the regulation stipulated much stricter evidentiary requirements, requiring the applicant to be evaluated by a professional accepted by the INS as an expert in the field. The expert's evaluation was the only basis for determining the validity of the claim and as such the whole case hinged on the verdict of the expert. The regulation also limited the notion of "experts" to licensed clinical workers, psychologists, and psychiatrists, thereby setting parameters within the mental health field that excluded many individuals trained in the area of domestic violence.

On the basis of these regulations, the whole process of seeking a battered spouse waiver on the grounds of extreme mental cruelty put tremendous pressure on the abused immigrant spouse. First, she had to have access to a mental health professional. Second, she had no choice but to confide what is often viewed as an extremely private matter to an outsider, one who may not be aware of the cultural subtleties involved in the mental cruelty. Third, she faced the possibility of misinterpretation if the evaluation was being conducted with the help of an interpreter. Finally, she had to bear the cost of this procedure. All these issues were raised by various groups and organizations, especially organizations addressing the needs of battered immigrant women.[15] Because the INS had not required such professional evidence in any other form of immigration adjudication, such a restrictive position for claims of mental cruelty could only be understood as first, the attribution by the INS of different degrees of importance to physical abuse as compared with mental abuse, and second, as a response to the service's fear of a potential onslaught of fraudulent claims to obtain immigration benefits.

Most problematic was the fact that the 1990 Immigration Act still allowed the abusive spouse to exercise considerable control over the alien spouse. It was still within his power to withdraw the initial petition he filed within the conditional status period. If the petition is withdrawn, the alien loses her legal status in the United States, thereby making it illegal for her to work and subjecting her to possible deportation. Most important, the battered spouse waiver in the 1990 Immigration Act failed to address the problem of undocumented aliens trapped in an abusive situation. There was no respite for an undocumented abused spouse whose citizen or LPR spouse failed to file the petition that initiated her conditional status. Nor was there any respite for the nonimmigrant, who came to the States as a tourist, later married a citizen or LPR, but did not change her immigrant status, thereby becoming undocumented upon the expiration of her nonimmigrant visa. Although attempts were made in the act to alleviate some of the power and control that citizen or LPR spouses had over their alien/conditional resident spouse, it did not yet fully address the problem of the spousal power or the structural impediments that a battered alien spouse experienced.

Violent Crime Control and Law Enforcement Act of 1994: Another Step Forward

In November 1993, after increased pressure from various organizations and public recognition of the pervasiveness of domestic violence, Congress proposed the Violence Against Women Act (VAWA).[16] The act attempted to focus on the prevention of violence against women by making it an important law enforcement priority. Immigrant rights organizations and those addressing domestic violence, especially among immigrant groups, pressured members of Congress to include provisions for immigrant women. While the House of Representatives proposed specific provisions to protect immigrant women and thereby rectify the limitations of 1990 act, the Senate version had no such provisions. When legislators from both houses worked out the final immigration-related provisions, VAWA was included in the Violent Crime Control and Law Enforcement Act passed into law on September 13, 1994.

Previously an alien spouse was dependent on her citizen or LPR to file a petition for resident status on her behalf, thereby giving him enormous control over her. One of the most important immigrant-related components of VAWA is the "self-petition" provision in Title IV. This provision allows an alien spouse to petition on her own for an unconditional permanent resident status on behalf of herself and her children without depending on the sponsorship of her citizen or LPR spouse. This can be done: (1) if she or her children have been battered or subjected to extreme cruelty by the citizen or LPR spouse during a bona-fide marriage; and (2) if she has been married and has resided with the citizen or LPR spouse for at least three years and he has failed to file a petition on her behalf.[17] To qualify, an alien spouse must show that: (1) she is a person of good moral character; (2) she has lived in the United States with her citizen or LPR spouse; (3) she is currently residing in this country; (4) she married in good faith; (5) she or her child was battered or subjected to extreme cruelty by her spouse during the marriage; and (6) she or her child would face extreme hardship as a result of deportation.[18]

The law also included other important provisions in favor of an abused alien spouse. First, some of the earlier restrictions in demonstrating that deportation would lead to extreme hardship were removed through a new provision stipulating that the attorney general take into consideration any credible evidence pertinent to the petition, thereby broadening the scope of factors that could potentially be included in demonstrating extreme hardship. It also allowed an alien spouse to fulfill the "extreme hardship" provision if she could demonstrate that her deportation would cause "extreme hardship" for her child. Second, to avoid an abu-sive citizen or LPR spouse's ability to weaken the chances of his spouse's self-petition under the "immediate relative status" category by a divorce, the act included a provision that prevented the revocation of a self-petition solely on the basis of the termination of a marriage.[19] Third, there was a change in the usual criteria of seven years of continuous presence in the United States to be eligible to apply for the suspension of deportation. A new provision was set that allows an abused alien to be eligible for the suspension of deportation if she has stayed in the United States for three years and if she is subject to deportation because her husband did not file the initial petition or refuses to cooperate in meeting the requirements of the joint petition to move her from condi-tional resident status to that of an LPR. To do this, an abused alien/con-ditional resident spouse needs to prove that: (1) she has been physically present in the United States for at least three years prior to application; (2) she has been battered or subjected to extreme cruelty by her citizen or LPR spouse; (3) she is of good moral character; and (4) deportation would cause extreme hardship for her or her child.

There are still many problems with VAWA. First, legislation such as VAWA does not take into account women who experience abuse within the first three years of marriage, as was the case for some of the women I interviewed. In addition, as Weinstein (1997, 121) puts it, "The civil rights provision in particular is troublesome because it is only relevant to middle and upper class battered women who have the resources to bring claims against their batterers and who have wealthy batterers from whom any potential recovery would be meaningful." What happens to the abused immigrant woman who does not have her own resources or lacks other structural support to attain legal assistance? Many of these issues leave the abused immigrant woman very little legal recourse and thereby compel an alien spouse to stay with her abuser or risk deporta-tion. Second, there is always a hiatus between legislation and the re-sulting regulations. Often the regulations are so restrictive that they make the legislation ineffective. Third, attempts by the government to address the problem of the immigration status of an alien spouse are diminished when it is presumed that there is also ongoing fraud among immigrants in general that requires strong preventive measures.

Problems increased in the mid-1990s in a socioeconomic climate where there was considerable anti-immigrant sentiment and a general belief that Third World immigrants were not only taking away economic viability from mainstream American families but were also changing the color and the moral fabric of white America. The result was targeted discriminatory policies such as the 1996 welfare reform legislation, which "denies legal immigrants access to federal, state and local benefit programs [thus forcing] thousands of battered immigrant women to remain in abusive relationships" (Vohra 1995, A22). This legislation was one more way of denying immigrants basic human rights and perpetuating violence against immigrant women. Many of the women who came as dependent spouses and were in an abusive relationship were now again faced with the daunting prospect of staying with an abusive spouse or leaving with no structural support due to a punitive approach taken by the United States. Immediately after the 1996 legislation was passed, abused immigrant women who had taken the courageous step to leave their abusive husbands and were on welfare, began calling the SAWOs asking what would happen to them. Changes in the Immigration Act of 1990 combined with the 1996 welfare reform legislation do, however, allow for battered immigrant women, previously unqualified for aid, to become eligible to receive benefits within the parameters defined by each state. However, the process itself places a considerable burden on the woman, as she has to demonstrate proof of being battered (Pillai 1997, 10). In order to receive welfare benefits, the "battered unqualified immigrant woman must also prove a 'substantial connection' between the need for the benefit to be provided such as Temporary Aid to Needy Families and the battering."[20] To attain such proof, abused women often need legal assistance that they may find hard to get and thus this becomes another impediment in attaining the aid they desperately need.

It is ironic that at a time when Congress has taken one of the first significant steps in confronting coverture in immigration law by providing the self-petitioning provision in Title IV of the Crime Bill, it has simultaneously undone some of these gains by passing discriminatory, anti-immigrant legislation. This legislation minimizes the effectiveness of any comprehensive program to end domestic violence.

The complexities of immigration policy affect immigrant women, in multiple ways. Their problems of abuse are made worse by the capitalist, racist, and gendered policies and practices of U.S. immigration. Such policies contribute to spousal domination, which can lead to marital violence.

4 Isolation

Alone in a Foreign Country

He took off for a day after I came. The next day, when I went to the door as he was leaving, he told me that it wasn't necessary. He shut the door and locked it from outside. Actually it could be locked from both inside and outside. I could have opened it from inside [but I didn't know this]. He used to come around at 6:30 and eat dinner around 7:30. So the whole day I was alone in the house. I spent my time watching TV. When I asked about a job, he said that he didn't want me to have any small job. If I got a good job, then I could do it. When I asked for English classes, he said that he didn't have any money. He told me if I had money, then I could go and take English classes. I did not know how much he earned. He used to do all the shopping and spending. He had never even taken me for grocery. He told me not to go because it wasn't a good neighborhood.

—Shahida

Cultural change is usually hard for immigrants (Sluzki 1979; Brislin 1981; Dyal and Dyal 1981; Moon and Pearl 1991). As was true for Yamuna, leaving behind nearly all that is familiar and coming to a foreign country for the first time is an extremely difficult experience. Having left a familiar culture and socio-economic system, immigrants may experience a deep sense of loneliness in their new environment, often compounded by social isolation (Kang and Kang 1983).

Research indicates that social isolation is "strongly related to the risk of wife abuse" (Gelles 1997, 86). The more socially isolated a family, the greater the risk that there will be marital violence (Fagen and Browne 1994). Melvin Seeman (1972, 492–494) defines social isolation as "the individual's low expectancy for social inclusion and social acceptance." According to Seeman, this form of isolation is found among minority members and is usually accompanied by loneliness. Social isolation also refers to a lack of social interaction and social integration (Hughes and Gove 1981, 50), where social integration refers to "the existence or quantity of social ties or relationships" (House and Kahn 1985, 85). Although there is considerable evidence in the literature that social isolation of the family is a factor in domestic violence, almost no attention is paid to how it functions for ethnic minority immigrant families, and how it lends itself to the invisibility that immigrant women experience in the United States. The familial and cultural support systems available to an abused wife in her home country are often removed in the shift to a new unfamiliar land.

For South Asian women, especially recent immigrants who come to the United States as dependent spouses, isolation is one of the most painful manifestations of the marital abuse perpetrated against them. Here, isolation refers to the individual's experience, both in perception and in reality, of being emotionally and socially alone, economically confined, and culturally disconnected. It is the feeling and fact of not belonging or having a meaningful relationship(s). This social isolation functions at three levels: first, in terms of the quality of a woman's relationship with her spouse; second, in terms of the frequency and quality of social interaction in informal networks of friends, relatives, and coworkers; and third, in terms of access to and participation in formal organizations such as community organizations or economic, legal, and political institutions.[1] Here I will discuss the first two levels. The third is considered in chapter 6.

Through the experiences of some of the women I interviewed, we will see how marital abuse in the immigrant community can appear nonexistent due to the invisible wall of isolation that arises from multiple factors. These include the power tactics used by the abuser, lack of geographic mobility, cultural constraints, language barriers, financial dependency in a new environment, and lack of friendship networks, social contacts, and emotional support. Men also restrict their wives' friendships with others because they fear their "Americanization." In addition, isolation can be increased by the structure of American society, where race, class, and ethnic divisions leave little room for social interaction that cuts across such differences in the complex realities of people's day-to-day experiences. Isolation is also exacerbated by the immigration policies discussed in chapter 3 that discriminate against immigrants and force women to stay in abusive relationships for fear of deportation.

Isolation by One's Spouse

Not knowing anyone and not having anyone to talk to is one of an immigrant woman's most lonely experiences. Her isolation is heightened when the only person she depends on for social interaction is her husband and he too isolates her. This was the case for Shahida. When I first met Shahida, she was thirty-four years old and had been living in the United States for three years. Although she could speak English, she was not very fluent in it and was more comfortable being interviewed in Hindi. Dressed casually, she looked much younger than her thirty-four years when she met me at a mutual friend's house. She worked as a chemist in a large pharmaceutical lab, earned approximately $250 a week, and lived alone in a studio apartment.

Shahida is a Muslim from Pakistan. Her father, like many Muslims, migrated from India to Pakistan in 1947 during the India-Pakistan partition. He is a doctor and businessman in ———. Shahida's mother died in 1983. She has two sisters and two brothers and is the second oldest among the siblings. According to Shahida, her family is upper middle class in Pakistan and has a good lifestyle. Although her older sister remained unmarried, Shahida married her first cousin, Ahmed, who is eight years older than she, in 1989, and came to the United States in 1990. Ahmed's mother and Shahida's mother are sisters. Prior to his marriage to Shahida, Ahmed was married to a white American woman with whom he had a son. Two years after his divorce from his first wife, Ahmed returned to Pakistan and married Shahida.

> When Ahmed was going to come again [to Pakistan], my aunt came again with the proposal. My father asked me again. He wasn't sure what I was feeling inside. But none of my siblings wanted me to marry him. He came to Pakistan and we got married within thirteen days.
>
> We were together for one month. On the whole, we had a very nice time during that month. He came back to America after one month. Now when I think back, the other people used to tell him to take me with him [to America]. They said I would have been able to leave within the six weeks, as he is a [U.S.] citizen. But he didn't want to bring me with him. He said he didn't have all the divorce papers of his first marriage with him. He said he would send me the papers once he came to the U.S. People said that I could have gone within six weeks of his going back, if he wanted. But he took about a year to send all the papers.
>
> When I called America after I got my visa, he said, "Why don't I [Ahmed] come over there [Pakistan] instead of you coming here." So I asked him why he made me go through all this [red tape for a U.S. visa]. We have to go through police clearance

and this and that. I had to take all these four or five things [clearance tests] and stand in a line at the U.S. embassy and go through all these troubles. I told him, now that I have all these things done, you are saying that you will come back. Even then I didn't realize that he had other things going on here [in the United States].

I got married in February 1989 and came here in mid-February 1990. For my journey he sent tickets by KLM which came directly to ———. But for that I had to go through [another country] and I wasn't able to get a transit visa for that [other country] in Pakistan. Then his brother changed the bookings to arrive in New Jersey. Ahmed did not come to receive me in New Jersey. I had to stay a night in a hotel in New Jersey.

I just asked people. I kept calling his number. Nobody was answering it and the answering machine was on. I didn't leave a message as he hadn't told me about it [the answering machine] and I didn't know what to do. You see answering machines are not very common in Pakistan. He knew I was coming. He even knew that I was coming to New Jersey, but the flight to ——— was canceled due to bad weather.

When I reached [him] the next day, he didn't welcome me at all. When I smiled at him, he didn't smile back. I didn't mind that too much, as I thought he was upset because I had changed the flight. It had taken me two days to reach here. I hadn't eaten anything on the plane. So when I reached home, I asked for something to eat, like milk and cookies. There was nothing in the house. He cooked some rice and lentil. We ate it and then he told me to sleep and left. When he came back after three or four hours, he had lot of groceries. But there was nothing when I reached. If you are expecting somebody, you should make some preparations. The beds were unmade, the sheets were not changed. One can live whatever way one wants, but if he is expecting somebody, like his wife, he should make some arrangements.

Shahida's problems with Ahmed began with the question of her coming to the States as his wife. Although Shahida got her visa, Ahmed's subtle attempt to force her to stay in Pakistan is one form of rejection that women waiting to join their husbands experience. In some cases the husband may not even file for the wife to join him, and the abandoned wife is forced to stay in South Asia with her in-laws or return to her parents' home. This circumstance is related to the restrictive U.S. immigration policies that force women to wait until their spouse decides to file on their dependent's behalf. In some cases, rather than file for his wife's green card, the absentee husband occasionally returns to his home country to symbolically acknowledge some form of social or filial obligation to his parents. Thus the wife is forced to continue to live in South Asia, hoping that one day her husband will take her to the United States or that he will return permanently to South Asia.

Shahida, despite Ahmed's efforts to dissuade her, did come to the United States, but was soon to experience considerable isolation. For an immigrant woman like Shahida, who had led a relatively sheltered life, to arrive at an airport in a foreign country and not find anyone to meet her is an extremely intimidating experience. Other women too recalled their arrival at the strange and unfamiliar environment of an international airport, even when someone was there to meet them, as intimidating and lonely. It heightens the feeling of being a stranger, of being different, and of being in a situation where one has little control due to lack of familiarity with the surroundings. Often the impersonal environment of the airport becomes the first site of difference for immigrants. For Shahida, the lack of warmth and insensitivity shown by Ahmed on her arrival initiated her feelings of rejection and isolation. From then on, these feelings were exacerbated by Ahmed's behavior toward her, as she found herself totally dependent on him for social and economic support during the course of their marriage.

From the time Shahida arrived in the States, Ahmed ignored her except when he needed her and instead spent most of his time with their neighbor Jen, an Italian American. When Shahida questioned Ahmed after three months, he tried to beat her and punished her. He increased her sense of isolation by forcing her to sleep in the living room and not talking to her. Shahida recounts:

After our fight, he had come and put my comforter and pillow in the living room. For the first two nights he slept there. Then he told me that that he couldn't sleep very well and had to go to work early so I had to sleep there instead [in the living room]. For a few days I slept on the sofa but I could not sleep like that. So I started making the sofa bed and sleeping. We stopped talking completely, to the extent that, when I was cooking in the kitchen, he used to be in the living room. After I kept food on the dining table and left, then he would enter the dining room and eat. We had no communication.

In July he had to undergo surgery. He had some problems with piles and had to get operated. So he took leave. One night when I was sleeping, he woke me up and said he had some accident and to clean it up. I did. Then slowly he started talking to me. See! When he needed my help, he came and woke me up and talked to me. The doctors had given medication for a bowel movement before surgery but he had dirtied the bed and wanted me to clean it. I cleaned everything from bedroom to bathroom. Then he started talking a little . . . .

He went to the hospital for surgery with Jen. I had wanted to go with him but he said that there was no need for that. He wanted me to go and stay with B [Ahmed's South Asian friend's wife] for three days and I did that. . . . Even on the day he came back, despite his doctor's warning he walked to Jen's house. He couldn't even walk properly, but still he went there, walking very slowly. I told him not to go, as we lived on the third floor. He said that his doctor had advised him to walk so he went for a walk with Jen around the block. I said I wanted to come too but he said no, the area was not nice, lots of blacks etc. But he is my husband and I am not going out alone. I was going to be with him. Later, I went for a walk with him for a couple of days but he used to go with her for walks. He said that he gave her company, as she was alone. I didn't tell him that even I was alone and needed some company. . . .

I did not go out because Ahmed had forbidden me but these friends told Ahmed to let me go to the public library. He said, fine and took me there. It was about two blocks away [from their house]. Then I used to go and get books from there. . . . One day I had gone to the library and on the way back went to that neighborhood store and bought some cards. When I came back the front door was locked. There was a woman on the second floor, but she never locked the door, so I knew that Ahmed had come back and locked it. I rang her bell and she opened the door for me. When I went up [to our apartment], he was there in the bedroom. As soon as he saw me he got very angry with me. He demanded to know where I had gone. I still had the books and cassettes in my hand. So I told him I had gone to the library. He wanted to know why I had gone to the store when he had forbidden me to do so. He said that the woman sold drugs and I would get involved in that. I don't know whether she sold drugs, but I think he was scared that this woman's aunt was Jen's neighbor and I would come to know something. Ahmed said that if I couldn't stay the way he wanted me to then I could go back to Pakistan. . . .

After that B called me and asked me where I had been as

> Ahmed had called her to find out where I had gone. I had gone
> to the library at three o'clock. It seems that he had a doctor's
> appointment and had come home early. I had no idea about the
> appointment, as he never told me anything. We had no com-
> munication.

Being in a strange, unknown country forces Shahida to be emotionally dependent on her spouse, who is totally insensitive to her loneliness and need to be a part of his social environment. Leaving Shahida
alone in the home and spending most of his free time in the evening
with Jen was one of the mechanisms used by Ahmed to isolate Shahida
and make her feel inadequate. Such treatment has consequences in the
context of sexual abuse, as will be discussed in chapter 5. Not letting
her come to the hospital to visit him and later going for walks with his
neighbor was another way of making Shahida feel inadequate in an environment where she was already struggling to make the adjustment to
an unfamiliar culture and country. Ahmed used stereotypes of blacks
as potentially dangerous or others as drug peddlers to compel Shahida
to stay within the confines of the home. This is typical of an abuser's
use of power when he knows that a woman like Shahida is vulnerable,
given that she is in an unfamiliar surrounding with culture and language
barriers. That she had to cook for him and clean up after he acciden-
tally defecated on the bed is indicative of his perception of her role in
their relationship, that of someone who would fulfill the instrumental
role of cleaning and cooking. From what Shahida describes, there was
no intimacy in the relationship and a complete breakdown in any communication. Much of Shahida's loneliness arose from her lack of social
inclusion and acceptance. Having a husband who devotes considerable
time to others and ignores his wife's need for company is an example
of one type of isolation that dependent immigrant women experience
at the interpersonal level.

The very nature of intimate relationships exposes individuals to one
another's strengths and weakness (Wolfe, Wekerle, and Scott 1997). An
essential element of intimacy is the willingness of people within a relationship to self-disclose and be open to each other with mutual trust
and respect. The difficulties of intimacy with a partner who often lacks
interpersonal skills and is insensitive to the nature of dependency created in the marital relationship in the immigrant context contributes in
significant ways to social isolation. Such isolation also removes the potential restraints of cultural and familial mechanisms of social control
on an aggressive husband, as he does not have to be socially accountable to the woman's family. It is not surprising that South Asian women

whose dependence on their spouse is high and who have few resources at their disposal are much more vulnerable to the power exercised by an abusive spouse.

In Shahida's case, isolation tactics are deliberately used by the husband to increase his power and control over his wife in a social environment that is alien to her and in which she depends primarily on him. The husband appears to control all of the woman's activities and contacts. He locks the woman in the house so that she cannot get out, forces her to cook and clean up all day, monitors all telephone calls, leaves her without any money so that she is forced to stay at home, constantly questions her actions and whereabouts if she tries to go out, uses racial stereotypes to scare her about the dangers of leaving the house, and threatens to shame her by sending her back to her family if she does not adhere to his wishes. These tactics were mentioned by other women I interviewed as well.

Like Shahida, Geeta also talks about her isolation in the United States and the mechanisms of control of her husband, Ramesh. Born in South India in 1963 and raised by her grandparents, Geeta went to medical school in India and came to the United States in 1988 to join her husband. She had been introduced to him through a friend's brother. Five years older than Geeta, Ramesh came to the United States as a student and later worked for a private company. Having lived in the States for six years, Ramesh returned to India to get his green card and get married. Prior to marrying him, Geeta had called her uncle in the States to inquire about Ramesh. Her uncle informed her that "some of the people, the Indians, [say] that he is a wonderful person—if you miss him, you won't get such a guy again." Ten days after their marriage, Ramesh returned to the States with his green card, and Geeta followed him two months later with her provisional green card as his dependent. Geeta describes her isolation and the intimidation in her marriage:

> After three days [after Geeta's arrival], he invited some people for dinner. The people who recommended him to me, he started liking them as I had told him about them. They thought we were newlyweds and wanted to leave us alone. They said it is O.K. there is no hurry you can invite us later. . . . They thought that I didn't know any cooking, they told my husband why trouble her. My husband started yelling at me, why is that man saying that it is trouble for you, when are you going to cook. I didn't feel like cooking. But he wanted them to come. On that afternoon he had invited them, I wore a dress and he started fighting about that. He told me that I don't like this black dress or

pink dress whatever it might be. He started yelling, "how many times I have told you not to wear that dress." I was there for just three days, it was the first day I wore it. I started crying. I was in a new place. Everything was new to me. I was living with a new person. I started crying.

In the beginning [when he yelled] I used to cry. He didn't react to it, he would stay away in another room. He never apologized. I am the one who would apologize. I would say I am sorry, I made you do like that. He wouldn't say anything. It [The yelling] went on like that. His nature is like that. Everyday before he goes he would tell that I had to clean the walls, a big list of things. I used to take a shower before he came, and get dressed because I thought that I was newly wed. As soon as he came he would push me into the shower. I tell him that I have just taken a shower, ten minutes ago, but he won't listen to anything. He will just tell me go and take a shower, whatever dress I wear, he will point out and say it is not nice. He will make me change ten dresses. He won't pick a dress and say, "Wear it." Simply, that this is not good, this is not good. Before leaving [in the morning] he would give a big list. I just had two cooking vessels. He used to work for a private company. He took an apartment. Whatever clothes I wear, he would make me change all the time. . . . He used to check, whether I am studying or not, whether I am sleeping. . . . I called my uncle and told him. He didn't say anything.

Emotionally weakened by the separation from their families and the reality of being in an unknown environment, immigrant women like Geeta and Shahida are forced to deal with their spouses' abusive behavior on their own. In addition, given that transnational marriages allow very little time for couples to get to know each other and given the delays in obtaining a green card for the dependent, couples are faced with a long distance marriage that allows no growth of intimacy or bonding. In most cases couples are coerced into learning each other's personalities after the dependent spouse has moved to the United States and where there are none of the traditional support systems for the couple. For immigrant women like Shahida and Geeta, the husband is usually the only person or one of the only persons she knows, and she is compelled to rely on him in the early stages of residence in her new country. Thus she is dependent emotionally, socially, and economically on her husband despite his being a relative stranger to her in many ways. She is eager to please him in the hope that the quality of her interpersonal relations with him will reduce the anxiety of being in a foreign country and help negotiate the difficulties of transition, both in terms of married life and in terms of living in a culturally and structurally alien society. The husband in turn often takes advantage of this relative powerlessness. Geeta tells me:

> After fifteen days I realized that he is doing all that purposely. Before marriage, I had told him, that if we have any differences, we should sit and talk it over and work out the differences, not keep it inside pent up. So I called him up at his office, and told him, "I have been observing your behavior for the past fifteen days. It always seems I am at fault, how would you like me to be? I asked him all these questions. He said that I know the doctor wives like to twist their husbands in their little fingers, so I am being careful. So I asked him, "If you are so cautious, why did you get married to a doctor." He said, "Why did you get married to me? I know you didn't get married to a doctor, because you can't twist him. You got married to me, because you thought you can twist me." I asked him, "Do I look like a person who would want to twist their husband?" It was only fifteen days that we had been together. . . .
>
> No, we can't predict him. If you live with a person, you know what he likes and what he dislikes. He was very unpredictable. I don't know when he will be happy and when he will be angry. I used to try different ways to make him happy. I used to think that if I do like this he would be happy. I used to keep vows. I used to clean. I used to think that if I wear this saree he would be pleased. I used to think that as he cared for his family a lot, he is a caring person and that eventually he would start caring for me. He would fall in love with me. He would start liking me.

While abused women use various strategies to alleviate their isolation, their abusive husbands use multiple strategies to increase their wives' isolation by systematically minimizing their contacts with the outside world. The isolation that abused immigrant women face is compounded by economic deprivation. Many women talked about financial deprivation as a major source of isolation and powerlessness. One important way an abusive husband isolates his immigrant wife and literally makes her "nonexistent" to the outside world is by controlling all the finances, giving her no money and thereby restricting her freedom of movement, holding her accountable for every penny she spends, and excluding her from any bank accounts and any movable or immovable assets. Shahida says:

> He gave me no money for household expenses. . . . He used to
> do all the shopping and spending. He never took me for gro-
> cery. He told me not to go, because it wasn't a good neighbor-
> hood. . . . I had no slippers to wear at home, so I asked him for
> one. He bought me one that was one size bigger. So I was in a
> state, that I couldn't even go out to buy a pair of slippers. . . .
> During Ramzaan, I had kept Roza, but he did not. You know I
> couldn't eat anything the whole day. He never got fruits or any-
> thing for me. It was very hot those days. I had found a bag of
> coins in a drawer. I didn't know that they were old rare coins. I
> took a couple and bought orange juice. Later he told his friend
> that I had stolen his money.

Although Geeta's husband put her name on their bank account, he never
let her withdraw any money. Her name was on the joint checking account, but she was never given any checks. Interestingly, however, when
they went grocery shopping, he used to make her write the checks, which
could have been an attempt by him to outwardly present another image
of himself than what he actually was. He never gave Geeta any money,
and no money was ever left in the apartment. Thus he forced financial
dependency on Geeta as a mechanism of isolating and controlling her.

Isolation is not limited to women who come as dependents or to
any specific class. Through Malti's narrative we see the intersection of
class and gender in the way women experience isolation and intimidation as well as the cultural constraints that some South Asian women
face as immigrants. At the time I interviewed Malti she was in her late
forties and had lived in the United States for more than twenty years.
Divorced at the time I interviewed her, Malti had had to give up her job
when she married a doctor in a love marriage. For both of them it had
been their second marriage, although Malti did not know about his first
marriage when she married him. When Malti married for the second time,
her parents were so upset at her violation of Hindu tradition—first by a
divorce, and then by a second marriage—that they stopped talking to
her and moved in with her brother's family, who took the same approach
to Malti. The only supportive family member had been her sister. One
year and two months into her new marriage, she had a daughter, much
to her husband's disillusionment. From then on he began abusing Malti,
especially by isolating her. Recounting her isolation, Malti said:

> It started getting from bad to worse. When he was home, it was
> constant criticism. I could never be right. He would get up in
> the middle of the night. He stopped taking me out anywhere,
> whether it was a party or people's house. I was probably becom-

ing like an unpaid maidservant at home. . . . Within a period of a week it would happen three or four times [intimidation]. He said I couldn't go anywhere because I wasn't working. He would say that I have no support because I had married him. I could not make any phone calls. The rules of the house were very strict. I couldn't call anyone. He would call the house often to see whether the line was busy. If the line was busy any particular time, I had to tell him why the line had been busy at that time. If I had received a phone call, that was O.K., but his argument was that he is a doctor and the line should always be free for emergency calls, which I could understand. He would check the mileage in the car before he left and after he arrived to see if I had done any local trips. The garbage and the refrigerator were checked. He wanted to find fault in everything I did. He did not want me going anywhere.

I could not call anybody. I hadn't seen my friends. I hadn't been in touch with any of my friends during this time. I don't think any of the neighbors knew anything. These were huge houses. We had a four-bedroom, five-bathroom, indoor swimming pool. People looking from outside were thinking that I was leading a lavish life, but I had to account for everything even when I spent my own money [that she had saved from her previous job]. Every move of mine had to be explained. I was becoming very tense because I did not know what would turn him off. I didn't have anybody to go to. I started feeling very uncomfortable about that. I couldn't call my sister who was in [a southern state]. She did not realize anything was going on. Since I was not calling her, she wouldn't call me often. Because it's a reciprocal thing. You call somebody and they call you back. If you don't call them at all [they don't call you back]. I didn't have anybody to talk to. Every time I had to get out of the house, I had to make some sort of excuse.

However, as we will read in chapter 7, Malti managed to hold on to her job and finally left her husband one evening when he was still at work. Her case demonstrates the way in which the lack of a support system can have serious ramifications for abused women and makes them more prone to isolation and control by an abuser. Malti had deviated from the normative order by divorcing and remarrying. This was most likely seen by her parents as a great source of family shame and a loss of honor for them in their community. In the South Asian culture, where the family is so important, the lack of family support places women in an extremely vulnerable situation. Through Malti's narrative we see both the cultural and the structural constraints that women can face.

In some cases, cultural limitations combined with gender role conditioning make even highly educated and financially independent women feel pressured to be accountable to their spouses and their families. Economic alienation occurs when a woman feels a sense of exclusion from basic economic decisions and control over her wages (Abraham 1998). This is described here by Usha, a thirty-year-old insurance agent, whose narrative I will focus on in greater detail in chapter 6. According to Usha, her husband and his family took all the money she earned, giving her only $20 a week. She says:

> And then they [her husband and in-laws] would give me twenty dollars a week. With this I had to pay my gas and for all my lunches. Things kept getting hard because when you go out and all, you have to contribute to other things. You have to maintain your attire. . . . First I started talking that I need some more. Then the father-in-law started interfering. Then the brother[-in-law] started interfering more and more. If I go for grocery, why did I spend it? They would open my groceries and go through everything. How much I spent on it. Whatever I do at home is wrong.

In an attempt to gain some economic independence, Usha opened an independent bank account. When her husband found out, he put pressure on her to close it. When she did not initially comply, he beat her and threatened to call his father and brother to also beat her. By controlling the finances, men ensure that immigrant women remain isolated and abused due to a perceived, and often real, inability to leave owing to their lack of viable alternative options as dependent immigrants. Most important, the inability to seek financial support from their own families back home and the lack of any source of financial support in the United States other than their husband exacerbates isolation through financial entrapment and increases the abuser's power over his wife.

Isolation by and from Family and Friends
For immigrant women, isolation stems not only from one's relationship with one's husband but also from the lack of friends and familial support in a foreign country. For immigrants, culturally appropriate mechanisms of intervention in family problems by respected kin or valued others frequently do not exist, thereby making it difficult to seek help and leading to an increased sense of social isolation and alienation (Lum 1998). In nearly all my interviews, the women spoke

about their isolation in terms of both the lack of mechanisms of social control over their abusers and the limited emotional and instrumental social support that they themselves received while in the abusive relationship. Back in their own home country, for Shahida, Geeta, and other such South Asian women, a husband's lack of interpersonal interaction may be compensated for by social ties to their own family, their friends, or other members of the community. Members of families and friends may act as a buffer against stress and abuse. Through their relative physical proximity, family members and friends can act as a mechanism of social control on an abusive spouse and reduce isolation.

Many immigrant men and women find themselves in the United States without any equivalent friends or supportive relatives who can be such buffers.[2] For immigrant women who come as dependents, the situation is made more difficult because the social interactions with friends, relatives, and in some cases co-workers that the couple tends to have are primarily with the husband's friends. For example, although Shahida had a cousin in the States, she had not been able to contact her. It was only when Ahmed threatened to send Shahida back to Pakistan that Ahmed's friend's wife (B) took the initiative and contacted this cousin. Shahida says:

> When B heard everything, she said that this has gone too far. She told me not to go back to Pakistan. I have a cousin in ———. B took her phone number, as she wanted to contact her. So they talked to each other. I had never spoken to this cousin. Ahmed had forbidden me to talk to anybody. I have quite a few relatives, but he usually criticized them and told me not to talk to them. I think he knew that if I did talk, then all this would come out. So I was completely cut off.

When the friends are primarily the husband's, their loyalty frequently rests with him, thereby increasing the woman's sense of social isolation. This was the case for Geeta. Within four or five months of Geeta's arrival, Ramesh began battering her when she did not speed up the process of completing her medical qualifying exams so that she could support his family back home and sponsor them to the United States. Geeta says:

> He asks me, "When are you going to pass the exam? They [his family] want to come to States." I told him I don't want to pass the exam for some other thing and I need one year for each paper, because there is no need for me to work right away, he is earning and we have one support. Then he threw me on the bed and he started stamping his feet all over my body. After that again

one day, he put oil on the stove to heat to pour on me. When he started boiling oil on the stove, and he said he would pour on me, I screamed and went to the bathroom and called my friends. I was screaming. The neighbors heard me screaming, and they called the police I think. The police came and my friend's husband came at the same time. At that time, I didn't know how the police here look. I thought they were the security people of the apartment. The police said that they have to talk to me. My friend's husband said that it is nothing, only a wife and husband matter. They said that the lady has to tell us. My friend's husband told me in my language to tell them it is nothing, and I said it is nothing. So I told them and they left. I didn't know that they were police. The friends took me to their house, they started talking like it was my fault the police came. They said that if the police come, he [Ramesh] will lose his green card. He used to play according to them. He used to spend money on them. . . . In the beginning I didn't seek [help] because when I told someone, he used to be nice to them. When I told my friend [Ramesh's friend's wife], he would take her shopping and spend money on her. She used to tell me what a nice person he is. He is God. He is very sensitive and you have to treat him like this and this. . . .

Once he threw me out of the apartment. I held to him strongly, so that again I would go inside the room. It was winter and the middle of the night. The area where we were living was not a good neighborhood. It is not like here, the apartments open outside. He used to bang the door. He would take the telephone with him so that I could not make any telephone calls. He threw away all my clothes. If I made any call, when the bill came he would start shouting. For every small thing, he would pick up a fight. I told my uncle. He said that it is usual between wife and husband.

In Geeta's case, her only relative in the States trivialized the abuse by saying it was common between spouses. Her only other source of support, the couple that Geeta and Ramesh socialized with, not only denied the abuse but actively supported her husband by compelling her not to say anything to the police and blaming her for jeopardizing her husband's green card status. Thus immigrant women often find themselves socially isolated as friendships are centered around the abusers' interests and needs with the dependent wife having little or no say in the matter. Not having anyone to talk to, answer questions, provide basic information, or support her against her abuser increases a woman's sense of vulnerability and social isolation as a new immigrant. Given the collectivist orientation of South Asian culture, the importance of social interaction with friends and family and its importance to a woman's social well-being cannot be underestimated. This sense of community is often lacking for both immigrant men and women in the United States, thereby contributing to isolation and abuse.

Isolation by the Ethnic Community and Other Formal Institutions

Social isolation for recent immigrants and ethnic minorities in general occurs in complex ways at the most impersonal and outermost level of social interaction, based on their ethno-gender positioning. Every society has its normative expectations and mechanisms of social control. For ethnic minority immigrants, the sense of social isolation at the outermost level is often increased, given the contradictory and conflictual relations that arise from the intersections of ethnicity, class, and gender in the United States. As a function of their position as an ethnic minority in the United States, members of the community often find themselves socially isolated both because of the stigma attached to their ethnic identity and because of the discriminatory practices of dominant groups and institutions. Excluded from attaining mainstream jobs, ethnic minorities often work in the ethnic subeconomy, where immigrant entrepreneurs are still less willing to do away with traditional gender-role divisions than U.S. middle-class couples (Min 1992). For the individual, whether he or she works in the mainstream or the ethnic subeconomy, the nature of American capitalist society allows little time for socialization. Work is all consuming, and the stress of remaining in the work force is so high that it leaves little time for social interaction. When a woman works outside the home, it is seen as an extension of her domestic obligations. Usually little or no time can be devoted toward building friendships, thereby increasing her sense of isolation (Mazumdar 1989a).

Given that the structure of American society contributes to racial, ethnic, and class-based divisions, there is little social interaction that cuts across these divides. In addition, the perceived cultural hiatus between South Asian and mainstream American culture, coupled with ethnic stereotyping by the dominant society, indirectly forces immigrants to seek out their "own people" to gain a sense of belonging in the new country. For abused South Asian women this seeking out can become problematic. Not only do they experience the isolation and dependence stemming from leaving behind the support system of the larger family back home, but they also have to deal with the lack of support from institutions as well as the cultural chauvinism within their own communities (Narayan 1995). In the rhetoric of cultural chauvinism, the mainstream South Asian community elevates their cultural values, especially in terms of gender relations, as the best and to be upheld at any cost. Often this is at the cost of not addressing domestic violence as it erodes the model minority image of South Asians in the United States. Dasgupta and Warrier (1996) discuss the way in which the larger community condones violence against women by ignoring or dismissing their problems so as to portray the immigrant community in cultural-specific ways. Such strategic silences exacerbate abused women's social isolation, as will be discussed in greater detail in chapter 6.

For abused immigrant women the pain and loneliness of coming to a new country, the lack of familiarity with the new environment, the separation from family and friends in the home country, the emotional, social, and economic dependence on the citizen or lawful permanent resident spouse, coupled in some cases with language, cultural, and structural barriers, increase the sense of isolation in a foreign country. These factors, combined with the anonymity of immigrant families, make it conducive for South Asian immigrant women to be trapped in abusive marriages and help enable their perpetrators to remain unaccountable for their actions. Immigrant women's unfamiliarity with formal American institutional support systems contributes to their perception that they are unable to cope on their own in a new country and as such increases their dependency on their abuser (Abraham 1995, 1998; Krishnan et al. 1998; Lum 1998). The result is that frequently women who are victims of marital violence have no family or friends of their own to turn to in a crisis situation and thus experience social isolation not only at the interpersonal level but also at the community and societal level.

For many of the women, isolation is one of the most painful and disempowering aspects of marital abuse in a foreign country. The isolation stems from many factors, including fear about their legal status, economic dependency, lack of proficiency in English, restricted mobility, and the lack of information about viable alternatives. Cultural notions of the consequences of leaving an abusive partner and the probability of cultural labeling within the community deter some women from seeking help and increase their sense of isolation. Thus isolation tactics deliberately used by the husband to increase his power and control over the wife in a social environment that is alien to her, the privatization of the home and atomization of South Asian women in the United States through lack of social interaction or community support, and the marginalization of ethnic minorities in the dominant American culture all have major ramifications for immigrant women's lives. As a result, a violent space is created through the institution of marriage, a cultural chauvinist community, and a racialized society whereby men can silence women, use coercion on women's bodies, and not be held accountable for their violence.

5 | Sexual Abuse

In many cultures, levels of sexual aggression deemed acceptable by men within marriage often normalize women's experiences of sexual abuse. Sexual abuse is often tolerated by institutions and by cultural beliefs that uphold the superior position of men, the sacredness of the family, and women's socioeconomic dependency on men (Dobash and Dobash 1992; McWilliams and McKiernan 1993; Maynard 1993). Sex is an important mechanism of power and social control in an abusive relationship and is used by men as a way of attaining and maintaining a relationship of dominance and subordination that is central to the patriarchal order. Within marriage, men have traditionally had more power than women have. Given the asymmetry of spousal power relations and cultural notions of sexuality, sexual abuse within marriage is often the hardest to name.[1]

In this chapter I explain how women define and understand their own experience of sexual abuse.[2] Sexual abuse is defined here as a range of sexual behavior used by an individual to exercise power and control over another. It includes sex without consent, sexual assault, rape, sexual control of reproductive rights, and all forms of sexual manipulation carried out by the perpetrator with the intention or perceived intention to cause emotional, sexual, or physical degradation to another person. Using an ethno-gender perspective, I argue that South Asian immigrant women's experiences of sexual abuse within marriage should be explained by incorporating gender, class, ethnicity, and immigrant women's positioning or social location based on a bicultural context (Abraham

1995). The interactive effect of gender and ethnicity should include an understanding of how sexual interaction can be physically and psychologically coercive to immigrant women as they renegotiate their lives in a new country.

In South Asia, violations of a woman's body, particularly within the institution of marriage, are frequently justified through cultural values. These values make violations, particularly rape within marriage, "ethically permissible" (Mazumdar 1998, 130). South Asian immigrants frequently transport some of these cultural beliefs and patterns from their country of origin as part of an effort to re-create an authentic community ethnic identity in the United States and thus avoid assimilation (Mazumdar 1998). This has major ramifications for the social construction of immigrant women's ethnic and gender identity and has implications for their experiences of sexual abuse. Abused immigrant women may also feel discouraged from speaking about or reporting sexual abuse owing to their perception and experience of ethnic, class, and gender discrimination in the United States. Thus the dominant ethos of marriage and family as sacred and the relative isolation of immigrant women in the United States render the silence around sexual abuse pervasive in South Asian communities.[3]

Drawing upon Liz Kelly's concept of a "continuum of sexual violence" as a means of discussing the range of sexual abuse that women experience, I include South Asian women's narratives of sexual abuse that do not always specifically use words such as sexual harassment or marital rape (1988, 115). This is appropriate given the South Asian cultural milieu and the different languages used during the interviews. On the basis of my analysis of the narratives, I focus on three forms of sexual abuse: (1) marital rape and sexual assault; (2) sexual control through manipulation of reproductive rights; and (3) sexual control through the construction of the "sexual other." These forms are not exhaustive; rather, they are some of the important ways sexual abuse occurs. I also briefly describe sexual abuse by significant others besides the husband in the immigrant context.

Masculinity, Femininity, and Sexuality in South Asian Cultures

In traditional South Asian culture, patriarchal authority and the control of female sexuality are important values related to the construction of masculinity and femininity, and are often interpreted within frameworks structured by major social, economic, political, and legal institutions. To understand the different manifestations of sexual abuse experienced by South Asian immigrant women, it is therefore essential to understand what comprises South Asian masculinity and femininity. We also need to understand the norms of sexuality and marriage, since the iconicization of South Asian women has a major impact both within their nation-states and internationally.[4] These norms and values are frequently the foundation for sexual relations within marriage and get transferred in complex ways into the immigrant bicultural experience in the United States.[5] What we are is not always what we would like to be, but to some degree what culture makes of us, through the regulation of norms (Thapan 1996). What we are is also based on cultural validation by the institutions of that society.

Femininity in South Asia is defined in terms of both submissiveness and power. Unlike the Judeo-Christian ideology, female sexuality in South Asian culture is associated with female power (Mernissi 1987; Wadley 1994; Mazumdar 1998). Drawing from her interviews, Susan Wadley states in her study of Karimpur:

> Female power is allied to female sexuality. Two themes emerge here: first that there is a relationship between digestion/eating and sexuality, and second, that women have greater sexual power than men—they can "digest" (*Hazam karna*) twice as much as men. Although many of the comments made by the village residents focus on men lusting after women and women seeking to escape, the greater digestive capacities attributed to women are markers of phenomenal female sexuality and female powers more generally. (1994, 41)

Similarly, Dasgupta and Warrier point out that "the concept 'Shakti,' femininity in control of her own sexuality, and its real life translation, 'Virangana' (warrior woman), is a pervasive image that is widely accepted in Indian society" (1996, 255).

Despite these more powerful images, however, there is a general tendency in mainstream South Asian cultures to primarily construct femininity in terms of submissiveness, inferiority, self-sacrifice, nurturing, good moral values, docile demeanor, social dependency, and chastity.[6] This is particularly so in the socialization of females and especially so in the realm of sexual relations, with its emphasis on female virginity.[7]

South Asian cultures ascribe a high value to women's purity. This is especially understood in terms of premarital virginity. Most women are socialized to believe that loss of virginity prior to marriage means shame, loss of family honor, and social ostracization if it becomes known. The sexual purity of the woman is a measure of the male honor of her family and kin as it ensures caste purity and/or legitimate heirs to propertied classes (Yalman 1963; Uberoi 1996). Hence there is considerable pressure to harness women's sexuality by limiting their social interaction with other men. Sexual relations prior to and outside of marriage for women are taboo; family honor is closely linked to controlling women's sexuality.

Sherry Ortner (1978) states that all complex agrarian societies have some form of a "virginity complex" based on the importance of the connection between inheritance and legitimate birth as a criterion for determining status inequalities. The construction of female sexuality is closely connected to the maintenance of the social order and legitimate inheritance (Ortner 1978). A man's honor and his own legitimacy rest upon the control of his female relatives, while a woman's honor is linked to her own sense of shame. Sexual transgression on her part can jeopardize her position in the material, spiritual, and social world (Young 1993). In some segments of South Asian society, this leads to young women's seclusion for fear that other men will taint their sexual purity. The assumption is that women's sexuality must somehow be controlled, since female premarital virginity is an essential cultural prescription that benefits men. Thus men in South Asian culture are taught to be controllers of women's sexuality (Wadley 1994).

Until recently, for many South Asian women, especially for those raised in South Asia, open discussions of sexuality and sex with parents, elders, or at school were relatively rare and somewhat forbidden in the socialization process. This is not to assume that all South Asian women have the same experiences growing up or to minimize the differences that arise based on women's location in terms of class, religion, status, or region (urban/rural). In fact, these differences play an important role in power relations and issues of the sexual accessibility of women. Rather, it is to indicate that the overarching culture in South Asia is one in which there is not much open discussion of sex, and women as a gender category are discouraged from being sexually active prior to marriage. Irrespective of material specificity, the one image that is central in the dominant religious and cultural rhetoric is that of the "true" South Asian woman in terms of purity, docility, keeper of cultural traditions, and family unity (Abraham 1998b; Dasgupta 1994; Mazumdar 1998). It is this image that is then extended to the immigrant context with little attention to the ongoing contestation of such images by the women's movement in South Asia.

Since the normative order denigrates sexual activity by unmarried females, understanding one's own sexuality and the nature of sexual interaction at times is drawn from stereotypes from popular culture and in some cases individual experiences of sexual interaction or sexual coercion by a family friend or relative.[8] Until recently, popular films continuously presented icons that focused the viewer's attention on the relationship between men and women, portraying specific qualities such as self-censored sexual repression as essential for women, glorifying chastity and condemning premarital sex (Dasgupta 1994). These popular culture images, especially in South Asian films, illustrate punitive outcomes, both personal and societal, for sexual transgression. Thus the representation of women on the social-structural level, through popular culture, is potentially replicated within each individual and becomes the basis for sexual knowledge, values, and behavior (Collins 1990). Sexual purity is understood as the burden of women for the honor of men, family, community, and country.

Masculinity in mainstream South Asian cultures is defined to a large degree in terms of men's power, virility, and ability to control women's morality and sexuality. If an important component of femininity is sexual purity, a defining feature of masculinity is sexual virility. South Asian men are socialized to believe sexual virility is an indicator of masculinity and that male sexual needs are natural. The fact that access to women is controlled through the larger culture of virginity and chastity brings forth complex intersections of class, caste, and religion in men's contact with unmarried women. Therefore men's sexual knowledge prior to marriage may be drawn from pornography or limited sexual interaction with women who are constructed as the sexually exploitable other, based on their caste or class status or a man's perception of a woman's morality.

In South Asia, the traditional normative order socializes men to believe in their sexual prowess and socializes women to believe in the need to fulfill their husband's sexual desires without really addressing their own sexual needs. South Asian men are socialized to have expectations of their sexual needs and assumptions of female accessibility that justify forcing sexual access, especially within the context of marriage. This sexual access is supported by legal, religious, and social definitions of women as male property and sex as part of the obligation for exchange of goods (Bart 1979; Bacchetta 1994; Uberoi 1996; Abraham 1998b). Male domination and the fulfillment of male rights are thus an essential component of gender relations. This has consequences for women and men's sexual relations within marriage and can lead to sexual abuse, particularly marital rape.

Forms of Sexual Abuse: Marital Rape as a Male Marital Right

The sexual repression of women in South Asian cultures compels both men and women to view sexual intercourse for women as acceptable only within the confines of marriage. Traditionally, men are taught that sex is their masculine right as a husband, and little attention is placed on socializing them to fulfill the sexual desires and needs of their wives. As the dominant cultural rhetoric upholds the subordination of women by men as an integral part of the gendered construction of the family, the socialization of both males and females in the context of sexual relations within marriage emphasizes sexual gratification for men and the suppression of women's sexual needs. Given the notions of masculinity and femininity, men assume that it is their responsibility and marital right to take control of sexual interaction and affirm their sexual prowess. This can result in marital rape. Marital rape can be defined when a husband forces his wife to have sex against her will. It may involve genital intercourse, sodomy, or fellatio.

Notions of natural male sexuality and ordinary sexual intercourse within marriage often normalize rape within marriages. Given this cultural ideology, many South Asian women subjected to sexual violence by their husbands find it hard to reveal the abuse. They have not only been socially conditioned to acquiesce to the needs of their husbands but are silenced by the larger culture and structure that legitimate men's dominance and women's subordination in the patriarchal order. As Stanko puts it, women "learn to define their worlds and thus their experience as less important than men . . . [and therefore] . . . internalize and silence many of their experiences of sexual and/or physical intimidation and violation" (1985, 17). Among the women I interviewed approximately 60 percent spoke of being forced to have sex with their husbands against their will.

Yamuna's story about marital rape is not an uncommon one for many South Asian women. Yamuna explains:

> My first contact with him came after the wedding. That's when I realized what a horror the whole thing was. You know that it's not the easiest thing being in a hotel, I mean being with someone you don't even know and you are starting off a new thing. I think I must have been nervous actually. He started off very aggressively. . . . He was very aggressive. I mean the whole act was like,—I, I almost felt like I was raped or something like that. It was very aggressive. He knew that there was no response from me but he continued obviously. He said, "You should not be shy". He just took it to be shyness. . . . I just couldn't get myself to talk. I think if I had spoken, I may have just said no. Then he turned off the lights and all. And I thought, um, one has to go through this sort of thing—your mind is prepared for some

things but your body just isn't. And I couldn't say no. I didn't say no and I went through it all. . . .

I guess I felt violated. The way he treated my breasts, not only was it painful, uh, uhh it was very painful, definitely just very painful. I don't know what I had expected. It's not as if I did not know anything, but I was without any sexual experience. It's not as if one had read enough, one had talked enough of these things to know what things are like. But I guess I didn't expect violence. And definitely I must have expected tenderness and some kind of gentleness. This aggression really threw me off. It was fortunate that next morning my parents, my mother didn't see. After that, we went to his sister's place. The next morning I was in a state of shock, I just could not get myself to say a word to him. And then at some point I said O.K., I mean I am married to him now.

Many women are sexually inexperienced when they get married and are emotionally unprepared for the wedding night. Although women often know that they will engage in sexual intercourse, they anticipate that sex will at least fulfill some need for intimacy. Their concept of sexual intimacy is based not on practical observation or experience but on elements of popular culture such as films and books that romanticize and idealize the wedding night. These films and romantic fiction often portray the wedding night as the coming together of mind, body, and soul, where sexual pleasure and intimacy is felt by both parties. Often the images portrayed are of women demurely but eagerly waiting for their husbands to show them the pleasure of sexual intimacy and ultimately the joy of motherhood. Since the films are not sexually explicit, the concept of sexual intimacy in marriage remains relatively vague and left to the imagination of the viewer.

If the wedding night becomes sex without intimacy, many women like Yamuna feel empty, lonely, and objectified. The sexual act thus becomes one in which women are silenced, controlled, and subordinated. Often rape occurs in the first night with the husband justifying the woman's silence as shyness. As women are supposed to be virgins when they marry, men attribute a woman's lack of sexual experience, reluctance, or silence at his aggression to shyness on her part as a bride. The assumption that nonparticipation culturally implies shyness in the case of the woman and must be overcome by the husband is closely connected with cultural notions of femininity, masculinity, and gender role expectations. Women often keep silent out of shock, dismay, and because they have been socialized that a woman's ability to place her husband's needs before her own is the glue that holds their marriage together. Many of the women I interviewed talked of their lack of sexual knowledge and experience. Simultaneously, many expressed the pressure they felt to hold the marriage together, because marriage is an important cultural marker of a woman's identity and social status in South Asian culture. Thus rather than enhancing the marital relationship, the gender expectations within a marriage lead to power and control. These expectations are one of the first impediments to the development of a happy and egalitarian marital relationship and, later, the basis for continued sexual violence through the appropriation of the wife's body. Yamuna explains:

> We went to ———. We spent about four days there. He seemed to want sex endlessly—all the time. And I don't know the way he went about it. It was terrible, even if I tried saying no. The first night I was silent but by now I had kind of said let's not. He did not listen. He absolutely said no. He just put it down. He said you just can't be like this. . . . He always said the word shy. He said you can't be shy. You must be bold like them [American women] and do what I ask you to do because if you can't please me, I'll probably have to look for it elsewhere. Also sexually he would like to do things, like uh, um, like he would hurt me. Like say when he put his fingers in my vagina, like he would try putting fingers up my vagina. He would put two or three fingers. It would hurt. I said, "don't do it." And he said "no." There was no way [that he was going to stop]. I just couldn't physically throw him off—maybe I could have done it or something. I don't know. I couldn't just get myself to do this kind of thing. Maybe I was afraid that if I tried, if the slightest aggression on my part would make him more violent. Maybe he would beat me or things like that. . . . He would do things like I remember one occasion, he forced his penis into my mouth. I just wasn't prepared for those things. For him the whole thing was like a big game, like some big play. Once I remember, I was lying and he just squirted his semen all over my back and started laughing at me.

Studies point out that immigrant Asian women in the United States are at a higher risk of sexual abuse than their American counterparts because they may be socialized to believe that they have fewer sexual rights than their husbands (Ho 1990; Lum 1998). For men the assumption is that male aggression is natural and a normal part of sexual intercourse and sexual activity. As Yamuna recounts, rather than provoke her husband and risk his anger or desertion, she capitulated to his abuse. In

South Asia, consenting to marriage generally assumes consent to sexual intercourse with or without a wife's consent. Lack of consent within marriage is not treated as rape; the concept of marital rape is generally absent in the culture. Rinita Mazumdar (1998, 134) notes that marital rape has "ethical permissibility" in Hindu culture.[9] Using three different illustrations, she demonstrates that the justification for this permissibility is based on the following assumptions involving the notion of obligation: first, that entering into marriage obligates the female to fulfill all duties that her husband deems fit, regardless of her own wishes, or face the consequences; second, that entering into a marriage obligates a woman to produce progeny and therefore any actions on the part of the husband to achieve this goal are justifiable; and third, that marriage involves the complete transfer of ownership of the woman (a burden) from her father to her husband. This transfer of woman as property assumes that the husband has all rights and that the father gives up any rights and obligations in relation to this property. Mazumdar contends that it is from this notion of obligation that marital rape gets justified within the South Asian context.

The legal interpretation of rape in many South Asian countries is also extremely limited and affects individuals' social construction of marital abuse. In Pakistan, Islamic law does not view rape of a wife as a legal offense. Similarly in India a woman being raped by her husband is not a legal offense (unless she is less than fifteen years old). The law assumes that a man has a right to sexual intercourse and that the woman does not have the right to withhold her consent to it, as she is her husband's property (Lawyers Collective 1992).[10]

Under Indian law, rape is defined only in terms of achieved penile-vaginal penetration, thereby excluding nonconsensual acts such as vaginal penetration by fingers or other objects although these may cause considerable physical and psychological injury.[11] Cultural notions upheld by the legal system strengthen men's assumption that sexual abuse is permissible because there are no cultural or legal sanctions against such behavior. Although these laws may vary in the immigrant context, ignorance of the laws, the cultural chauvinism of immigrant men, and the relative isolation of immigrant women allow sexual abuse to continue. Like Yamuna, Jayathi, a forty-three-year-old woman, currently divorced and working as a staff person in a hospital, speaks of her husband's insensitivity, abuse, and assumption of sexual right in their marriage.

> He was just too quick, too rough, and too crude. He did not think about making my feelings more pleasant. . . . All I felt was pain. . . . After the children came, the kids and I would be in

one room [husband's decision] and he would be in another bedroom . . . whenever he felt like having sex . . . he would ask me
to come to his room. . . . After that he would send me back to
my room, go because the kids are sleeping there alone. It made
me feel cheap. Like I felt I was whoring myself for him. There
was no intimacy, no compassion, no friendship, no companion-
ship between the two of us. I always felt that I was the cook,
housekeeper, nanny, and then his prostitute.

Within the context of traditional South Asian patriarchal marriages,
men initiate the sexual act, define its nature, and determine when it ends,
while women rarely have any say in the matter. The lack of sexual gratification or sympathy leaves women feeling that there is no room for intimacy and caring. She becomes the object and sees herself as an unequal
participant in sexual activity. The sexual act is one in which women
are silenced, controlled, and subordinated and experience bodily alienation (Abraham, 1998a). Sex then becomes defined by men for their pleasure and for women's reproductivity. This is not to say that women do
not rebel and try to change their sexual relationship or that all men behave in this way. Rather it is to show that in an abusive relationship,
the baggage of an overwhelming cultural prescription makes the marital relationship unequal.

Marital rape and sexual control is not only justified by men in terms
of women's shyness but can also be a punitive mechanism. Like Yamuna
and Jayathi, Zakhia's husband felt it was his right as a husband to sexually control Zakhia. However, he did not justify marital rape and sexual
assault as shyness on Zakhia's part but as her punishment for his alle-
gation about her immorality. Zakhia, a thirty-three-year-old woman with
a seven-year-old daughter, migrated to the United States with her husband, who had been sponsored by his elder brother. Our interview was
conducted in Hindi.

Zakhia explains that her husband did not work and that it was she
who had to support the family with her low-paying job as a garment
worker. Although he had never abused her in Pakistan, three months
after his arrival in the United States he began sexually abusing and hitting her, claiming that she was sexually involved at her workplace. She
says:

My husband would bother me at night. He would accuse me of
doing immoral things at the job and for being tired at night. He
would beat me and then do whatever he wanted to . . . he never
asked me at all. He did whatever he wanted to do. If I refused
then fights would start. He would never apologize. I had to

apologize to him . . . he used to say, I am married to you, I don't
have to ask or apologize for anything.

Here aggression and violence are used to justify punishment for a perceived transgression as well as to reaffirm masculinity and a husband's
control over his wife's body. Zakhia's husband assumes that she is deviating from her role as his wife and treats his own behavior as a form
of social control, punishment, or revenge for her alleged infidelity.

A woman's sexuality is perceived as being under control within
marriage. Thus when the husband feels that he has no control over his
wife's sexuality and that there is the possibility that she may experience
her sexuality independent of him, he seeks to regain this sexual control
(Thapan 1996). Studies have also shown that when there is status in-
compatibility, that is, when the husband whom society expects to be the
head of the family has lower educational or job opportunities than his
wife, the risk of marital violence increases (Hornung, McCullough, and
Sugimoto 1981; Gelles 1997).

In the United States, the interplay among culturally sanctioned sexual
rights to a woman's body, status inconsistency, and the discrimination
based on the ethnic, class, cultural, and structural location of immigrant
men and women may indirectly exacerbate sexual abuse. Such abuse is
also partly connected to the larger culture of sexual violence in the United
States and assumptions by South Asian men that they must control their
women's sexuality in what they perceive to be a sexually permissive culture. At the same time, it is often the stereotyping of ethnic minority
women and men and the cultural prejudice of mainstream American society that silence sexually abused women for fear of the ramifications
of any protest for their families and communities. The racial, ethnic, and
class discrimination that minorities have to contend with from the institutions from which they seek help often deters abused immigrant
women from addressing their concerns. Torn between the gender discrimination within their own community and the racism of the dominant culture, many immigrant women remain silenced and continue to
experience sexual abuse.

Controlling Women's Reproductive Rights

A husband's assumptions of his right to control his
wife's sexuality often extend to include his power to manipulate her reproductive rights. We have seen that protecting women's virginity and
harnessing women's sexuality is linked in the larger South Asian culture to ensuring men's right to legitimate heirs. Here sexual abuse by
controlling a woman's reproductive rights implies controlling a woman's

body by controlling her choice of and access to contraceptives, her decision to have a child, or her right to an abortion. Control of a woman's reproductivity by South Asian men is viewed as part of their entitlement as husband and patriarch. It is important to note that regardless of a woman's choice in the matter, reproductivity is also closely linked with a man's power to deny or perpetuate the notion of motherhood for a woman. Some of the women I interviewed talked of the different ways that their husbands sexually abused them by forcibly impregnating them, battering them when they were pregnant, or forcing them to have an abortion.

For example, Zarina, who had four children in the first five years of her marriage and whose love marriage was described in chapter 2, explains how her husband controlled her sexual and reproductive rights.

> Most of the time he would force himself on me . . . he did not feel any guilt and would go about his activities like nothing happened . . . after my fourth child, my sister's friend suggested I go on the pill . . . but my husband was reluctant to buy them. He himself never wanted to use condoms or anything . . . and by making me pregnant time and time again, he was trying to tie me down to him.

For Zarina's husband, her pregnancies were a visible proof of his virility to the outsider. While confining Zarina to the home and motherhood, he himself sought other women to justify his normalized sexual needs, especially during the times that he sent Zarina to her parents' home for the delivery of their children. Underlying this sexual control through impregnation is the larger cultural belief that producing progeny is the natural desire of men and women. This belief is also the basis for defining a wife's sexual relationship as primarily oriented toward motherhood rather than toward her own sexual desire or gratification.

Tara also experienced considerable sexual abuse and battering. At the time I interviewed Tara, she was thirty-seven years old, working as a secretary, and had two children, ages twelve and three. She had left her husband a year earlier after having lived with him in an abusive relationship for almost fourteen years. Tara, who went back to South Asia to get married and who sponsored her husband's migration to the United States, explains the way in which her sexual and reproductive rights were controlled. In her case, her husband controlled her not by forcing her to have children but by forcing her to have abortions, thereby denying her the right to motherhood as well as causing her psychological trauma for going against her religious beliefs as a Christian.

Those first two years, I got pregnant three times. He didn't want to be a father at that time. Three times he forced me to go for an abortion, which I was totally against. But I couldn't do anything at the time . . . he said we can't afford it, we are not settled. We have nobody to watch the baby, things like that . . . when I finally got pregnant for the fourth time, I told him that I was not going back for the abortion. I convinced him somehow to keep the baby. He was not happy throughout the pregnancy but after my son was born he started playing with him . . . but a year later he said he can't stand this, he does not want to deal with the responsibilities, it is too much for him, he is too young for all this, he should be enjoying his life. He started going out and having an affair.

In Tara's case, her sexual abuse was accompanied by battering, especially when she questioned her husband's relationships with other women, thereby challenging his power and the notion of the obedience, docility, and subordination of a wife:

He slapped me. He punched me. I was already two and a half months pregnant at that time. I lost the baby. He punched me in my stomach several times and he kicked me. He would hit me in places where you can't see the bruises. Like under the thighs, under arms or my back. He will grab my arms real hard and in the morning you could see. With the dark skin I have, you could still see the marks. That day, he took my clothes off and hit me with a belt. . . . That same night, he also put some pins and needles between his fingers and he used to punch me with that. I know it is hard to understand that, but those little pins with a head on top [thumb tacks]. I finally called my sister, that day. She lives just two minutes away from me. . . . She came straight away and tried to stop him. . . . She called the police and then she said just get out of the back door . . . the first thing she did was take me to the hospital emergency right away . . . then I found out that I lost the baby.

This use of sexual and physical violence to deny a woman her right to have a child and to go against her fundamental beliefs is an extreme case of controlling reproductive rights. Four of the women I interviewed explicitly talked of the physical abuse they encountered during their pregnancy. A woman may be more prone to abuse when she is pregnant, because her husband may feel that there are competing interests inter-

Prema Vora, program director of Sakhi for South Asian Women, demonstrating against Syeda Sufian's batterer, Mohammed Mohsin. April 13, 1996. *Courtesy of Sakhi for South Asian Women.*

Syeda Sufian with Prema Vora outside the criminal court during the May 1999 trial. *Courtesy of Mathew Strozier/* India Abroad.

Members of SEWAA (Service and Education for Women Against Abuse) at a community outreach program in Philadelphia. *Courtesy of Lalita Krishnan of SEWAA.*

Two founding members of Apna Ghar, Prem Sharma and Kanta Khipple, at an evening of music, a mini fundraiser for Apna Ghar, Chicago. *Courtesy of Apna Ghar.*

Sakhi for South Asian Women with SALGA (South Asian Lesbian and Gay Organization) at India Day Parade 1994. Sakhi included SALGA, which had been banned from the parade, in its contingent as a sign of solidarity. *Courtesy of Sakhi.*

South Asian Task Force protesting FIA's ban on Sakhi's and SALGA's participation in the August 1995 India Day parade. *Courtesy of Sakhi.*

Sakhi volunteers placing posters outside a store in Jackson Heights, Queens, at a community outreach event, 1998. *Courtesy of Sakhi.*

Sakhi volunteers celebrating Sakhi's tenth anniversary on June 5, 1999. *Courtesy of Sakhi.*

Manavi volunteers protesting racism at a rally in Newark, New Jersey. *Courtesy of Manavi.*

Manavi volunteers Shamita Das Dasgupta, cofounder, and Sujata Warrier, board member, at the third annual fundraiser. *Courtesy of Manavi.*

fering with her loyalty and attention to him. Studies point to a high incidence of domestic violence during pregnancy (Schornstein 1997).

Flaunting the "Sexual Other"

In the South Asian immigrant context, a man sexu-
ally abuses his wife by manipulating the "other woman" factor as a means
of sexually intimidating his wife and exercising power and control by
sexually appropriating or rejecting her. By insinuating, threatening, or
actually having a sexual relationship with another woman, the husband
makes the wife feel sexually inadequate and alienates her from her own
body (Abraham 1998a). He also humiliates his wife by flaunting the fact
that others are sexually more desirable than she. In my interviews I found
this behavior closely linked to women's and men's notions of sexuality.
From the women's narratives it can be deduced that there is a double
standard, whereby a husband feels that he, but not his wife, is justified
in having extramarital sex. In some cases flaunting the other may be
linked to the notion that Western women are more sexually permissive
than South Asian women and therefore are easily sexually accessible.
This behavior may fit into the construct of woman as the sexually exploitable other, previously discussed. However, further research is needed.

Notions of what is perceived as western sexuality are superimposed
by some husbands on their wives while simultaneously drawing upon
traditional cultural values of the rights of a husband to demand sexual
gratification from his wife. For Yamuna this type of abuse took the form
of her husband threatening to seek sex elsewhere if she did not succumb
to his desires. Describing her wedding night, Yamuna says:

> He said, "I'm sure when you were told that someone from
> America was coming, you were expecting somebody with movie
> star looks, weren't you?—You sisters, you can communicate so
> well. I'm not so good, but you have married me now, so you
> have to live with that kind of thing." It was a very bad begin-
> ning. He went on about how things are like in America, how
> sex is like in America, how easy it was to get girlfriends, how
> easy it is to have sex in America and if I don't comply with what
> he wants, if I am shy, he would probably have to seek it else-
> where. I just couldn't get myself to talk.

Shahida experienced a somewhat similar situation upon her arrival
in the United States. In her interview, Shahida mentioned that her husband wanted her to watch pornography and perform oral sex and justified it as something that all Americans do. She says:

> He had dirty movies at home. I hadn't seen any before. He made
> me see them and wanted me to perform oral sex. Since I had

gone there, barring the time we had sex, he never kissed me or showed affection in any other way. He said he did not like those things but he wanted me to perform oral sex. After that if he wanted to do something he would. I told him that I did not like this at all. He told me that everyone does that in America. I told him I didn't like them [movies] at all. I had seen them a couple of times and when Ramzaan came I told him that I would throw them as they didn't contain anything much. I was willing to perform for him if he wanted but I felt like throwing up when I saw them. He told me not to talk nonsense. "If you don't want to see, don't see them."

Pornography often represents men in positions of power and influence over women. Russell (1993) notes that sexual objectification, typical in pornography, portrays human beings, especially women, as depersonalized sexual things. Pornography degrades women and sexualizes and eroticizes dominance and submission, which has ramifications for men and women's relationships. Further, exposure to pornography has a negative impact on attitudes, sexuality, and behavior (Moane 1996, 84). As such the view that the use of pornography is normal in the United States has implications for perceptions of sexual behavior on the part of both immigrant men and immigrant women and undermines women's ability to resist sexual acts that are against their will.

In Tara's case her husband had many affairs with both South Asian and non–South Asian women. Her confrontation of her husband only heightened his anger toward her and in one incident resulted in a sexual assault in front of her child and father-in-law. In the following narrative, Tara explains how her husband defines his relationship to other women and his anger at any challenge to this construction.

He always had affairs. . . . I found out about one of the girls because she called at home and she was looking for him. I said, "I am sorry that he is not at home." She said, "I am calling from the office." So I said, "If you have anything, call him at work tomorrow." So she says, "Who is this?" So I said, "This is his wife." She says, "Oh my God! But he told me that he was divorced." I said, "No, sorry." She started telling me, it was strange. That's how she started telling me things that he had promised her. That he was going to marry her and that he is divorced. His sister is living with him, with his little boy. I said, "It is not his sister, none of his sisters are here right now, but we have a little boy." He [her husband] was outside shopping.

After he [her husband] came back she called again. So he

went into the room. Every time anybody called, he would close the bedroom door. He used to ask me to leave, so that he would be in the room alone. After he hung up with her, he came out. He was furious. I was feeding my son and his father [her husband's father] was also sitting there. He came and grabbed me by the hair and said, "How dare you tell her that you are my wife." I said, "What am I supposed to tell her?" He dialed the phone and he said, "You tell her right now that you are not my wife." I said, "I can't do that." His father was sitting there and not saying anything. He started really abusing me. I was running from one room to another. We had a two-bedroom apartment. I was running from one room to another trying to escape. Then I went into the bathroom and closed the door. He broke the door. The frame came off. The lock came off. He grabbed me and pushed me into the tub. My son was four and half years old. He was watching, standing by the bathroom but there was no feeling there for me. He wasn't scared or crying, he was just staring. I was already hurt, like cut on my head and was bleeding. He finally called me to the phone, grabbed my hair by one hand and another hand was on my throat and said now tell that woman. He dialed the number. This lady was on the phone. So I said, "Mary, he is my husband holding me by the neck and asking me to tell you that I am not his wife." He got so angry that he hung up the phone and started abusing me, That night he abused me all night. . . . He ripped my nightgown, pushed me down on the sofa in the living room [and sexually abused her in front of her child and father-in-law].

In yet another instance of sexual power, when Tara was pregnant with her second child, she found that her husband was having sexual relations in their home with the daughter of a pastor who had come from India and was temporarily living with them.

Shahida explains how upon her arrival in the States her husband Ahmed made her feel inadequate and unwelcome by devoting all his attention to their neighbor, a divorced Italian American woman. In her case, we see how the construction of the other leaves Shahida feeling inadequate and alone in a foreign country.

He told me that there is somebody called Jen in the neighborhood. She is Italian American. He used to do his groceries with her. After two or three days [after Shahida's arrival], Jen invited us over for coffee and we had gone to her place. That day there were two of us and one of Jen's friends. Ahmed had brought his camera. The three of them were talking and taking pictures. I was sitting all alone. They asked me a few questions and then neglected me completely. They were taking pictures of each other. Even then I didn't mind too much, as I am not that jealous. I just accepted the fact that they were good friends but it was very awkward. They gave me two presents. One for my marriage and one for coming to America, but other than that they ignored me completely that day. After we went home, I asked him why he couldn't have taken a couple of pictures of me. He said O.K. and clicked a few.

Jen came to our house twice during the seven months I was there. Ahmed used to go there nearly every day. After dinner he would go. A couple of times, he asked me to come along and I went. But they sat and played cards and talked about their old friends. I used to sit there and read the newspaper. So I stopped going there myself and even he never asked me. But he used to go and have coffee. He used to go to Jen's everyday. He said that they were very good friends. She had helped a lot after his divorce and he helped her after her divorce and that they had a very good understanding. I said it is fine, but why don't we invite her to come here sometimes. We can sit here and drink coffee. But he never gave any reply to that. He used to come back around one at night. I could see from the kitchen door that her car wasn't there. So I knew that they used to go out together.

Once he tried to hit me with a brush but I managed to duck away, so he didn't hit me. I had asked him, why he got me here if he wanted to spend all his time with Jen. I would always feel that I was totally unwelcome. If I ever smiled at him, he would ignore me. I felt unwanted. I told him all this that day. He told me that I was misunderstanding the whole thing. I didn't ask him if they had any relationship. I just told him that he could take me out with them sometimes, when they went out. He knew that I was alone at home from morning. Whenever they went shopping or for grocery or anywhere, I could go along too. He didn't give any reply to that. He just banged the door and left. He had thought that because I didn't go out or anything I wouldn't come to know.

This process of using the "other woman" has multiple consequences. The South Asian woman finds herself experiencing not only loss of self-esteem but also a sense of emotional and sexual inadequacy. In some cases, she sees this as a failure in her role as a wife and feels compelled to have sex without any satisfaction for herself. In the immigrant context, the construction of the sexual other woman, frequently a non–South Asian as the foe/intruder/sexual competitor, diverts some of the resentment felt by the wife against her husband toward the foreign "other." The potential solidarity among women of different ethnicity and class is hindered by defining them as sexual competitors. This interaction of ethnicity, race, class, and gender plays a part in the process of immigrant women's experiences of abuse. Sexual competition among women in their relationships with men allows men to appropriate and objectify the body of both the wife and the sexual other, and as such allows for the continued sexual domination by men of women.

Sexual Abuse by Significant Others

Sexual abuse among South Asian immigrant women may not be limited to a woman's husband but may get extended to other significant males. This becomes extremely problematic in the immigrant context when a woman is isolated and is vulnerable because she lacks viable alternative cultural or structural support systems. Three of the twenty-five women I interviewed spoke of such experiences. They were Reena, Shahida, and Yamuna.

My interview with Reena was in Malayalam. Reena's mother and other family members (her father had died) arranged her marriage through a marriage broker. Reena's husband was a U.S. citizen. Raised in India and fluent only in her own local language, Reena came to the United States in 1986, only to find that her husband was already having an affair with his younger brother's wife. Upon questioning him about the liaison three days after her arrival, Reena was sexually coerced and beaten by her husband.

Reena's brother-in law and his family also lived with them. Having no support of her own and in a foreign country, Reena found herself more vulnerable to abuse by someone other than her husband. One day when the others were out, the younger brother-in-law sexually abused her. According to Reena:

> That night my brother-in-law molested me . . . [when the husband was away] he could not get too far but he told me not to repeat to anyone what had happened. But I repeated and he got angry. . . . I told my husband . . . when he [the brother-in-law] came to know and was questioned, he got furious and [later] beat me . . . when my husband was at work.

Although her brother-in-law never sexually abused her again, she was faced with the struggle of living in an environment where her husband continued with his affair, while she had no avenue for support in either her brother-in-law or his wife. For Shahida and Yamuna, the sexual abuse and harassment came from people who were helping them out of their abusive marriages. These women's dependency in an immigrant context made them sexually vulnerable. In Shahida's case, the husband of a couple with whom she was staying tried to take sexual advantage of her dependence on him. Shahida describes it:

> They had been very nice to me, even told my father on the phone that they were like my parents. They had helped me a lot, taken me to the airport, taken to the lawyer and all that. He is in his fifties. They told me to come over and stay with them. Since she [the wife] was studying, they wanted me to help them. The night before my meeting with an organization I was getting my papers, certificates and mark sheets ready for the meeting. She was putting their four-year-old to bed. He came into my room, sat down, looked at the papers, commented on my grades and as he was leaving tried to kiss me. I told him not to do all that and leave me alone. I was totally unprepared for this . . . he had said he was like my father. I couldn't sleep all that night. I was very scared that he might come in once she and the child were asleep. That day he had stayed home with sick leave while she had gone out. He asked me to sit down with him and talk. I did that. He said that he wanted to help me and not to think of it [of his sexual advances] as right or wrong. I told him that I couldn't do that because right is right and wrong is wrong. I knew how much his wife respected him. I was so scared as I had nowhere to go. I told him that I had to go and meet someone. He said that he was not happy that I was leaving without finishing my talk with him. When I rushed out he said that I was misunderstanding him and that he could take advantage of me if he wanted to. I told him that I wasn't blaming him for anything and rushed out.
>
> The next day on the way to the meeting he said that I shouldn't hide from him as he wanted to help me. He said that I fall sick because my body fluids were not circulating. I told him that I knew all that and that I used to be sick even before my marriage. I told him not to touch me at all. You see, he had started touching me with his hands whenever he passed me. I told him that he had never behaved like that when I visited them with Ahmed. As soon as possible I called [the South Asian Women's organization] and told them everything. They got me

out of there without making his wife suspicious. I could have told her everything but I don't know if she would have believed and I did not want to hurt her. Even now we meet although I hate him.

Immigrant women like Shahida find themselves being sexually abused first by their husbands and then by their friends. Significant others take advantage of these women's vulnerability and assume that they won't be held accountable for their actions. It is the abuser's belief that he has economic, social, and emotional power that allows him to take such sexual liberty.[12] In Shahida's case, a man counted on her silence, her affection for his wife, and her desperate need for support and dared to sexually abuse her. Under the guise of protector and confidante such men may sexually harass women, sometimes, as in Shahida's case, with the excuse that it would improve her health. In Yamuna's case, the husband of the family she lived with did not touch her but constantly looked at her in ways that made her feel sexually objectified. Financially and socially trapped, she had no alternative but to stay with this family. The experiences of these three women point to how significant others within the South Asian immigrant community also become partners in sexual abuse. They participate in the sexualization of women's bodies through their sexualized gaze, language, and action.

———

In this chapter, I have tried to show some of the ways in which sexuality is constructed for South Asian immigrant women and some of the forms of sexual abuse they experience. Although I have emphasized the cultural aspects, this is not in any way meant to put forth a cultural justification of sexual abuse of South Asian women. Culture does not imply ignoring the structural impediments that women experience in abusive relationships (Abraham 1995, 1998b; Dasgupta and Warrier 1996; Baig Amin et al. 1997). That many immigrant women look toward members of their own community for support in the United States is not only a result of cultural identification but arises from the reality of the race, class, ethnicity, and gender divisions that typify United States social relations. Hence, I caution here against reading this chapter as if cultural factors alone are the basis for sexual violence. Such a reading allows the appropriation of cultural constructs for political gain by those in power as well as further oppressing the disempowered both within one's own country and in the immigrant context.

6 Internal and External Barriers

It's Not Only the Abuser

Two years ago my friend called me to say that she had some sad news. Her friend Mary Mathew had died. I asked her, "What happened?" She said, "I don't know. Someone from the church called and told me. They were such a nice couple. He was a quiet man." My friend then went on to say that they had all lived in the same neighborhood at one time and, although she had moved, they had tried to keep in touch. The last time they met was about five years ago during Christmas. The day after my friend called me, I went over to her house to find out how she was feeling. She gave me a strange look and said, "It's not good news. It's a case of domestic violence. Apparently it had been going on for some time. The husband had lost his job and she was working a double shift as a nurse. They had slowly become isolated and, while her friends at work knew about the battering, she was not willing to report it."

On July 10, 1997, Mary Mathew, a South Asian immigrant woman from the Kerala Christian community, was battered in her home by her husband just before her fiftieth birthday.[1] Her husband, Thomas, called the police at 2:57 A.M., saying that there was a medical emergency (*India in New York*, July 18, 1997). Upon their arrival, the police found Mary's body in the bedroom. She had died from internal injuries caused by her husband's brutal battering. Mary's twenty-two-year-old son and seventeen-year-old daughter were at home when she was murdered.[2] According to the police, this was not the first time that they had been called to the Mathews' residence. Two weeks before Mary's murder, the police had been called to investigate a domestic dispute, but no charges were filed against Thomas Mathew. Two weeks later, however, he was to be charged, this time for Mary's murder.

Mary Mathew is one among many South Asian women who are abused daily, but this does not make Mary simply a statistic. Mary Mathew had a right to live a life free of violence. Some of us got to know about her murder from friends or from brief reports in local newspapers. While publicly noted, Mary's death did not lead to any major mobilization or social uproar in the community.

Mary Mathew went to a South Asian church, worked in a hospital as a nurse, lived in a good neighborhood, had friends and co-workers who knew of the abuse, had indirectly sought the help of the police, and had met with a counselor. Yet little seemed to have been done to prevent her murder. Often it is the failure of both individuals and the institutions they represent to provide the help battered women need that entraps them in violent relationships and, in cases such as Mary's, ultimately leads to their death at the hands of their batterer. In many cases no one ever finds out about the abuse. This chapter focuses on internal barriers to stopping domestic violence, such as parents, in-laws, and the South Asian community, and external barriers, such as the police, courts, and health care providers.

When marital abuse is discussed in the United States, the focus is primarily on the relationship between the couple. Such a framework assumes a specific family form, in which only the spousal relationship is important. It precludes an understanding of family forms in which other relations within the family may contribute to marital violence. It also does not take into account the multiple barriers that some women, especially ethnic minority immigrant women, may face from important others such as family members, friends, the larger ethnic community, police, the courts and health care providers. These issues, of course, exist for nonimmigrant women as well (Richie and Kanuha 1993; Campbell, Masaki, and Torres 1997; Gelles 1997). But we need to understand how certain factors other than the behavior of the abuser heighten the immigrant woman's vulnerability to abuse. Important others can become partners in crime through their passive or active participation or through their strategic silence on the issue of abuse.

Internal Barriers
Parents and In-laws

The absence or presence of parents and in-laws influences the dynamics of social relations within South Asian families in the United States. The persistence and changes in family values and structure among immigrant South Asian families can be a source of oppression, contestation, or support for women. Previous research has shown that inequality within the home and generally between women and men can diminish both social control and the cost of being violent (Laslett 1978; Gelles 1997, 135). For abused immigrant women, factors such as the privatization of the family in the United States, shifts in their socioeconomic status, and the social construction of the normative order in South Asian families can have a negative impact. In addition, competing loyalties stemming from their position as women and as members of an ethnic minority can become impediments in ending the violence perpetrated against them.

Examinations of marital violence in the United States are generally based on the assumption that the dominant family form is couple oriented and the notion that love is the predominant criterion for marriages. Such assumptions exclude the variations in family structure and the impact of the reorganization of family relations within the immigrant context.

The abuse that South Asian immigrant women in the United States experience often stems from the perpetuation of "traditional" South Asian cultural notions regarding the position a woman occupies in her husband's home. This construction of "traditional" is manipulated to serve the interests of the abuser and is based on imagery that frequently has little to do with the reality of the changing roles of women in South Asia. Added to this are the structural factors that ensure immigrant women's dependency and isolation in the interlocking systems of domination within the United States.

Parents and in-laws become partners in crime when they directly or indirectly partake in the abuse. To understand their role, we must first briefly look at the power structure within the South Asian home. Although there are ongoing changes in family relations in contemporary South Asia, there is a long cultural history whereby men have exercised considerable power and authority over women. However, while men have the primary power, authority, and decision-making ability within the family, they frequently delegate the control of younger women to older women (Fernandez 1997, 440). Traditionally, once a woman marries, her position is usually defined in terms of her conjugal family and is characterized by her subordination to the men in the family and to the older women, especially her mother-in-law. In South Asia, even when a young couple does not live with the husband's family, his family exercises control over the couple and especially over the daughter-in-law (Fernandez 1997). According to Mies (1980), in India a married woman's primary relationship is to her mother-in-law rather than to her husband, while her husband's is to his father. Therefore the mother-in-law exercises considerable power over her daughter-in-law on the basis of her position as the husband's mother in a patriarchal society.

The manifestation of a mother-in-law's power and control may include abuses such as limiting her daughter-in-law's free time, demeaning her by the type of work she is given to do within the home, and monitoring her activities. This power includes the freedom to say negative things about the younger woman's family and other overt or covert behavior that demonstrates her subordinate position. In part the mother-in-law seeks to prove to her daughter-in-law that despite the marriage, she, as the husband's mother, still has the ultimate loyalty and love of her son rather than his wife. Even when the mother-in-law exercises control, ultimately this power is indirectly controlled by and is in the interest of the men of the household. By promoting favoritism, and developing jealousy and conflicting interests between the women, there is an attempt to prevent a sense of solidarity among them. Daughters-in-law, however, realizing their common oppression based on their position, on occasion band together and support one another in times of need. In some cases, certain members may play a mediating role within a joint family. A woman's parents or siblings may also attempt to act as buffers against some of this possible violence and to use both cultural and legal mechanisms of mediation and social control to protect their daughter or sister.

Immigrant women, whose husbands have family members in the United States but who themselves come as dependents with no family support, find themselves more vulnerable to abuse from the husband and his family. When only the husband has family in the country, his family members often seize upon the wife's lack of traditional support mechanisms. Drawing upon South Asian values regarding gender, age, and relationship-based hierarchies as well as the woman's unfamiliarity with her new surroundings, these members exploit her. She is frequently emotionally and physically abused as a way of demonstrating their power and control as the husband's relatives. Since the woman is without the support of her own family, there is less pressure for the men and their families to be socially accountable. The lack of accountability on the part of the abuser's family reduces the social costs of perpetrating violence as a mechanism of power and control. This was the case for some of the women I interviewed. They were forced to conform to gender, age, and marital relationships assumed by the woman's in-laws as normative in South Asian culture. At the same time these relatives also exploited the fact that their daughter-in-law or sister-in-law could not seek her own family's help on a day-to-day basis because of geographic constraints.

In an important reconfiguration of power relations in the United States, it is frequently not the mother-in-law but the husband's siblings who actively abuse the woman. This can be partially explained as an outcome of the shifting patterns of authority stemming from migration and economic factors. Parents or in-laws in the United States tend to be retired, unemployed, or themselves economically and emotionally dependent on their sons. An outcome of this dependent relationship is some erosion of age as a source of power and respect, and its replacement by economic worth, particularly of the men. Thus traditional paternal authority, based on age, is diminished in the immigrant setting. There is a reconfiguration of familial authority and social relations within the family derived from individual male economic worth. This is exemplified in Usha's case. Usha was twenty-one when she came to the United States after marrying her husband in an arranged marriage in India. At the time Usha was married, her family lived in India and her husband's family lived in the United States. Her mother-in-law died prior to Usha's marriage and it was her husband, brother-in-law, and father-in-law who abused her. Although Usha's husband had his own home, his brother and father exercised considerable control over Usha's life, coming to the house on a weekly basis. Usha describes what happened:

> Everything which needed to be done in my house has to be okayed by his brother. His brother is like a father to him. He is almost twenty years older than him. He dictated the whole time—in the marriage and over here. His father wanted to have a lot of respect and everything, but nobody was willing to give it to him. So he would take out all his frustrations by yelling and screaming to anybody who is in front of him. Apparently I was the newest member in the family. The other sister-in-law was living here for twenty-five to thirty years. She didn't care. She had had it with them. She would just take a car and go outside whenever they started screaming and yelling. I was a victim of everything.
>
> One day I talked to my sister-in-law [a few months after her arrival]. She said, "You know Indian marriages, this is how it happens, since you married you are there for life. Look at me. I am suffering all the time and I have to do it." So I just crushed my feelings and thought that I got to stay here and I continued to stay.
>
> After the baby was born, things just continued to get worse. Somehow he was not happy. They were miserly people. If I spent any money or go out, it was very hard . . . I had to go to India

for my sister's wedding at one time. They said you can't do this, you can't do that. You can't spend so much money. I was making equally or more than he was but I had no right to spend. I was getting [given] twenty dollars a week and I had to do everything with that twenty dollars. . . . First I started talking that I need more. Then the father started interfering. Then the brother [in-law] started interfering more and more. If I go for grocery, why did I spend it? They would open my groceries and go through everything. . . . It was slowly getting very bad so I made the determination that I have got to do something. I opened a separate account. My husband got real upset. The whole family was very upset. They got physical at that time. . . . They started abusing me physically. They kicked me. Father-in-law came and twisted my arm and threw me in the family room. It was an everyday problem. They wouldn't let me go to work. They would close the garage door on me. They would lock all the doors so that I could not go out of the house. It was real, real hard. . . . When I was going to India for my sister's marriage they would not let me go. I had to call my neighbors to let me out of the house. Otherwise, I would have missed the plane. When I came back the same thing started again.

As we see from Usha's narrative, marital abuse for South Asian immigrant women is not just a dyadic relationship between a husband and wife but frequently involves other family members who exercise considerable power and control. This has numerous consequences for the abused woman, because the monitoring and control of her activities is not limited to one individual. The situation not only becomes doubly oppressive but more dangerous for the woman as she struggles to protect herself at various levels. Moreover, the frustrations of fathers-in-law over their diminished power in contrast to their sons is frequently transferred to a show of power against their daughters-in-law. But frustration is not the only motive.

Sometimes parents, especially those who live with their sons in the United States, feel emotionally, economically, and socially dependent on them and are reluctant to do anything that might jeopardize their own status. Often this is due to their relative sense of powerlessness based on economic dependency. Added to this is the traditional patriarchal belief that the parents' home in their old age is with their son's family. Thus patriarchal beliefs and economic dependency combine to contribute to a father-in-law's attitude toward his daughter-in-law's abuse. His complicity in the abuse perpetrated on a daughter-in-law takes the form of not actively stopping the abuse when it occurs in front of him or supporting the son by denying the abuse occurred when questioned by the authorities. This was the case with Tara's father-in-law. We read earlier that Tara, two and half months pregnant at the time, was being battered by her husband in front of her four-and-a-half-year-old son. Her father-in-law, who was living with them, did little to prevent his son's violence. It was only after Tara's clothes had been ripped apart by her husband and she had been badly beaten with a belt that her father-in-law even made a token attempt to stop his son. Tara says:

> Finally my father-in-law came and said, "Stop that." He was just saying Stop! Stop! But he was not really trying. He wasn't attempting to stop him in any way. Finally he came in the room and said Stop that! My husband said, "it is none of your business. This is my home. I will do whatever I have to do. You go and stay in your room." So he went and that was his biggest excuse. He said that his son had told him it wasn't his business, so he didn't get involved.

Later, despite the fact that Tara was clearly battered, her father-in-law supported his son by helping him clear up the mess created in the living room where the abuse occurred. Further, he supported, through his silence, his son's denial that anything had occurred when the police questioned his son.

Similarly, Mallika found herself as a dependent spouse completely under the control of her husband's family. In her case it was the sisters-in-law who were abusive, and one of the sister's husbands exercised considerable power. Here, power was based not solely on one's generation or relationship to the husband but on complex relationships connected to sponsorship and employment status.

Mallika is a thirty-four-year-old Indian from Gujarat. I interviewed her in Hindi. Mallika is the youngest among four sisters and one brother. All her family is in India. Her father was a farmer who died some years ago and her mother lives with Mallika's brother and sister-in-law. Mallika married her abuser in March 1990 when she was thirty-two years old. Her husband is six years older than she, and his family lives in the United States. It is the second marriage for both. Mallika came to the United States in the middle of 1991 as a dependent spouse. I interviewed Mallika at her relatively middle-class home in late 1992. One year and four months after Mallika's arrival, her husband walked out on her. A petite, friendly looking women with short hair, wearing a salwar kameez, Mallika met her caseworker and me at her front door. With typical South Asian hospitality, Mallika invited us to eat what she had prepared specially for us before I conducted the interview alone with her. Her husband had left a month earlier. With no means of conveyance and no income, Mallika continued to stay in their home, making a meager amount of money by cooking Indian dishes for members of the community which were collected and distributed by a volunteer from a SAWO. Mallika tells her story:

> My husband is forty years old. He has three sisters and he is the only brother. He is the second [oldest] in the line. He works for my brother-in-law [his sister's husband] in a store. He has been working in the store for ten years. He is staying in his sister's house. This is my second marriage and his second marriage too. . . . In the beginning his attitude was very good. After the marriage he was there in India for a week. His behavior was very good. Even when I came here, my husband never told me anything. But my sister-in-laws tried to run my life. When I told my husband about it his attitude changed towards me. . . .
>
> My sister-in-law would get the groceries in my house. Until recently, my sister-in-law used to buy the clothes for me to wear. [Mallika was given no money.] My husband would never take me to the stores with him. He wanted me to go with my sister-in-law. After six months I told my husband that I didn't want to live like that. These people bothered me all the time. I couldn't go anywhere on my own. My husband had instructed me to go out only with my sister-in-law. When they came to our house, there were times that they would talk to me, and other times they would just ignore me for no reason. One day I was in the kitchen making chapatis and my sister-in-law came in and snatched the rolling pin from me and started making chapatis on her own! It really surprised me, as I had never seen anything like that in my house.
>
> He would tell me to go out only with my sisters-in-law. If I got a pair of jeans, he would tell me not to buy such expensive clothes. [Later on when] he would take me to stores and if I picked up anything, he would not let me buy it. When we went for groceries, he wouldn't let me pick up anything that I wanted. But he never said anything when his sisters bought things for our house. I couldn't even turn on the heater at home. During the winter, I used to work in the second shift and come home at twelve o'clock at night. It was my first winter and I felt very cold. When I wanted to turn on the heater, he told me it was broken. So I told him to get it repaired. He said that he had got

it repaired and still it was not working. Actually most people think that when people come new to America, they don't know anything and won't understand anything. I asked a few people and came to know about the switch. When I turned it on I realized that the heater was working. I started the heater. My father-in-law and my husband didn't like this at all. So we fought about that too.

I used to work as a cleaner in a sewing company. I worked there for two months for half days. I have also done table work in —— company. Later my husband and brother-in-law made me leave that job.

When I started having fights with my husband, he called my brother-in-law over to our house. The brother-in-law said that I have no rights in this house. I can only live and eat here. Then my husband told him that I had opened a separate account. I told him that I had done it because he had refused to open a joint account with me. I was willing to give him my paycheck if the account had my name in it too. Then my husband said that I had to leave my job and close my account. So I left my job and closed the account. Whatever money was there, he took it away. I had four or five paychecks from my job and my husband deposited it into his account.

The two younger sisters-in-law used to work. They would come to our house in the evening after work and stay until six o'clock. They would dictate to me about everything. "Don't call anybody. Don't write to anybody." They would never say anything directly but indirectly they always made me understand that if I wanted to live in this house, I had to follow their commands. They would come to this house and tell me how to live in my own house. My father-in-law, my mother-in-law, or my husband would never tell me anything, but my sisters-in-law would always tell me how to live in this house, how to eat, and what to do. When I told all this to my husband, he told me that he didn't want to hear any complaints, but if I had to complain, then I should go and do it in the "big house." When I asked what the big house was, he said it was the eldest brother-in-law's house, the brother-in-law that had sponsored all of them. He said that I had to voice all my complaints to him. I told him, "you are my husband—why should I tell him?" I told him just because he sponsored us, that doesn't mean we have to live under his control. I am willing to show him respect, but I am not going to run my house according to his command. So the fights started. When I started complaining, my husband stopped talking to me. He stopped having any marital relationship with me.

The day he left the house he slapped me. What happened was—he used to bring back the lunch that I packed for him. He was very short tempered and would get angry with me over small things. Even when I spoke to him nicely, he would get angry. So I asked him why couldn't he speak nicely when I am doing the same. He told me that his nature was like that. I told him if he continued to behave like that, how could we develop a relationship between the two of us? We were having dinner at that time. He took a glass and smashed it and told me that if I wanted to live in his house I had to live the way he wanted and had to obey him. I said that I was willing to act according to his wishes, but why did he get angry with me for no reason, or scream and yell at me for no reason. He slapped me on my cheek. He went away and said that he would not come back to the house. The next day I called him at his sister's house but he didn't come back. He had three conditions. I had to obey his three sisters. I had to put all my money in his bank account, as there would be no joint account. I was ready to put my money in a joint account, but didn't want to put my money in his account. His third condition was that he didn't want any child. I didn't agree to all three conditions. Instead of living like this, I would prefer to live alone.

Mallika's narrative points to the complex ways that family and power relations become reconfigured in the United States for many immigrants.

In Mallika's case it was her husband who worked for his sister's husband's business. This employer-employee relationship permeated the power relationship within the family and contributed to Mallika's marital abuse. Mallika's husband was economically dependent on his brother-in-law. Mallika's sister-in-law therefore drew upon both cultural and economic mechanisms to exercise power over her. Women like Mallika thus find themselves confronted with marital abuse from multiple sources, including various members of their husband's family, due to the complex employment relations that shape the immigrant subethnic economy in the United States.

Racism in the United States often limits ethnic minority immigrants' work opportunities and has a negative impact on the family (Espiritu 1997). Lack of institutional recognition of the qualifications immigrants may bring from their home country results in downward occupational mobility for many. Language barriers and the lack of appropriate education or work skills required to get high-prestige or high-paying jobs force a sizable segment of the South Asian population to work in low-paying, labor-intensive jobs that exploit and oppress them (Mazumdar 1989a; Espiritu 1997). In an attempt to counter some of the labor market barriers, many South Asians, like other Asian immigrants, have tried to carve out a niche for themselves in small self-employed businesses such as small clothing stores, restaurants, vendor stands, and twenty-four-hour convenience stores.[3]

Either to make ends meet or to maximize surplus value and cut labor costs, the owners of many of these micro-enterprises employ their own family members or other more economically disadvantaged co-ethnic workers. For example, we saw in chapter 3 that Seema's husband was a harsh employer, forcing her to work as unpaid labor in the motel that he ran. She became the unpaid employee of her husband and was abused both at home and in her work.

The working conditions in these micro-enterprises tend to be extremely exploitative, with no opportunity for economic mobility. Yet many ethnic immigrants have little choice but to work in the subethnic economy due to the institutional and racial barriers they encounter in the mainstream economy. Although many South Asian women have been educated in their home country, they don't have the type of preparation demanded by mainstream employers to get a job that can provide financial independence in the United States. This too contributes to a woman's sense of dependency and financial entrapment within her marriage. Others find that their qualifications and training may be outdated because they have abided by the culturally prescribed norm and focused on their primary role as wife, mother, and keeper of the home. The resulting loss of self-esteem and confidence, especially in an alien country, deters them from seeking jobs or, in some cases, obtaining them. In addition, the long hours put into many of these micro-enterprises contribute to isolation for members who work in them, especially for those women who have to work both at home and in these stores. Working in stores and motels, as Mazumdar (1989, 17) says, "affords little time and opportunity for women who run them to develop other skills or establish close friendships."

Often the pressure and loss of status for men in the work force plays out in the home through marital violence. Job insecurities and racism affect not only the family life of those working in the subethnic economy but also that of professionals.[4] As Espiritu points out, "racism in the workplace threatens the employment security and class status of Asian American professionals and places an undue stress on the family" (1997,

71). Thus employment factors contribute to stress within the family, which in turn often contributes to marital violence.

Many immigrant women feel that some of the patriarchal forms within the family in South Asia have been carried over to the United States without the equivalent traditional support system of South Asia. Given the geographic distances, immigrant women feel that they lack the support of their family back in their home country. Physical proximity to a woman's family, however, does not necessarily mitigate marital violence. Often in South Asia these so-called traditional support systems are not very supportive, particularly if the situation involves a divorce.

New forms of oppression are added for immigrant women as a result of the position they occupy in the United States. Their vulnerability to abuse increases due to language barriers, inadequate information on available resources, and the limited accessibility of support systems coupled with the institutional discrimination they frequently experience as ethnic minority immigrant women. The inability to seek financial support from their own families makes getting a job imperative for these South Asian women, yet the dehumanizing qualities of the structural arrangements of the major institutions of American society become barriers. Often it is this vulnerability—being in a foreign country, invisible to outsiders, with limited institutional support—that allows a husband and his family to abuse without being socially accountable.

Rehana, a twenty-six-year-old Pakistani woman with whom I conducted an interview in Hindi and English, told me that her husband had beaten her, financially deprived her, taken away her passport, ticket, and green card and then ultimately abandoned her. She explains:

> I spent a year with ——— because of my lack of English knowledge. In spite of hating to stay there, cooking for him and working for him and his brothers. I didn't dare to go out, as I thought I wouldn't be able to survive without English. But then I took a bold step and now I am on my own.

Finally, in some cases, I found that women were initially hesitant to tell their parents back home in South Asia about their abuse because they felt that the physical distance prevented their parents from being effective mediators and that they would only cause their parents to worry. In other instances, women mentioned an initial reluctance to tell their parents about the abuse because they felt that they should first try to resolve the problem on their own. Later, however, as the situation worsened, the women told a sibling or relative who could personally convey the information to their parents. Often parents learned about the abuse when they visited their daughter or when she went back to South Asia.

The majority of the women I interviewed perceived the members of their own family to be generally sympathetic to their plight upon knowing about the abuse, but not all of these kin were initially comfortable with the option of a divorce. As most of the women pointed out, the importance of marriage for South Asians and the fact that women's social status is intricately tied to it make women and their families view divorce as one of the last options available. Often this is contextualized in terms of the implications of a divorce for the woman's children, her unmarried siblings, and her own situation, as she grows older. As Mallika mentioned, despite her own hesitancy, her mother and brother were keen that she marry again. They felt the life of a single woman to be problematic. For immigrant women, not having an economic or social support system coupled with the geographic distance from their parents can often be a drawback in parents' comprehending the gravity of the situation.

Friends

Family and friends, because of cultural, social, and economic constraints, often prevent abused South Asian immigrant women from seeking support services. Women's attempts to seek out friends and the community are shaped by the responses they anticipate or receive from such sources. Many abused women are reluctant to seek support from friends and members of the community after their initial attempts are either rebuffed or met with sympathy that is soon followed by advice to be stoical so as to preserve the family. In some cases when other women try to help the abused women, their husbands dissuade them from interfering in other people's family matters. For mainstream members of the ethnic community, protecting the sanctity of the immigrant home implies the protection of South Asian culture. Time and again the women I interviewed spoke about the closed-mindedness of the South Asian community and the reluctance of their South Asian friends to actively intervene in ways that would send the abuser the message that his abuse would not be condoned. Abused women fear that, rather than getting support from friends, they will be blamed for their abuser's behavior. At the same time, friends who may want to help fear the community's reaction to them for actively supporting an abused woman. Sometimes their reluctance also stems from a fear that helping an abused woman may entail providing temporary shelter in their own home with consequences for their family life. Thus women who are economically dependent on their abusers face a further obstacle in obtaining the support of friends who fear the economic and social ramifications. Usha explains:

> All my friends were O.K., but as they found out that I am going through a divorce everybody started disappearing . . . I think the community is very much closed about the situation [domestic violence]. Even though people see this is happening, the people are not aware. I don't think that they are aware at the 10 percent level of the things that are happening in people's home. And if it is happening, they are saying, "Oh no it is not me but somebody else." They think like this. They want to show the society that they are fine. It is just this society thing. They are deceiving themselves, telling that we are fine. In actuality, in everyone's home there are problems—some are workable, some are not. But they are just saying, this should be in the house, it should not be coming out. Lot of American families may still feel the same way but the percentages of South Asian and American people feeling this way varies a lot. Probably 30 [percent] of American families think that it [domestic violence] should remain in the home. However, probably 99.9 percent of South Asians feel that. I think it is education probably. I think that there are many different reasons. First of all we are new to this country—we don't know a lot of different things—how to act on it. Secondly, we are afraid, especially in the suburbs. Everyone thinks, "I am a doctor or I am an engineer and this and that." [They think] we are different from the poor. I think this happens for both Indians and Americans. People are afraid to change the status quo. They don't want to. They are afraid of change, what is going to happen. Who knows it might be worse.

The South Asian community attempts to put forth a collective identity that speaks to the great moral character of the community, especially as it pertains to the South Asian family. Given the public construction of the community identity in such terms, South Asian immigrant women struggle with the question of their social position if they speak out in public against their abusers. Abused women face not only gender barriers but also class and religious biases within their community.

Religion and the Community

For many South Asians, their religious institutions play a central role in defining their community identity. Temples, mosques, and churches establish and perpetuate a link with their traditional and cultural roots. Religious institutions are not places of prayer alone but, more important, are the arena for the construction and maintenance of the values, beliefs, and customs of the immigrant community (Rayaprol 1992). These centers of worship become the caretakers of tradition in an alien, modernistic society. The moral solidarity of the collective becomes of vital importance. Various social and cultural activities that bind the immigrant community are played out in this context. These religious institutions thus become the basis for social interaction and social cohesion.

The beliefs of the immigrant community collectively experienced and shared are created through social action within these religious institutions (Bhattacharjee 1992). They play a central role in the reproduction and maintenance of the gender identity of South Asian women in America as the caretakers and representatives of the traditional South Asian woman. They must be the perfect self-sacrificing wife, daughter-in-law, and mother, especially in an alien culture. Religious ideology frequently constructs family roles in ways that serve the interests of men, providing moral legitimacy by drawing upon religious texts. Religion also shapes people's perceptions of marital violence. It is frequently implicit that the primary burden of any adjustment in a marriage must come from the woman. From the perspective of most of the major religions practiced in South Asia, divorce is still perceived as a social stigma, particularly for the woman.

The importance of the woman as the glue that holds the family together is constantly reinforced by religious leaders. It is not uncommon for the clergy, when called upon in cases of domestic violence, to intervene in ways whereby the husband is lightly reprimanded but the woman is pressured to try to keep the marriage together at all costs. This is especially true in cases where children are involved. This is exemplified in Tara's case. After the severe battering that had caused Tara to lose her unborn baby, Tara pressed charges against her husband and began living with her parents. After four months of living apart, however, Tara's husband came back to Tara, pleading with her to return. In Tara's words:

> He started coming to my house and saying "I want you. I want the family back." He started crying. Every day he would come at work, call me at home to say how much he misses me and wants to see my son. He did that and some of the church elders got involved. His father once approached them. They started coming and talking. They said it is not good. There is difference but . . . Nobody could understand, nobody could understand. I kept telling no, I can't go back. They kept telling me

"No! No! No! You can't do this. You guys belong together. See he has apologized. He is not going to do this." So I went back.

Similarly, when Tara was going through the abuse, the pastor's wife, who had lived in the United States for seventeen years, said: "Tara this is your cross, bear it. We all have crosses to bear and this is yours. One day your kids will turn around and say it is your fault that now we don't have a father." Tara believed her for a long time.

In the case of Nadira, a Sunni Muslim, her husband, a Shiite, was able to use the support of some members of the Shia community and a Maulavi (preacher) to justify his treatment of Nadira. Nadira did not want a divorce or to return to Pakistan as she felt she would be socially stigmatized. However, the Maulavi supported the husband, saying that he could divorce her because she had not produced a child. Little attention was paid to the fact that he had been abusing Nadira and was using his religion to justify his treatment of her. All too often, rather than addressing the issue of abuse, pastoral support goes to the perpetrator on the basis of his religious affiliation.

The use of religious ideology to support the continued oppression of women in the immigrant context is largely a function of perceiving religion as the last bastion for the collective maintenance of traditional South Asian values. This is particularly the case in a Western society, where South Asians perceive there to be an erosion of morality, rights, and duties. Therefore, in the early 1980s, the problem of marital violence was simply not acknowledged, because it threatened the moral solidarity of the community. In Mary Mathew's case, we do not know how many of the church attendees knew of the issue or, if they knew, how many actively attempted to address the problem. Abused women use their religious institution for social solidarity and a sense of belonging, and their silence in speaking out against their abuser frequently stems from the possible social ostracism that may result from any form of public attention to the problem. My informal discussions with Kerala Christian women in the United States indicated that it is difficult to make inroads into the issue of marital violence in that community. The church takes a very strong position against divorce and emphasizes the need for solidarity in the community. This refusal to acknowledge the problem of domestic violence is not unique to the Kerala Christian community in the United States, but is also prevalent in other religious communities. Thus religious institutions that could play a role in addressing the problem of marital violence, because of their own patriarchal practices and their position on marriage, make it difficult for South Asian women who identify with their religious institution to leave. It has only been with the initiative of South Asian women's organizations that South Asian religious centers have begun paying some minor attention to the problem of marital violence.[5]

External Barriers
Police

Negative attitudes in general toward ethnic minorities demonstrated by police may influence an ethnic immigrant woman's decision to seek their assistance. If battered women feel that the response of the police will be shaped by the officer's perceptions of the victim's ethnicity and socioeconomic status, the chances are reduced that she will call the police. In addition, a victim's fears about her legal status, compounded by cultural and gender stereotyping on the part of police officers, inadequate training programs for officers responding to calls from abused women, and the officers' reluctance to arrest abusers, become major obstacles in the protection of abused immigrant women.

The literature indicates that responses from law enforcement officers to domestic violence are inadequate (Field and Field 1973; Pirog-Good and Stets 1986; Caputo 1988; Hamlin 1991; Ferraro 1993). Despite considerable change in laws, policies, and training pertaining to intervention in battering, many problems remain to be addressed (Ferraro 1989, Dobash and Dobash 1992). In the context of domestic violence in ethnic minority and immigrant communities, the responses of police to cases must be carefully scrutinized, because gender bias is not the only problem in the criminal justice system. There is increased repression of people on the basis of race, class, and sexual orientation (Ferraro 1993). According to Ferraro, "rates of arrests are much higher for low income and racial ethnic minority groups, and pressure to increase arrests may exacerbate the use of police force against these groups" (1993, 168).[6]

Saunders and Size (1986) note that officers who had traditional perspectives on women tended to take the least amount of action in domestic violence situations that needed intervention. For South Asian women, the situation becomes even more problematic. Their fear has many components, including fear of the police's attitude toward minority groups, fear of the individual police officer's apathy or insensitivity, and fear of the inability to successfully communicate the nature of the abuse to the police officers. Some South Asian women who are in violent situations in their homes but are not proficient in English are thus reluctant to seek the help of the police. In some cases, the inability of a woman to communicate her situation to the officers because of language barriers results in the officer's letting the abuser become the communicator of the situation. As a result, the abuser may avoid arrest.

Negative experiences in obtaining the support of the police can deter immigrant women in seeking their help and thus cut off one important avenue to end the violence perpetrated against them. For example, Zakhia's two encounters with the police left her feeling that the police were unresponsive to her needs. She recalls the first time she sought their help:

> He was hitting me very badly. Then he started threatening to take my life. Somehow I escaped from him and went and hid in the bathroom. Then I went outside and called the police and they came. [A female and a male came to the site.] They asked me questions but I don't remember anything. They asked him but he said that he hadn't done anything. They said that they knew that he had beaten me up, because I was lying down and bruised all over. They told him that this [is] America and you can't hit anybody here. If you hit like this then you can be arrested. He still denied beating me. I told them that he had beaten me, but he kept on denying it, saying that somebody else had beaten me up. . . . I was not able to give a full statement as I fainted, so they didn't take him. . . . I don't know what happened after that. They took me to the hospital. When I regained consciousness, I found that I had tubes going into me . . . at the hospital [they did] nothing. They just filled up some papers. Later when I became well I came back home. The next day I went back to my job, and it just continued like that. . . . I never called the police again. Why should I call them? After all I have to live with him as I am married to him. Then the people will say that she has got her husband arrested.

Zakhia left her husband twice. The first time she returned to him:

> I had nowhere else to go. I don't have anybody here. I thought if he becomes better, then I would be able to live somehow. He had asked for forgiveness in front of about six or seven people. I thought that I should give him the benefit of doubt and went back to him. After a couple of days the same thing started. Again the fights started. I had nowhere to go. All the people were seeing the fun.
>
> The second time I left I stayed with a friend for two weeks. Also my American boss supported me. She saw my husband hitting me in the street near my place of work. Then one day he came and hit me at work. I went to the police station but the police didn't listen to me. They just asked me to wait. So I went

back to work. Then my boss asked me about my problems. I said it was nothing but my supervisor said that he had seen my husband hitting me and as I was going to the police station, my husband was following me and cursing me. Even then I said it was nothing. Then I just broke down and started crying. I told them that I didn't know what to do. They told me to go to the police station. I said I had gone there but that the police were not willing to hear anything and nobody is there to help me. Then my boss helped me. She called the police and she got all the paperwork done. I stayed with a friend for two weeks. She was a Pakistani. She was not very comfortable keeping me in her home. She was scared that I would stay for a long time. She started telling me of all her problems. So I left her place and went away. Then my American boss contacted a SAWO who then helped me.

In Zakhia's case, her boss's class status and communication skills had a stronger impact on the police. One wonders if Zakhia would have sought police assistance again had the supervisor and boss not actively intervened. Zakhia's case is one that leads us at times to question the police's treatment of different classes and ethnicities. When the police take an apathetic or casual approach, many immigrant women's preconceived notions of the negative attitudes of the police are reinforced and thus become a barrier in seeking institutional help. It is imperative that police engage in building rapport and a sense of trust in the community areas where they work. In addition, the process of arrests must be scrutinized. Police interaction with an abused person should not deter her from reporting such incidents.

Some important changes have occurred in the last decade. Nearly all the states have initiated new civil and criminal legal remedies to address domestic violence (Gelles 1997, 146). States have developed programs to train police officers in the appropriate way to handle domestic violence cases and, in general, stronger action against abusers seems to be the trend. It is also important that the police increasingly get the input of organizations that address domestic violence in their communities so that they can develop a more comprehensive picture of domestic violence.

Recently I was a speaker at a domestic violence awareness and prevention program sponsored by the police department in Hempstead, New York. Such programs are an important step and demonstrate the increasing attention being paid by the police to domestic violence and its criminalization. However, responses to particular issues by the audience, particularly by abused women, indicated that the police still have some way to go in understanding the complexity of the interconnections in race, class, and ethnicity in women's experiences of domestic violence and the institutional barriers they encounter in seeking help and leaving the abusive situation.

Courts

Negative perceptions of or experiences within the court system also make it difficult for women to leave abusive relationships. The emotional, physical, and financial struggles that abused women have to go through make women like Usha dislike the legal system and the attitude of the police. As she says, "It sucks. Nobody cares, nobody cares. It is your life. Nobody cares." It is such experiences with the legal system and the associated high costs that act as major deterrents for women seeking legal recourse. If victims' experiences lead to a perception that the courts are prejudiced, that cases will be long and drawn out, that there are low rates of conviction, and that the likelihood of the victim's obtaining justice is minimal, then there is less incentive to seek legal recourse. It is rarely the case that in any crime other than domestic violence the victim is compelled to live with her abuser due to the inadequacy of the court system. Usha recounts:

This friend I had was an Indian also, however, she grew up in London and Canada. She was more like a second or third generation here. Her husband grew up in London and was fifth-generation Indian. So it was a little bit different. They supported me. As a matter of fact they knew before that. Before I went to work, he would jog around to see if it was safe for me to go out. They helped me a lot. However, they did not say I should do one way or the other. They said, "Weigh your things, whether you can tolerate it or can't and conclude what is going to happen." So I basically sat down, read these books. I was very concerned for my daughter, because she was seeing all these things. How was it going to affect the rest of her life? She was just two at the time and it came out that it is not going to be good for her. She is going to be in the same vicious cycle and she is going to see life as this. This is not what she should be seeing. She was a major reason for my decision. I could be strong or I could have done anything—but to break that marriage was very important for the child. She should not see the family as this. I spoke to friends at work about getting a divorce. One of my friends went through a divorce. She is an American girl. I have lots of American friends who supported me, even neighbors. You wouldn't believe how much support they have given.

My friend told me about a lawyer. With my luck, I didn't screen too many lawyers because I didn't have much time. I just went in and said this is the situation. I want to file. Actually, first I went not to file for a divorce. I wanted an order of protection, so that these people could not beat me. But the lawyer said that he would do everything together. I didn't know anything, that there could be some other way. So I told him. O.K. Go ahead and do everything that needs to be done. That's how the proceedings started.

I was staying in my home. I had an order of protection served. It was just hell. All three of them were served—father-in-law, brother-in-law, and ex-husband. My ex-husband was at work and my father-in-law at home. I didn't come home till midnight. They didn't know how to handle it. Later I heard that his brother had advised him [the ex-husband] not to say anything to me and to go to all the banks and clear out everything. That is what he did, the first thing. My lawyer had put a court order against all the banks but somehow it did not cover all. He had accounts in eleven different banks. So he took out the money from several and there were some that were locked. After that it was just hell, story of hell. It took us about two years to get the divorce case settled. It was just hell. I cannot describe what hell it was.

He would come out and just to make the house dirty—he would take dirt from outside and throw it on the floor and put juice on it—so that I had to come and clean it. He would go to the bathroom and not flush it, so that I had to. The judge would not let [make] him go out of the house, so we had to live in the same house. Because both attorneys were very strong. The case was from county to county. We were living there and traveling back and forth. It was hell for me and my daughter. I did think of moving out but I didn't know much about the judiciary system and my attorney said, "Don't move away from the home, they can take away your child from you." I was just sitting there, living with him in the same house for two years. It was just hell. After the order of protection, I had to call the police many times. He had been arrested after that. He violated the order of protection. They would arrest him and take him and leave him after a day or two. That is about it.

He would not give me a divorce. I had to take a no-fault divorce, because he would not do it otherwise. And it was fifty-five thousand dollars for both the attorneys. We were going through a lot of money. It all came out from the equity of the home and other savings. . . . I got [child custody]. We had to go through one psychologist. He proved that he [the husband] has no brain. The only concern in my husband's life is money and doesn't think the custody for the child [should go] to the father. He does have visitation rights. Every other weekend, he comes and takes her. But the responsibility is mine. He has only three decisions where I have to ask him. If I have to go through a major surgery, if I want to change my religion, or if I want to send her to private school, Catholic or something. Otherwise I can be independent as to what I do with her.

Negative experiences such as Usha's become a major deterrent to women wanting to use the legal system to protect them. Ferraro and Boychuk (1992) found that victims are less likely to follow through with prosecution if they find that most cases result in dismissal or a sentence of probation. This in turn incorrectly influences prosecutors' beliefs that it is waste of time to prosecute batterers. Abused women's noncooperation in prosecuting, however, is due to multiple factors. As Ferraro (1993, 172) aptly puts it:

There are many factors that influence women's request to drop charges against the abuser. Many women are dependent on men's economic contribution for support of children. Imprisonment eliminates current employment and endangers future opportunities. Several months usually pass between the violent incident and the court hearings. Most offenders are released from custody during this period and find ways to intimidate and manipulate women into dropping charges against them. Some battered women have other legal problems, such as immigration status or outstanding traffic warrants, which lead them to be wary of involvement with the courts. Women who ask for incarceration may believe that prison will lead to an increase in violence upon the abuser's release.

In some cases women, aware of the racial and ethnic discrimination in American prisons, do not want their abusers to spend time in jail. In addition, judges have also been criticized for being an impediment to a woman's receiving a fair hearing. Schecter states that advocates for battered women report that in some cases judges have inadequate awareness and "inaccurate information" about protection under the law. She says, "If the legislature has recently enacted new laws, ignorance tends to multiply" (Schechter 1982, 168). Often the courts are not aware of the marriage customs among the various sections of the South Asian community, such as the lack of legal documentation of marriages, dowry and gift-giving traditions, and sexual mores. As a consequence, women who are victims of marital violence and attempt to obtain a divorce are at a disadvantage in some rulings because lawyers and judges lack an understanding of the cultural dynamics. In addition, inadequate provisions are made for South Asian language interpreters in U.S. courts; particularly problematic is the frequent use of South Asian men whose own gender biases may influence their interpretation and seriously damage the case an abused women has against her perpetrator.

The Sakhi February 1993 newsletter described a case in which a volunteer had to explain to the judge that the South Asian male interpreter had incorrectly interpreted the information to the abused woman. More recently, in another case, however, the Immigration and Naturalization Court judge impressed me when she adjourned the proceedings upon realizing that the male interpreter was misinterpreting and that the victim was stressed by her inability to convey her testimony. In this particular case, the judge requested another interpreter, preferably a woman given the nature of the case. It is only when the court and its representatives make a serious commitment to show the public that the justice system is not biased and is sensitive to diverse needs that victims will increasingly seek a legal remedy. It is not sufficient to have policies addressing domestic abuse if they do not truly address the different needs and experiences of abused women.

Health Care Providers

According to Sherri Schornstein (1997), for many abused women victims the medical community is the first major institution from which they seek help. In my own research I found that, with the exception of extreme battering, most women who were battered and needed medical attention rarely mentioned the real source of their injury to their physician, nor did the latter inquire further into the matter. In her study of the records of fifty-two cases of women with clear signs of abuse, Carole Warshaw found that neither the doctors nor nurses addressed the issues the battered women brought to the emergency room. Although it seemed that these providers appeared aware of the abuse, this information seemed to be deemphasized or obscured in their reports. Little attention was paid to documenting the events leading to battering or finding out information that could result in more appropriate and comprehensive intervention (1993, 134–145). I also noticed that women did not identify the health care system and its providers as a potential source of intervention in ending the violence perpetrated against them. Usually their interaction with the health care system was the result of serious injuries they received from their batterers. For example, for Seema it was only when her husband poked her eye out of its socket and the police took her to the hospital that she came into contact with the medical system. Similarly, Tara was taken twice to the emergency room due to severe battering.

For immigrant women, the stereotypes, negative attitudes, and false perceptions of ethnic minorities by providers of medical care can lead to insensitivity toward the victim and an apathetic attitude toward the type of intervention she is offered. In a participant observation study of the responses to battered women by emergency department staff in four metropolitan hospitals, Demi Kurz (1987) found that the medical staff's intervention was influenced by their perception of the abused woman. For example, she found that intervention was more likely when the staff saw the abused woman as a "true victim," that is, an individual who had no "discrediting attitudes," was polite in demeanor, and was looked upon by the staff as in immediate danger. She also noted that staff members were more sympathetic and proactive to abused women who were pleasant and who were actively attempting to leave their abuser.

In some cases, communication problems can also result in incorrect diagnoses or the victim's feeling a lack of understanding by the provider. As stated by Hamlin (1991, 403), "negative behaviors exhibited by health care providers toward victims lessen the victim's willingness to seek help." In most of my interviews I found little mention of the role of health providers. Six of the twenty-five women had to seek medical help due to severe battering. Yet none of them ever spoke about going to the hospital on their own; rather, they were taken by police officers, relatives, or friends. Similarly, when asked, women spoke about the importance of counselors but invariably mentioned their preference for South Asian counselors. They felt this was important, as the counselors would be familiar with South Asian culture and therefore more likely to be sensitive to their issues. According to Usha:

> Both my daughter and me had some counseling. I didn't care much about it, because it is very important for the counselor first to understand which culture you are coming from. My counselor was American and she didn't know much about it [Indian culture]. And it was real hard for her and I had to explain to her. She would not come up to the level of what I am feeling,

which is hard. It is very hard to find a counselor who does not have preconceived notions.

Although the women I spoke with did not focus much on the nature of intervention by the medical community, my discussions with volunteers in women's organizations indicate that the receptivity of health care providers to the problems battered women experience is essential to the well-being and life chances of these women. Negative perceptions of health care providers by abused women are influenced by predetermined attitudes by health care providers about immigrant families, apathetic treatment, and the reduction of a battered woman's experience to medical facts. For immigrant women, some of whom may face language barriers, a doctor-patient relationship which clearly reflects asymmetrical power or a lack of sensitivity to the victim's emotional needs can result in negative perceptions of the health care system and deter them from seeking help in the future, thus endangering their lives. This asymmetry of power relations is also experienced by nonimmigrant abused women. In the last few years, health care providers have become much more sensitive to the well-being of abused women.

Schornstein (1997) provides an excellent overview of what the medical response to abused women should be. She explains that members of the medical community are in a unique position to gain the trust and confidence of their patients and that this gives them the power to assist domestic violence victims. By showing women that their well-being is valued, providing nonjudgmental support, asking pertinent questions, providing complete documentation in medical reports, educating patients about domestic violence, providing information regarding options and resources, and providing follow-up, the medical community can play an extremely important role in the empowerment of battered women.[7] Given the diversity of needs, it is also important for hospitals to build a network with community organizations, sensitize staff to possible cultural issues, and develop comprehensive programs that educate them against race, class, ethnicity, and gender biases.

———

While marital abuse cuts across all socioeconomic segments of the South Asian community, the South Asian immigrant woman's lack of a social support system in the form of friends and community increases her vulnerability to abuse. In addition, language barriers, unemployment, or exploitative work conditions place tension on the immigrant family and appear to exacerbate marital violence. (As we saw in chapter 3, not having a permanent green card also becomes an obstacle for women seeking economic independence from their abuser.) Although the police have become somewhat more sensitized to abuse issues, the general treatment that abused immigrant women, especially lower socioeconomic class women, experience at the hands of some police, courts, and medical practitioners is a barrier to ending marital violence. Financial constraints, procedural delays, ethnic and gender stereotyping, language barriers, and a general lack of sensitivity are all a part of the immigrant women's experience of abuse. Thus it is not just the abuser's behavior but the internal and external barriers that contribute to immigrant women's abuse. While there has been an overall increase in the public and institutional awareness of the problem of domestic violence, we still have a long way to go. Cultural chauvinism within the South Asian community coupled with the persistence of ethnic, race, and gender-based discrimination by the major American institutions result in multiple obstacles for abused South Asian immigrant women. As one abused women put it while I drove her and her children back to their home after my interview, "You know Maggie, in our community in the United States it is just not the husband, it is everything that adds up and becomes a wall that we have to really struggle to climb over."

7

Fighting Back
Abused Women's Strategies of Resistance

There are people who hear of incidents of domestic violence and respond: "Maybe it was her fault. It can't be just his fault. What is wrong with these women? Why don't they fight back? They are not children! They could have gotten out or done something about it! Why do they go back? I don't understand these women, why do they just lie down and take this stuff? Why do they suffer in silence?" Often it is easy to blame women and assume that they passively accept abuse. Studies have shown, however, that abused women do employ a number of techniques in an effort to stop the abuse, to get assistance, or to leave the abuser (Pagelow 1981; Bowker 1983; Gelles and Straus 1988; Mehrotra 1999). My research too indicates that despite the lack of resources and relative isolation, abused South Asian women engage in a variety of strategies of resistance that challenge assumptions of passivity and submissiveness. Sometimes these acts of resistance are for immediate gains, but ultimately they are a part of the empowerment process that helps many women retain or regain a sense of self (Lempert 1996.

In this chapter I focus on individual women's strategies of resistance—all the tactics that a woman uses to challenge her abuser's power and control and prevent her abuse. Although I use incidents as examples, it is important to keep in mind that women's strategies of resistance cannot be reduced to specific incidents but must be understood in the context of the multiple strategies most women use in a relationship. Class, ethnicity, legal status, socioeconomic viability, and the accessibility of alternate support systems also play a major role in determining a woman's use of strategies of resistance and their efficacy. It is not only the patriarchal relations within the marriage that influence abused immigrant women's strategies of resistance in the United States. Issues such as perceptions of ethnic and class discrimination shape women's response. For example, while a woman may resist her abuser by talking back or by seeking the help of a South Asian friend, she may be more reluctant to call the police, if her perception of them is that they are racially or class biased. In addition, the need to belong to one's ethnic community may sometimes take precedence over gender-based abuse within the marriage. Thus, for various cultural and socioeconomic reasons, many South Asian immigrant women initially feel that it is important to try to keep their marriage together or at least to try personal strategies prior to seeking informal or formal help. Initially some are also torn between their resentment toward their abuser and their sympathy to the economic and social frustrations that the abuser experiences because of his ethnic and class position in the United States.

This is not to say, however, that abused immigrant women do not use multiple strategies of resistance against their abusers from early on in the marriage. Rather their strategy is partially determined by the resources and alternative opportunities they have available. Although the decision to get out of a relationship permanently usually did not occur until the woman felt the situation was untenable, nearly all women I interviewed did take the courageous step of leaving the abuser. Thus they not only resisted their abuser but also challenged the normative order that assumes a married woman's place is with her husband and his family. Throughout the marriage these immigrant women used creative ways to challenge their abuser, seek help, or leave the abusive relationship. They strategically navigated within the cultural and structural constraints to end the violence perpetrated against them.

Time and again in my interviews, I heard of the great risks abused immigrant women took to challenge their abuser despite their relative isolation and the limited resources available to them. Women's strategies of resistance included silence, avoidance, confrontation, hiding, talking back, hitting back, challenging the abuser's fiscal control, contemplating and resisting suicide, and seeking informal and institutional help. Often women had to resist not only their abuser but also those others who deliberately or inadvertently contributed to the abuse.

With some variation within categories, I will draw on Lee Bowker's (1983) threefold typology to categorize strategies of resistance. These are: (1) *personal strategies*, such as talking, promising, hiding, avoidance, and passive or aggressive defense; (2) *using informal sources of help*,

such as family members, in-laws, neighbors, friends, and shelters; and
(3) *using formal sources of help*, such as the police, social service agencies, and lawyers. To Bowker's personal strategies, I have added contemplating and resisting suicide and challenging the abuser's fiscal
control.

Personal Strategies
Placating and Avoidance
One of the most common strategies, especially in the
early stages of abuse, is to placate the abuser, particularly when the abuser
is the husband. This is done by trying to do what he wants, praising
him, apologizing to him, wearing the clothes he likes, cooking what he
desires, and generally engaging in the activities most perceived as minimizing the abuse. Many of the women I interviewed initially used this
strategy of resistance with the hope that it would make the abuser feel
good, diffuse the tension, and reduce the probability of an immediate
abusive episode. This was particularly the case with women who came
to the United States as dependents. This strategy of placating should not
always be seen as passivity or merely giving into the abuser. Rather, it
is a type of resistance women engage in while trying to negotiate a relationship in a new country where they are isolated, dependent on their
abusers, and perceive themselves as not having many other viable options.

For example, Geeta, an economically dependent spouse in an alien
country, tried to placate her husband in the early stages of their marriage by dressing the way he liked. Often he would make her change
her clothes a number of times before deciding what she should wear.
To appease him she adhered strictly to his demand that she cook daily
for him and be bathed before he arrived back from work. With no family support and what she perceived as extremely limited options, she
used this behavior as a strategy to attempt to reduce the probability that
her husband would abuse her. In reality, such a strategy is rarely effective and most women move away from it once they realize they have
other options.

In a couple of cases, placating as a strategy of resistance was an indirect method of disproving the abuser or enhancing a woman's own
self-worth. For example, for Mary's husband, George, the notion of Mary's
large student loan, common in the United States, was a culturally alien
concept. The debt, when translated from dollars to Indian rupees, seemed
a tremendous amount and was a constant source of tension in their
arranged marriage. George had married Mary believing her to be professionally well placed with a corresponding level of earnings. The realization that she had a huge loan, coupled with his own occupational

downward mobility since arriving in the United States, brought on a large degree of marital discord. Thus when Mary's husband used the loan as a catalyst to abuse her, Mary attempted to placate him by promising that she would somehow drastically reduce the amount of the loan. To do so, she saved as much as she could from her salary and borrowed a large sum of money from her sister. This from Mary's point of view was not just a way of placating her husband but also a strategic way of taking away what she perceived to be a major source of tension in the marriage.

In some cases the strategy of placating is combined with avoidance, as was the case with Shehanaz, a twenty-two-year-old Muslim woman married to her thirty-nine-year-old cousin.

> He would verbally abuse and also hit me. I had become so used to this that I considered it trivial. I used to try and please him. Whenever we got that junk mail, saying you have become a millionaire, tell him that. But he would still keep fighting with me. Sometimes when I couldn't take it anymore, I would go out for a walk hoping things would calm down by the time I returned. Sometimes he would be in a pleasant mood when I came back.
>
> . . . Then he started bothering me to take up a job as all his pay was going toward the mortgage payment. It was very difficult for me to apply as the phone was disconnected and he never gave me money for bus fare. I tried to do whatever I could by walking. He used to get very angry saying everybody works and I was sitting home. I asked this person I knew to help me but he had bad intentions. He tried to take me to a motel. I somehow ran back home . . . I could not talk about it to anybody as they were already against me.

Other women I interviewed employed the strategy of avoidance by using another room, trying to minimize the time spent in common space. Often women's language barrier, isolation, and lack of money compel them to find ways to resist within the constraints they encounter. Many abusers take advantage of a woman's lack of familiarity with the new country to intimidate her and instill unnecessary fears about unknown others, including neighbors and the police. Thus placating and avoidance are the first line of resistance for abused women who do not have a support system and are dependent on their spouses. They feel that the least confrontational approach at this stage, though limited, may be the only viable strategy. Here again language barriers and lack of a sense of community play a role in compelling the woman to work and resist within the parameters of the spousal relationship. At some point in the relationship, however, the abused woman usually realizes that placating is not always effective because there is no way to predict the abuser's actions or reactions. Thus she begins using additional strategies.

Talking Back

Many of the women I interviewed also resisted by talking back. Talking back here includes all forms of verbal resistance. It involves questioning the abuser's attitude and behavior, denigrating his family if he has denigrated hers, telling him to stop the abuse, screaming, and confronting him about his relationships. For example, Reena says: "When my husband forced me to have sex I would say to him that he was a dog. I would tell him that I was not a dog. . . . He would say nothing. Just do it." While Reena's denegration of her husband did not have much of an impact on him, it is still an important form of resistance. It articulates her disgust at his behavior and communicates her need for respect. In another instance, Malti, who tried to appease her husband by doing things the way he liked and tolerated his emotional abuse, talked back the first time her husband physically abused her. She recounts:

> He was in the family room and got a call from his answering service . . . he said the telephone number aloud. I was cooking and I did not pay any attention. As soon as the answering service hung up, he said, "What was the telephone number?" I said, "I don't know. . . . " He got so furious, that I have no brains, I am not of any use. I think that was the first time he hit me or he did something violent. I told him at that time. This time I will tolerate this because it is the first time, even the second time probably I would let you go. The third time you touch me I am out of this house.

In Yamuna's case, when all her pleading and placating did not stop her husband from sexually abusing her, she resisted by scaring him with her screams. She recalls:

> All the time I was thinking of how to get out of there and then one night when he initiated sex, I just couldn't take it. I just screamed. I mean I started getting hysterical. I just started screaming and that frightened him a little bit, I think. I said, Don't come anywhere near me. I think I must have been down on the floor. I think he did not know what was happening. He called his brother and that's when things got out of his control and I guess he was helpless. The brother was upset and called my parents and that started the ball rolling.

Many of the women I interviewed, including Mallika, Geeta, Jayathi, Shahida, Wahida, Usha, and Mary, talked back to abusers. One of the strongest cases of talking back among my interviews, however, and one that resulted in one of the most serious cases of battering, was that of Tara. This type of talking back, though extremely dangerous, shows the extent to which a woman resists her abuser.

In chapter 5 we saw that Tara, despite her husband's brutality, challenged his demands and talked back to him by saying she would not do what he asked. She defied her husband by telling his woman friend that he was coercing her to lie. Nearly all the women I spoke with resisted by talking back at some point in the relationship, although not many talked back under the type of conditions that Tara did. Talking back is an important strategy of resistance because it voices a woman's resentment at her treatment and challenges her oppressor's power and control. Among the women I spoke with, talking back had varying effects on the abuser. In Malti's case, it led to her husband's taunting her by asking where she would go with a baby and no job. For some of the other women it resulted in their abuser resorting to some form of further verbal denigration or violence. In general, however, the women rarely took a submissive attitude and often at great risk to themselves resisted their abuser's attempts to exercise power and control.

Challenging the Abuser's Fiscal Control

Another extremely important personal strategy of resistance and one much more difficult for immigrant women, especially dependent spouses, is to limit the power exercised by the abuser through his financial control. Many women mentioned the abuser's complete control over the finances as a major mechanism of abuse and an obstacle in getting out of the relationship. Yet some of these women resisted their abuser's control by trying to open a separate bank account, using money from a hidden stash, seeking money from a relative or friend, or appealing for and obtaining some personal allowance.

As we saw in chapter 4, Usha challenged her husband and his family's control of her finances by refusing to close her independent bank account, even when her husband beat her for asserting her independence. Shehanaz, similarly resisting her husband's financial control, demanded that he give her the money her father had sent for her. Shahida too resisted her husband's financial control by first taking money from his secret stash for an emergency and, later, when her husband accused her in front of his friends of stealing, explained to them her state of penury. As a result, her husband's friends were able to persuade him to give her an allowance that she was not accountable to him for. Prior to this, her husband

had not even given her a dollar. Such personal strategies, especially shaming, though at times dangerous, can be an effective form of resistance,
given the constraints under which these women live.

Some of the women resisted by demanding joint accounts. Though
not always successful, the very process of insisting on a joint account
challenges the abuser's financial control. In addition to the husband's
financial control, the need for a minimum balance and other banking
costs are structural impediments that limit women's chances of starting
independent accounts, especially for those who have very little money.
Such structural impediments make it harder for women to resist the financial control of the abuser. Michael Strube and Linda Barbour's study
(1983) found that women who are economically dependent are more
likely to stay with an abusive husband. Strategies are needed through
which abused immigrant women and lower socioeconomic women can
obtain financial benefits such as no minimum balance requirement and
free personal banking.

Hitting Back

A few women defended themselves by hitting back,
but this strategy was least used. This could be because women were afraid
to use physical force or were intimidated by the sheer physical strength
of their abuser. It could also be that a woman feared that taking a more
aggressive defense tactic such as hitting back might exacerbate the violence against her, with a greater chance of jeopardizing her own life. This
issue needs further research. Only three of the women talked of hitting
back. Tara was one of them. One day when Tara's husband began sexually abusing her, Tara, after months of encouragement from her young
son, finally began hitting her abusive husband. She recounts:

> He was starting to force me to have sex, and I said no. I don't
> want you to touch me. He started asking why do you have a
> new boyfriend? I said no. Actually I had my periods at that time.
> I gave him that excuse but it didn't work. He still started forc-
> ing me. He pushed me down. I said no, the reason I don't want
> you to touch me is because you have touched that girl and I saw
> you, and that is enough. He said you have no proof. She was
> just there to borrow some money. So we had verbal confronta-
> tion back and forth.
>
> Then he started pushing me down, I started pushing him
> back, I started punching him back, for the first time, after all
> these years. I started kicking him back. That strength actually I
> got it from my son. . . . Actually September till December I was

abused, three days a week. Every time he abused me, my son would say, mom why do you take it, why don't you hit him back. All these three months he brainwashed me. So when he hit me that time, I hit him back, I kicked him with my feet, I punched him, I tried to bite him.

Tara's attempts at hitting back only exacerbated her husband's violence against her, and as a result she had to be hospitalized with a ruptured bladder. Thus while hitting back is a strategy of resistance, its outcome can be extremely dangerous. Tara's experience, however, did lead to police involvement and to her finally leaving her husband.

Suicide

When escape tactics fail, in desperation some women contemplate or attempt suicide. Usually this occurs when women are feeling extremely depressed, isolated, and appear to have lost hope of either changing the relationship or getting out. Isolated and alienated, the women I interviewed who contemplated suicide perceived this as a last resort when all else seemed to fail. Yamuna, Wahida, Jayathi, and a young woman called Deepa, whose husband had not only been abusive but also at one point decided to leave her, all contemplated suicide. Jayathi was the only one who attempted it, although she did not succeed. Contemplation of or attempting suicide demonstrates the sense of desperation that some of these women feel and their perception that death will release them from their abuse.[1] Suicide here is an extreme strategy of resistance, and a tragic one. Some women contemplate suicide because they see it as the only remaining means of ending the abusive relationship. This is especially the case when women perceive themselves as having absolutely no external alternative support system. As Yamuna comments: "All I needed was to get out of there. Whether it meant killing myself or running away to a safe place. I needed to get away from that place and from this man."

Similarly, Jayathi explains how three months after her arrival in the United States in 1982, frustrated and depressed, she tried to commit suicide as a way out of her oppressive life with her husband.

He had been to [a coat store] to buy him a coat. He came back and said something to me. I yelled back at him. I was just waiting for an opportunity like this. I gobbled down all the pills, including the sleeping pills. Of course, because we had had the fight I was sleeping with the children in the other room and he was in the master bedroom. . . . I told the kids. I had my son on one side and my daughter on the other. I told them that mommy is going. Please be good. God will watch over you. I will watch you from upstairs. . . . the pills must have started reacting. I was moaning and groaning. He heard me from the next room. He came and called the ambulance and the doctor at the same time. They took me and pumped my stomach and I was at the intensive care unit for four or five days.

Jayathi's suicide attempt was diagnosed as a drug overdose from depression. Counseling was recommended for her and her husband, but her husband only attended one session, where he was questioned about his abusive behavior. Despite the recommendation for continued counseling, Jayathi was forced to stop after the twenty sessions covered by her insurance because her husband was unwilling to pay for more out of his own pocket. Once the counseling stopped and most probably knowing that her avenues of support were limited, Jayathi's husband started abusing her again. Jayathi, on her part, slowly began resorting to multiple strategies, including silence, avoidance, and finally obtaining a divorce. In this case noncompliance by the abusive spouse with strategies of formal intervention and the abused spouse's lack of financial ability were a major hindrance to the prevention of abuse.

Wahida's contemplation of suicide poignantly reveals the way in which women, even in the depths of desperation, cling to the possibility of more viable options for themselves. At the time Wahida contemplated suicide, she felt that she was no longer getting any support from her family. She had struggled to get off welfare, get vocational training, and had found a job that barely provided for her chilren. She had left her husband and gotten herself an apartment, only to have him come back into her life and destroy all that she had struggled to build. To make matters worse, he was slowly trying to alienate her children from her. Desperate, lonely, and demoralized, Wahida contemplated suicide as a way out of her misery:

There was so much mental abuse, so much torment, and so much emotional abuse. He started accusing me that I want to go out to work, because I want to flaunt around, I want to play around with guys. He couldn't stand to see that I was supporting my kids and myself. His manly ego couldn't sit there and take it. He used to purposely make me late to work. I used to try very hard. I wanted to keep this job. No matter what the pay is, I want to keep this job. I started out at fifteen thousand. It wasn't enough for the kids and me but it was something. Something is better than nothing. It was better than welfare. I said, no, I have to go. There was so much, so much, so much, mental abuse now.

So much emotional abuse. I couldn't take it any more. He would say bad things to the kids. He would say your mom is no good. Your mom is bad. He would tell me that your kids hate you. So I said, now you are trying to turn the kids away from me. And he was driving me so insane, that I thought that I was going insane. I was totally mad. It was not even six months of my job, and I was totally mad. I said I can't take it any more. He drove me to commit suicide.

In 1991, I left the kids. My oldest had gone to school, I left the other two with him at home, and I walked out. I thought that I was really going to kill myself that day. And I went and just sat on the lake. It was a cold February morning, below twenty degrees weather, cold and snow. I didn't think of anything. My mind wasn't thinking straight. I was so distressed . . . I had given him hundred and fifty dollars, and he said that he is going to give it back right away, as he had to pay the lease on his cab. I said O.K. I am giving it to you, but I need it back, I don't have a single penny to go to work. And he promised me that he would give it back to me. He didn't [and I could not go to work that day]. I was so frustrated. On top of it, he is talking all these things with me, trying to torture me more. I didn't have anything. He wanted me to lose this job. He wanted me to be helpless again. He wanted me to be dependent on his way of life and I refuse to do that. I didn't want to lose the job. I thought that I was just going to kill myself. So I went to the lake, sat there for three hours. I sat there thinking and thinking and thinking. I thought I am really going crazy.

Then I thought I am not the one who is crazy. He is. I work too hard to get here, to be on my feet again, and I am not going to lose it. The kids are small. I constantly kept thinking of the kids. The kids don't deserve him. Because if something happens to me, my mom is not going to take them in. He will just take them to India, dump them in his parents' house and he will be off. So I thought about the kids. I thought that I am not going to prove to the world, that I was really crazy, and he is all right. I said that I am not going to do this. I was sitting there, and I remembered I read it in Indian newspaper about an association started for Indian domestic violence women. So I walked into a SAWO and [a staff member] was there. I told her what I was about to do. She was glad that I came in. First thing she told me, go get your kids. So I went and got my kids. And stayed in the shelter for two months. I left the house. All I did was take my immediate belongings, and some important documents, like my passport, citizenship paper, and the kids' birth certificates. I just took my immediate clothes, and some of my work clothes. I didn't take anything else and I went back to work.

Although some of the women I interviewed contemplated suicide, none of the women took an aggressive defensive stance such as threatening their husband that when he was not on guard that she would kill him, as did the women in the studies of Bowker (1983) and Pagelow (1981). The most aggressive threat I encountered was an effort to intimidate the abuser by telling him that she would call the police.

Using Informal and Semi-Formal Sources of Help

Despite their lack of resources and extreme isolation, many abused immigrant women, feeling the inadequacy of personal strategies, begin trying to get help from informal sources. This is usually the first level of looking outward as a strategy of resistance. Among the women I interviewed, many repeatedly tried to get external help. Some were successful; some partially successful; and some unsuccessful. The success depended on various factors, including the geographic distance of the persons whose help was sought, their attitudes, and the type of assistance they were willing to give. Almost all the abused women who sought help went first to South Asians, their families, friends, neighbors, or community members, at least in part due to a need for cultural sensitivity or support from one's own. Here the notion of "one's own" varied, based on social ties and accessibility.

Family

With the exception of two of the women, women who had their parents or siblings in the United States sought their families' support in their strategy of resistance. Women were more likely to contact their families, temporarily move in with them, or seek their support during a crisis or in its immediate aftermath. Family members intervened and used the family as a mechanism of social control and accountability against an abusive husband in the case of Mary, Tara, Shehanaz, and Mala.[2] In Tara's case, while her family members, particularly her sister, were always there for her in a crisis and in its immediate aftermath, they made no active attempt to dissuade her when she returned to her husband. In contrast, Mary's family was willing to actively intervene. Her brother even took an aggressive defensive position, saying that he would "settle" her husband by intimidating him with a baseball bat. Mary herself was against such intervention, however, as she hoped she could still salvage her marriage and change her husband's behavior. Although the process of seeking the help of family and demonstrating to the abuser that a woman has options is an important strategy of resistance, it is limited depending on the family's response and the woman's current attitude toward her abuser.

Some of the women who did not have any family or friends in the States reluctantly sought the help of their families back in South Asia. As we saw in chapter 6, however, geographic distances make it hard to explain all the issues or to get concrete help. What was extremely interesting were the ways women whose own family members were not accessible strategically used informal sources of help such as in-laws, their husband's friends, and neighbors.

In-laws

I found that some immigrant women, despite their isolation and lack of social networks, sought the assistance of others, including the abuser's kin or friends. While not always successful, seeking such help illustrates women's efforts to engage in resistance by whatever means possible. For example, having faced three months of abuse from her husband and with no support network of her own, Reena stayed temporarily with her husband's aunt. This aunt, her husband's mother's younger sister, was sympathetic to Reena's plight as she had been abused by Reena's father-in-law twenty years earlier when he sponsored her to the United States. While Reena was staying with the aunt, her husband came demanding that she return to him. Reena explains:

> He asked me to come back to the same house but I refused to return. I continued to stay with the lady. He used to come and curse. He said I didn't like him and liked the man of this house instead. He told me, "You like him. Is he your husband? I know he already has one wife and now he wants a young girl." The couple was old. When he said all this I felt unwell [fainted]. The ambulance came and took me to the hospital and from there we later went to stay with my father-in-law. However, my father-in-law would get upset if I cooked something that he did not like. I was pregnant at the time and so we parted on bad terms.

Reena left her husband three times, once with her daughter, whom she then left in India for three months while she tried to organize her life. All three times, Reena stayed away from her husband for a period of time, only to be ultimately persuaded to return. When I interviewed

Reena, her husband was living with her and their child, violating the court order that prohibited his contact with them. She told me that this time her husband called on their anniversary and took her to the temple. There he gave her a new *tali*, a symbol of marriage, and vowed that he would treat her well. Reena told me that her decision to return was determined by the belief that her husband was a good father and that her daughter was being deprived of his love and attention. In my interviews I noticed that the impact of the abuse on a woman's children and the husband's attitude toward the children played a major role in determining whether to stay or leave the husband.

The notion of staying with an abusive husband or returning to him can be partially explained as a type of attitude that Ola Barnett and La Violette (1993) call "learned hopefulness." The battered woman continues to believe that her partner's abusive behavior will stop and that his personality will change for the better. I also believe that in the immigrant context, the reason why women such as Reena frequently return to their abuser can be attributed to the ethnic and class barriers women encounter in their day-to-day lives. For immigrant women, language barriers and lack of social interaction can create a sense of loneliness and a need to identify with someone, in this case, even the abuser. This is especially true when the abuser manipulates this loneliness so that the abused woman begins to hope that the relationship will improve and alleviate her loneliness, as with Reena.

Like Reena, Yamuna too tried a range of strategies to protect herself, including an unsuccessful attempt to persuade her mother-in-law to come and live with them in their studio apartment. She hoped that the elderly woman's presence would act as a buffer and prevent her husband from sexually abusing her.

> I tried to get my mother-in-law to come and stay with me. I told her that I am new to this place and I have never set up house and things like that. Why don't you come and stay with me? She said, it is not practical since it's a studio and also her eldest son has small kids that he needs her to be with. I literally begged her to stay.

However, unlike Reena, Yamuna was adamant that the abuse should stop immediately and that there was no way that she could continue living with her husband. Thus all her strategies were aimed at somehow getting away from her abuser's control.

Friends and Neighbors

When parental support was unavailable or inaccessible and in-laws were unhelpful, women sought the help of friends, acquaintances, coworkers, or neighbors.

Tired of her husband's abuse and his threat to send her back to Pakistan as a failed wife, Shahida sought temporary assistance from her husband's friend and his wife. Initially wary of seeking their help because they were primarily her husband's friends, Shahida gradually sought their assistance as the wife became sympathetic to Shahida's plight. For Shahida, getting the help of her husband's friend also entailed resisting this man's efforts to take advantage of her vulnerability. In general, however, friends in the community who empathize tend to help within the purview of what they think is culturally or socially desirable. A narrative that demonstrates the creative ways used by immigrant women to seek informal help is that told by Mallika:

> I don't have any relatives here. I know somebody in [another state]. Even my husband has no friends here. Even my father-in-law has no friends. He has three daughters and his daughter has three sisters-in-law. We only interacted with these six families. They are his relatives, so they won't help me.
>
> My husband has never taken me to anybody's house. Therefore I don't know anybody. By God's grace, I thought up this idea. I took the telephone directory of my area, and made a list of all the Indian families listed there. I thought I would call them and somebody could help me. I talked to Mr. S. I told him that I don't know anybody in America. I don't have any relatives and I am not aware of all the things here so I need some help and could he help me? He said that he empathized with me, and he would talk it over with his wife and call me over to their house and discuss the ways that they can help me. So I went to his house.
>
> I was alone. He wanted me to compromise with my husband, so that we could start our life together. Usually people are not for divorce. He said that he would call my husband over to his house and we could talk. From what I told him, he could make out that my husband did not have any friends, that we never visited anybody. He said that he would invite us and also introduce us to other people. He thought that once my husband started having his own friends and saw how other people lived, he would change and my life would be better.
>
> Later I talked to some woman and she gave me the phone

number of a SAWO. I called the president of the association. She asked for all my history. She works with women who come to this country and are abandoned by their husbands. She helped me a lot.

Mallika's narrative is a good example of the way in which women, despite tremendous obstacles, do not passively accept abuse but actively engage in efforts to end it. Often the attitudes and behaviors of those from whom they seek help impede their resistance. In Mallika's case, the limited support she received from the family she approached did not deter her from seeking further help. The notion of abused women calling a friend or someone within the South Asian community for support is closely linked to an immigrant's notion of an imagined community. By calling someone within the community, abused women hope to place some social pressure on their husband to be accountable in a context where there are frequently no other traditional buffers to stop the abuse.

For some women, the problem is not only resisting their abuser but also not succumbing to those individuals who try to persuade them that the issue is not marital violence but a matter of adjusting as a new immigrant. Yamuna narrates:

> I don't know what would have happened if the brother [of her husband] had not called my parents. My parents called me back. Of course they tried talking to me. I said I want to come back home. My father said, "Don't worry, this is a new country and I will come in a month and stay with you for a couple of months." For me this month was an unendurably long time. I could not take another day, let alone another month to wait for somebody. I knew I couldn't talk to them. So, later when my husband was not there, I made a call to my friend and asked her to talk to my mother and tell her this is very important. She did that. Then my parents called me right back and said O.K. you can go to [the home of an acquaintance in another city]. They called my in-laws and politely said she is not well, so let her go to [this person's place] for a while. In the meantime, they called this friend, no not a friend but somebody we happened to know and these people sent me a ticket. . . . I went and stayed with them for a while.

At some point, all the women sought some informal help, including shouting out for neighbors or calling a friend when the husband was not home. Seeking informal help has multiple effects. It not only allows a woman to go beyond personal strategies but also indicates to the abuser that there are others beyond the abuser and the abused woman who know about the violence. This can act as a partial deterrent in some situations.

South Asian Women's Organizations

South Asian organizations were usually the most important contact for abused immigrant women.[3] These organizations, for those who approached them, usually became the first source of culturally identifiable collective support. They not only provided tangible support but also by their activities challenged the silence surrounding domestic violence within the South Asian community. Chapter 9 is devoted to these organizations.

Formal Sources of Help: The Police and the Courts

While informal sources were the primary source for seeking external help, a few of the women did call the police. More often, however, the police were called either by neighbors, a family member, or a friend. Women who were at least partially raised in the United States or who were more familiar with the institutional services available tended to be more likely to seek the help of the police or to threaten to call the police. For example, when Mary's husband hit her, she threatened to call the police and told him that in this country the police would not tolerate such things. Similarly Malti, who had lived and worked in the United States for some time, called the police when her husband physically abused her and his stepson:

The third time [Malti was physically abused] my son [from a previous marriage] had a phone call after 11 at night and [my husband] did not want anybody to call my son, period. He told my son to make a list of all his friends, with all their telephone numbers. So that he can call them and warn their parents to tell their children not to call. My son was in college and thought this was too childish. So I said, "Let us drop this." So my husband pushed me away with his hand. My baby was sleeping. My son said, "You can do anything to me but do not touch my mom." I think he pushed me again and my son got furious. He pushed him and said, "Get away from my mom, don't hit her." My husband got hold of my son's hand. I don't remember what happened but he bit my son to the extent that it was bleeding. I didn't know what to do. I called the police. The police said he could be arrested for that. They asked me whether they could arrest him and put him in jail for the night. I could not see that, so I said no. But they said he can't stay here for at least twenty-four hours. My husband said I should get out of the house. The police said no. She is with a baby. She will not get out of the house. Somehow he got out and came back after twenty-four hours. He could not forgive me for not sticking up for him. He thought I should have told the police that he could stay here.

Once when Malti could not get to the phone, she alerted the police by pressing the silent house alarm in her home, knowing that would bring them. In general, however, women rarely called the police directly. Multiple factors may be involved, including concern about the outcome, wariness stemming from beliefs about negative police attitudes toward minorities, and fear of ostracism by the community. I asked many of these women why they did not call the police and some replied that they simply did not think of it or were worried about the outcome for themselves or their children. Women's hesitancy in calling for formal sources of help probably also stems from both a cultural preference for informal mediation and negative perceptions of police attitudes in their country of origin. Even Malti, who called the police, was reluctant to have her husband spend even one night in jail.

However, when women decide to leave the relationship, they usually contact a lawyer at some point. Of the women I interviewed, fewer than a third first contacted a lawyer on their own. Many of the women sought a lawyer with the help of a South Asian women's organization. Women who did not contact lawyers on their own were primarily deterred by financial constraints, lack of information and accessibility, language barriers, cultural conceptions about divorce, and the difficulties of negotiating their way through structural barriers as new immigrants.

Taking Control and Getting Out

Although some of the women I interviewed did hear about South Asian women's organizations and used their support in getting out of their marriages, women like Malti, Prema, and Usha did not have such support as these organizations had not yet been created. In the next chapter I include the narratives of women who sought the help of South Asian women's groups; here I will focus on women who left their relationshps prior to the creation of these organizations. These women resisted their abusers and worked out ways to leave and regain control over their lives without much community support. For women like Prema and Usha, the need to get out was also motivated by the impact of the abuse on their children. For Malti, it was the emotional pres-

sure. Their narratives are testimony to the types of struggles women encounter and their will to resist their abuser's control even without any
major source of external support. Malti describes how she finally got
out:

> Once when there was a conference, he left town. I went to my
> previous work and said I needed my job. It was already a year
> and half since I had left it but fortunately they had an opening.
> I filled in an application and my boss said to take me in. But I
> had to explain this to my husband. When he came back I told
> him, my job called me. They have an opening and they want
> me to come back. He said, "No I don't want you to go back." I
> said, "They said at least for a month I should go and help them
> until they find a replacement. Since I know this place why don't
> I help them out." At that time my daughter was a year and a
> half. He said, "What are you going to do with the child?" I said
> that I would find somebody to take care of her. He said that I
> had to leave home just half an hour before work and be back
> half an hour after work. During lunchtime I took the opportu-
> nity and started looking for an apartment. I didn't tell him it
> was a permanent job. He did not know anything. At lunch I
> would say I am at the cafeteria. People would say she is out for
> lunch. Nobody knew that anything was going on.
>
> I secured an apartment. You know how apartments go
> through your credit check. They asked for my current address.
> I gave my work address. They did not know it was a company.
> Twice a week in the evenings he would go to another place to
> work. On that evening I went out to a truck place, rented a van.
> There was an office building near where I worked. I went here
> and parked the van at seven at night. I walked home with my
> baby. The next morning I had taken a day off from work. He
> did not know that. As soon as he left, I had my son and two of
> his friends come and help me remove some stuff, put it in the
> truck and moved out. I said that I am leaving and I left [almost
> three years after the marriage]. . . . He called me at work. He said
> he wanted me to come back as this is not the way things should
> be. He said, "I have nobody to help me." I said, "I couldn't care
> less." I couldn't take the pressure anymore.

Similarly Prema, who had been abused by her husband for a number of years, finally realized that the only way to stop her husband's abuse
of her and her children was to take back control and get out of the marriage. Married in 1962 in India, Prema left India in 1964. Her husband

initially had a job in England and later they migrated to the United States. She has worked in the same company for nineteen years. At the time I interviewed her she was completing her undergraduate degree and working as a program analyst, earning approximately $30,000 a year.

Prema's husband had started abusing her very soon after the marriage. From 1968 until the time she left him, Prema's husband did not work. Prema was the sole earning member of her home although her husband controlled the money. The South Asian community itself was quite small, and she mentioned in her interview with me that the family was relatively socially isolated. They did not have many friends, and most of the time there was only her husband, their two children, and herself. Over a period of time, Prema began seeking ways to get out of the abusive relationship. In 1967 and a couple of times later Prema had tried to seek counseling and leave the marriage. Ultimately in 1982 she succeeded in getting out and began rebuilding a life for herself and her children. The process of getting out was not easy, as she explains:

In 1980 I started taking control, slowly. I started taking control of the money. I quit the second job I had, from which I was making good money because it was an overtime job. I quit that job and started staying home more. Staying with the kids. The more I stayed home, the more control I took over. He lost control of the kids, over the money, over me. So that got him real angry. So the fights instead of being every month or every other week were now every day. And the beatings really accelerated and suddenly everything went haywire. . . . Then I planned I was going to leave him. I had to get some money first. Collect some money of my own. He wouldn't give me any money that was in the bank then. It was all his. It was fine. I don't want it. I opened my own account. Savings account and checking account and started saving money. I paid the rent, whatever needed to be paid I paid and I gave him the money. That is when the fights accelerated because I would ask him why he wants to eat outside when he could eat in the house and then go out instead of spending ten dollars on lunch everyday. Which he wasn't spending anyway. I think he was saving. He just wanted to take it from me. . . .

In 1982, I told him I am getting an apartment, since he is not going. I had got an apartment, paid security deposit and a month's rent on it. I went into the apartment, cleaned it, packed my boxes over at his house and I was going to move. This friend of mine he was going to help me move. He is my best friend's husband. He came to the house and my husband told him that he can't do that. You can't take my wife and kids away from me. You can't move my furniture from my own house. I wasn't moving furniture. It was just my personal things. Otherwise I will have you arrested for taking my wife and kids. So this man couldn't do anything. He was scared and he left me right there. So I said, well, if he is not going to help me, I am going to get out of this place with my kids, with or without these things. Then he knew I was determined. So I had another friend come over, we rented a van and we were going to move out. He told her the same thing but he did promise her that he would go for counseling. The same thing happened with counseling. I went for counseling and the counselor told me that there was no help for him because he is not willing to get help, so what you need is to go ahead. If you want to get divorced, go ahead and start planning. So this was in September 1982. I started looking for an apartment in January, because he had stopped counseling and was getting worse. He had beaten up my kids by then. He had really beaten them up.

He had beaten up my kids and I talked this to a counselor, and he reported it to my doctor and my doctor reported it to [the authorities, and their] people came in. I had to either give up the kids, or leave the house. That was the choice. I told them I was going to leave the house and that I had already tried once. . . .

About February or March [1983] I started looking for apartments without telling him. I felt I was committing robbery every day of my life after that. I couldn't tell him anything because if I told him, he would have a plan of his own and would ruin my plan. So I decided I was going to move out of this place, without telling him, without taking anything. Just me and my kids. Find another apartment and start all over again. I looked for apartment for two months, February and March. Finally in March I did find an apartment that was going to be vacated by May. I paid the lease and one month rent and moved into this place. That [getting out] was another experience in itself.

Trying to get out of there, just getting your personal things out was really bad. We didn't think he would let us get out first of all without beating us up. He was there when we moved but I had got legal help in February . . . through the yellow pages and talking to lots of other lawyers. The people at work were very helpful. I told them what was happening toward the end.

They couldn't believe it. They said, "We thought you had a perfect marriage." I said so did I. . . . After that it was easy going.
He was served the day after I left. He found out and didn't show
up at the court or anything. Within six months, I got my divorce.
I signed off all my rights. I didn't want anything from him for
my kids or for myself. I just wanted to get out of his life. I wanted
to get out of his life.

While Prema's and Malti's narratives point to the physical and emotional trauma involved in the process of getting out, they also show that
getting out is most effective when a woman ultimately recognizes that
the abuse must stop now. The departures of Prema, Usha, and Malti,
though extremely difficult, were partially possible because they were
economically independent, had no major language barrier, and were citizens or LPRs. Economic independence and the ability to communicate
in the dominant culture must be considered when assessing women's
ability to get out of an abusive relationship in the immigrant context.
Thus class position must be linked to ethnicity and gender when addressing women's strategies of resistance.

––––––––

The narratives in this chapter clearly contradict assumptions that South
Asian women passively accept their abuse. Rather, they actively engage
in resisting their abuser. The internalization of norms surrounding the
institution of marriage coupled with external economic, social, legal pressures and cultural dislocation all have to be taken into account in seeking to understand the strategies of resistance abused women use. All the
women I spoke with resisted their abuser at some point. The amount of
time they stayed with their abusers was, to a large extent, contingent
on both cultural factors and practical constraints. Isolation and the inability to obtain access to effective informal and formal sources of help
influenced the choice of strategies of resistance.

In my interviews, I found that the decision to stay or leave was based
on a number of factors, including children, perception of alternate economic options, fear of loss of legal status, fear of deportation, impact
on the family, and perception of the lack of availability of resources and
support systems. Not having their own bank account, being forced to
give up their entire salary, financially relying on their abuser, and all
forms of economic dependency impede abused women's strategies of resistance. Women do resist, but it is difficult to fight a battle on one's
own, especially when one faces both cultural and structural constraints.

Often it is not that women don't reach out for help, but that the help
they receive is symbolic or inadequate. Many women not only have to

resist their abuser but also must overcome cultural disapproval for violating the sanctity of the institution of marriage. However, such attitudes are slowly changing. In the 1990s there has been a gradual shift in the South Asian community toward greater sensitivity to gender roles, especially to the problem of marital violence. There are many individuals, particularly other South Asian women, who do care and want to help abused women. These individuals are often limited, however, by their own socialization in certain cultural values, their lack of knowledge of available resources in the United States, and their inability to provide tangible help given their own socioeconomic circumstances.

One of the common themes throughout my interviews was an abused woman's need for support within her community. That many South Asian women in the early 1980s did not come out in public to denigrate their abusers thus should not be misconstrued as passivity. Their silence was rather due to the atomization of immigrant women, their individual struggles to redefine their cultural and material lives in the United States, and the lack of public acknowledgment of domestic violence as a social problem by the South Asian community.

The immense increase in the number of women who reported domestic violence in late 1980s and the 1990s, including most of the women I interviewed, can be attributed to the birth during this period of South Asian women's organizations that address domestic violence. Their emergence marks a shift from private individual struggles to a more collective, publicly oriented system of resistance against marital abuse.

8

Making a Difference
South Asian Women's Organizations in the United States

This chapter looks at the rise of a new set of South Asian women's organizations (SAWOs) in the United States whose center of focus has been South Asian women. Although I incorporate the narratives of the women I interviewed, the primary analysis is drawn from data gathered from six SAWOs between 1990 and 1993. I examine some of the factors that determined the creation of these organizations, and explore their role in bringing about change at the individual, community, and societal levels. I see these organizations and the activities they engage in as part of a growing social movement aimed at enhancing the efficacy of the larger effort to end violence against women.[1] By intersecting ethnicity, gender, and class, these organizations play a pivotal role in addressing marital violence at both the micro and the macro levels.

The Emergence of South Asian Women's Organizations in the United States

Two movements form the background for the creation of the organizations examined here: the battered women's movement in the United States and the United Kingdom and the women's movement in South Asia. Prior to the mid-1970s, marital violence was perceived as an individual problem and little attention was devoted to it. In 1971, on the outskirts of London, a grass-roots organization of women organized the first shelter for abused wives, thereby initiating the battered women's movement (NiCarthy Merriam and Coffman 1984; Pagelow

1992). By the mid-1970s, leaders of the feminist movement termed marital violence unacceptable and created the battered women's movement in the United States. Its efforts were central in transforming marital violence from a private individual problem into an important social problem. Movement activists put forth the view that the abuse women experienced in marriage was a reflection of the unequal status that women had in society. They blamed the existing social structure for defining male aggression as acceptable and frequently desirable (Walker 1979; Schecter 1982). In the process, the battered women's movement shifted the attention from individual abusive men to men as a class who are a product of their socialization in a patriarchal society (Schecter 1982; Stordeur and Stille 1989). This definition produced a movement focusing not on the treatment or punishment of the individual husband, but on creating shelters for women and providing them with legal intervention, economic and social resources, and alternative living situations (Adams and McCormick 1982; Davis 1987). The movement also increased public support for the protection of battered women. A consequence of this was the creation of more shelters and pressure for legislation to protect women from marital violence.

From the late 1970s and early 1980s, Third World feminist groups began addressing the "woman question" in their own countries. Various women's organizations were created to examine the issues that had an impact on women. They focused on the global and internal oppression and exploitation of Third World women. Special emphasis was given to the various forms of violence that occurred in their countries, including rape, widow burning, dowry deaths, female infanticide, female foeticide, and marital violence (Everett 1979; Liddle and Joshi 1986; Kishwar and Vanita 1986; Bush 1992). Movement activists questioned the normative structure and culturally prescribed values within the institution of marriage and family. Most important, they initiated legislative changes that protected the rights of women. They advocated for social change and were central in bringing the problems of Third World women to the fore, making them an important issue for Third World women residing in Europe, Canada, and the United States. Until the 1980s, little attention was paid to the structural and cultural context in which marital violence occurred within the South Asian community in the United States.

The 1980s witnessed the rise of SAWOs in the United States. What was the basis for the creation of these organizations? Although South Asian organizations existed prior to 1980, they were a symbolic representation of ties to their home country; they helped in the maintenance of a national culture in a foreign land through cultural, social, and religious activities (Bhattacharjee 1992). South Asian men had greater visibility in these organizations and tended to be in positions of control. These organizations did not address the different experiences of immigrant men and women (Vaid 1989). In fact, the gendered division of labor was re-inforced within the institution of the family and the social and religious organizations of the South Asian community. At the same time, the spe-cific concerns of ethnic minority women had frequently been excluded by white U.S. feminists, thus marginalizing women like those who have immigrated from South Asia. There was an increasing need felt by some South Asian women to organize and address the problems faced by the women in their community. This need is described by Shamita Das Dasgupta, a cofounder of Manavi, the first SAWO to address domestic violence:

> Discarding the security of the mainstream movement was not easy. Neither was my conscious decision to wed my feminist agenda with my ethnic identity. Until then my relationship with my Indian community had been based on my birth; now my re-lationship became an act of choice. As a symbol, I gave up wear-ing all Western clothing. However, this was not enough. I had to develop a feminist agenda in the context of the South Asian community.
>
> I realized I was not alone in my efforts. Serendipitously, I came together with five other Indian women, all runaways from mainstream feminism. Reclaiming our community was an in-tricate task. We had to dig through its surface crust of conser-vatism, absolutism and androcentrism. In turn, the community had to receive us in our many faceted roles: mothers, activists, professionals, students, wives, feminists, single women. (Dasgupta and Dasgupta 1993)

Similarly, Mallika Dutt, one of the five founders of Sakhi for South Asian Women in New York, states:

> I've worked for many years with the woman's movement in the United States, predominantly around issues of women of color and sexuality. I have also done some work around violence in general . . . we [Dutt and another founding member] started get-ting to a point where we really felt we wanted to work with other South Asian women because all of our work had been done in the larger context of sort of mainstream America. We started hunting for an organization in New York and couldn't find any-thing. We finally found out about Manavi and originally thought that we would work with them . . . [this did not work out] well

apart from the logistic hassle of trying to get there and being an organization in New Jersey, we also began to realize that there was a huge problem in New York and that the South Asian community was really located in New York.[2] (interview, April 24, 1991)

Kanta Khipple, one of the founding members of Apna Ghar, another SAWO, spoke to me of how she and other women who were working with service organizations felt that there was a dire need to provide services within the South Asian community. According to her, no South Asian organization was doing such work in Chicago at the time. Ethnic organizations were not really providing any services for abused women. This made it difficult for them to get any real help from the community, and many were trapped in abusive relationships. The lack of such services and the complexity of some cases at the time became the impetus for the creation of Apna Ghar.

Such beliefs, vision, and commitment by the founders and the initial volunteers resulted in the emergence of a new set of organizations in the United States beginning in 1985 whose focus was South Asian women. In a short span of fifteen years, many SAWOs were established as a part of a growing social movement to address the problem of violence against women in the South Asian community. These include Sakhi for South Asian Women in New York, SEWAA (Service and Education for Women Against Abuse) in Philadelphia, Apna Ghar in Chicago, Sneha in Connecticut, Maitri and Narika in California, ASHA in Washington, D.C., Saheli in Austin, and many more in different parts of the United States. These organizations created a space for South Asian women to discuss issues that were pertinent to them as women and as South Asians in the United States and provided tangible support and services for South Asian abused women. Intersecting gender and ethnicity by their very existence and in the issues they articulate, these SAWOs attempt to protect and empower South Asian women while simultaneously demarginalizing them from the larger movement to end violence against women.

Organizational Ideology and Structure

The success of a social movement is contingent on its ability to convince its potential members, and sometimes the larger public, of the merits of its ideology (McAdam, McCarthy, and Zald 1988). Organizational ideology is a set of ideas and values, socially constructed by organizations, that forms the ideational framework; this framework defines the basis for a group's membership, organizational structure, goals, and strategies. The organizational ideologies of the SAWOs in the early

1990s fell in three categories: *value-oriented, diffused,* and *unspecified* ideologies.[3]

Value-oriented ideology can be defined as organizational ideology with a set of core values that are explicit and directly correspond to the structure, goals, and activities of the organization. Four SAWOs (Sakhi, Manavi, Maitri, and SEWAA) fit into this category to varying degrees. Their value orientation was explicitly feminist, with the struggle against patriarchy seen as central. These organizations worked to organize women for empowerment by linking personal and political aspects of a range of issues, especially the ending of violence against women. Empowerment involves the power to attain internal strength and the right to determine one's choices in life, to achieve self-reliance, to free oneself from any form of coercion or violence, to reject the existing structures that discriminate on the basis of gender, race, ethnicity, and class, and to influence the direction of social change. An important part of empowerment is the need to redress any form of change that did not include an acknowledgment of cultural diversity in influencing the direction of change. The underlying premise was for South Asian women to attain greater control over their own lives and exercise more power. As they did so, they would be able to break down many of the elements that resulted in their multiple oppression in the United States. The unit of focus was the South Asian woman.

Diffused ideology emphasizes more dispersed values that loosely form the basis of the structure, goals, and activities of the organization. This is not to say that such organizations did not have a set of values, but one central value did not determine all their dimensions. For example, while the problem of male dominance was addressed, the struggle against patriarchy was not an explicit core value that defined all other dimensions. Rather, a set of selective values such as the dignity of women within the institution of the family, economic equality, and the protection of children of abused women pervades the organization. While bearing elements of a feminist framework, this ideology was more diffused and included more clearly the components of the family violence perspective, as opposed to a feminist perspective on violence. The attempt was to address issues pertaining to women's rights while simultaneously providing services that made the family viable as an institution. Apna Ghar was an example of such an organization, as Kanta Khipple described in an informal conversation with me in the fall of 1992.

> At Apna Ghar, our goal is to help women address the abuse they face. We support them, provide them services, and try to get them out of an abusive situation. For many women, the family is very

important and it is not always easy to leave an abusive situation. Divorce is not always accepted in our communities, and not all women are ready to leave their husbands. So we carefully consider the ways to support these women, provide counseling, and work through the issues with them. In the process some of us become like an alternate family to some of the women, especially in a situation where they don't have their own family members.

Organizations with *unspecified ideology* have an amorphous set of values. Such a perspective results in a perception among the organizational members that there is no specific value or set of selective values that directly corresponds to their structure, goals, and activities. The organization Sneha fit into this category. In the early 1990s this organization perceived itself primarily as a service agency that assisted individuals in need, without regard to the articulation of a specific organizational value or set of values. More recently, however, Sneha has shifted from this perspective, as we will see.

Although the SAWOs I studied varied in their ideology to some degree, a common theme that bound them together was their underlying philosophy of support for South Asian women. Most important, they did not emphasize gender systems alone but also situated themselves so as to address the intersection of gender and ethnicity.

The SAWOs tended not to have branches, and contact with their membership was direct. Common to all the SAWOs was a structure based on voluntary membership. Their central commitment was to address the problems of South Asian women in the United States, specifically marital violence. Many of these organizations were officially incorporated and obtained nonprofit status. Their ideology, however, created some structural variation. Organizations based on a value-oriented ideology tended to be predominantly nonhierarchical and were characterized by a less formalized structure; volunteers divided tasks among themselves on the basis of their interests or their areas of expertise. The lack of a traditional hierarchical structure in most derived from the belief, unarticulated, that such hierarchies were to some degree the reflection of asymmetrical power relations under patriarchy. Monthly meetings were held to discuss issues and update members on the various activities. The emphasis was on collectivity. At the same time, these organizations did not lack leadership, and conflicts from latent leadership did arise. Leadership in most of these organizations tended to be based on two criteria: the central role played by the founders of the organization; and active involvement in and commitment to the activities. None of the value-oriented SAWOs had sought state funding, since they believed this would demand some degree of compromise of their values (this has partially changed in the late 1990s). However, they were well networked with other nongovernmental organizations that addressed domestic violence or immigrant rights. There was an emphasis on coalition building as a vital means to bring about social change. More recently, some have been undergoing structural change. For example, in 1997 Sakhi, after a bitter organizational struggle, underwent major changes, some of which will be discussed in chapter 9. Today, while having achieved considerable success, Sakhi is in a stage of transition, still trying to work out its structure and processes, particularly in terms of the roles and relationships among the board, staff, and the larger body of volunteers.

Organizations with a diffuse ideology tended to be more formally structured. Among the organizations studied, Apna Ghar was the only one that had a shelter and was funded by the state. Using state resources meant working to some degree within the confines of bureaucratic structures, since the organization had to conform to state-defined specifications for the allocation of funds and use of the shelter. In Apna Ghar, these circumstances necessitated including non-South Asian representatives as board members. Issues of ethnicity and gender were addressed through a service-oriented approach, and the organization was extremely successful in networking with other service organizations and making inroads into the South Asian community. Apna Ghar has undergone changes too.

The one organization with an unspecified ideology, Sneha, was differentiated in structure from the rest by its smaller membership. As a consequence of having a limited number of active members in its early stages, its nebulous structure evolved from the selective services provided at a given time. These were primarily support, listening, providing information, and referrals. Today, however, Sneha defines its ideology as "a more holistic form of activism":

> Sneha follows a more holistic model of activism than the models typically defined as feminist. While one part of our activism consists of helping people who call our 800 number because they need help, our other activities are focused on changing the context of South Asian women's lives. Hence we focus on different ways of networking, through book discussions, through workshops on issues of interest to the South Asia community, through Golden Socials (for older members of the community) and getting together to celebrate women. We strongly feel that unless the context changes, and there is sufficient interlocking

networks in the community to understand women's issues as COMMUNITY ISSUES, helping women after they are already in distress does not sufficiently address the problem of social change. In evolving our model we relied on women's networks we were familiar with in India—aunts, sisters, grandmothers, mothers who were strong women, outspoken in their challenge of family/community wrongdoing. While our model of activism does not fit the conventional domestic abuse models of activism, where the solution is focussed on the individual first and the collectivity as an associated target, we focus on the community as strongly as we are committed to those in distress.

As part of our focus on the larger focus we also regularly address racism and stereotyping on part of mainstream society, through networking with mainstream organizations. Dispelling myths about South Asian women are part of this model of changing the context within which women from South Asia are framed and categorized.[4] (Bandana Purkayastha, Sept. 28, 1998)

Although all these organizations are focused on South Asian women, organizational membership criteria tend to vary. Some of these organizations included only women as members; others included both men and women. Membership, meaning those individuals who were active members within the organization and not the larger mailing list of individuals who subscribed to the organizations' newsletters or financially contributed to them, was predominantly South Asian, with Indians forming the largest group.

A common feature of the organizational structure among the SAWOs was the connection between the direction of the growth of membership and the identity of the founding members. For example, the New York organization, started by young women professionals, tended to have predominantly young women professionals as members. The Philadelphia organization, initiated by South Indian women, was predominantly composed of South Indian women professionals. The Chicago and New Jersey organizations were a mixture of older professionals and homemakers. This dimension should not be overemphasized, however, since membership was also partially linked to the profile of the South Asian population in these areas. In the last few years, many of these organizations have seen increased participation from second-generation South Asians.

Unlike other women's organizations in the United States, the SAWOs, though woman-focused, addressed the cultural factors that differentiated the structure of immigrant families. They also addressed the tactics of control used by the abuser within the immigrant context, such as the green card factor, language barriers, and the lack of information or access to support services.

Organizational Goals and Strategies

The goals of a movement are to some extent collectively defined. The success of a group's goals cannot be discussed without simultaneously addressing organizational strategies, since individual participation depends to a large degree on the perceived usefulness of the goals and the feasibility of goal achievement (Klandermans 1993). The goals of the SAWOs could be divided for analytical purposes into three categories, although they were all interconnected and were prioritized differently within each organization: *organizing South Asian women; ending domestic violence;* and *community education.*

Organizing South Asian Women

Until last two decades or so, South Asian women in the United States have been relatively atomized or marginalized, remaining voiceless and powerless. The "dual marginalization" of South Asian women through the exclusion of gender issues by mainstream South Asian organizations and the relative exclusion of diverse cultural contexts by mainstream women's organizations led to a lacuna that needed to be filled. By speaking of their most intimate relations, South Asian women began to organize around their individualized and atomized experiences. As in the broader women's movement, by defining and sharing their private problems and experiences as South Asian women in the United States, some realized the need to mobilize to combat the oppression that South Asian women experience as women and as ethnic minority women.

There was and continues to be a need to address sexist violence and ethnic marginalization by challenging and reforming institutions such as the family, the economy, education, law, the state, media, and politics that perpetuate violence against women in general and against immigrant women in particular. Marital violence within the community provided a concrete issue around which to organize. Central to these organizations was the belief that organizing South Asian women would lead to solidarity and empowerment. Although varied in their approach, most tried to bring women together to grapple with issues pertinent to their lives, particularly those aspects that resulted in inequality and oppression. This focus on organizing was a particularly important aspect of value-oriented organizations. Mallika Dutt of Sahki says:

> We are very aware of gender issues, of power around gender. We're also both very aware of the connections between sexism,

between sex and race and class and sexual orientation and a whole range of other things. We saw and felt very much the need to organize around domestic violence, to organize around South Asian women and to organize within our community because there wasn't anybody doing the work around women at all at any level whatsoever. There was AIWA [Asian Indian Women in America]. . . . But in terms of our political voice, in terms of a voice that really challenged some of the cultural norms and some of the sexism and patriarchy that exists in our communities, we didn't see anybody doing that work in New York.

So we decided that we needed a mechanism through which we do the consciousness-raising work and to do the organizing work. Domestic violence seemed to be one of those issues, which allowed women to come together across class, across race, across sexual preference. I mean violence against women is generally an issue around which women come together I think most easily. Also there was a huge need. I mean we kept hearing horror story after horror story of battered women in the community and you know nobody knew where to go, nobody knew what to do. So that was the motivation behind having a focus on domestic violence because we didn't think that we could be all things to everybody. But I think the idea was that domestic violence would be the hook through which we raised larger issues about women. That it wouldn't end at domestic violence. We also didn't want to be a service organization. I mean, we were very clear that we were a political group. I mean that we did have a political consciousness. (interview, April 24, 1991)

An important way of organizing women has also been to bring them together to publicly demonstrate against abusers. This was effectively done in the case of Syeda Sufian, as we saw in chapter 1, and more recently against employers who abuse domestic workers. There has been an attempt to link women through group opposition to the multiple forms of oppression. This approach has been pursued particularly by value-oriented organizations such as Sakhi.

Ending Domestic Violence against South Asian Women

For most of these organizations, the problem of marital violence in the South Asian community became a concrete basis through which South Asian women could address issues that were of specific relevance to them. Although domestic violence occurs all over the world, it occurs with cultural and structural differences. An important goal of these SAWOs was to address the problem of domestic violence among South Asians in the United States at the *macro* and *micro* level.

Macro level At the macro level, the strategy for many of the SAWOs was to engage in advocacy on issues affecting women's rights with a focus on immigrant women's rights. The attempt was to bring about legislative reform and cultural sensitization in law enforcement and medical care systems. Heretofore U.S. legislation and policy had generally been broadly based, lacking sensitivity to the distinctiveness of different immigrant groups. The SAWOs, especially those with a value-oriented ideology, developed strategies to rectify this imbalance.

High-quality legislation, legal enforcement, and legal assistance are essential requirements for victims of marital violence, because they provide protection and safety for women. As shown in chapter 3, a wife's legal dependency (in terms of her immigration status) often places the husband in a position of dominance and control and becomes an obstacle for many dependent wives in their efforts to attain economic independence from their abusers.

The need to protect immigrant women's rights led SAWOs to participate in coalitions for "immigrant rights" and "women's rights" and to actively pressure members of Congress to pass legislation protecting the rights of women, including immigrant women, such as the Immigration Act of 1990 and the Violence Against Women Act (VAWA) of 1994 (Barai 1998). As we have seen, VAWA contains provisions to protect immigrant women such as the important "self-petitioning clause." Such legislation has been a big step in removing a major structural impediment forcing abused immigrant women to stay with their spouses. Through coalition building, organizations with value-oriented ideology played an important role in combining gender issues with immigrant rights.

All the SAWOs developed strategies to sensitize police officers to the needs of South Asian women by providing handbooks and addressing gender and culture specific issues with mainstream services. SAWOs provide courts with expert witnesses who explain the cultural aspects of cases that required such information. They also work to remedy the inadequate provisions for South Asian language interpreters in U.S. courts, including the frequent use of South Asian men whose own gender biases influence their interpretation and may seriously damage the case an abused women has against her perpetrator. To counteract this gender imbalance, whereby South Asian men become the voices for South Asian women who are victims of marital violence, SAWOs such as Apna

Ghar, Sakhi, Maitri, and Manavi developed two strategies. They made South Asian women available as interpreters and also acted as watchdogs, alerting the judge when the interpreter inappropriately translated the proceedings. For example, the Sakhi February 1993 newsletter discussed a case in which a volunteer explained to the judge that the South Asian male interpreter had incorrectly interpreted the information to the female victim. Apna Ghar and Manavi also provided interpreters for cases when deemed appropriate. In the late 1990s, under the initiative of Sakhi's Program Director, Prema Vohra, Sakhi was in the process of developing a court interpreters' campaign. Vohra states:

> Sakhi plans to launch a gender equity campaign to protest the current system of court appointed interpreters within the New York Family Courts. In our work over the last several years with South Asian survivors of domestic violence we have found that the translation and interpreting services provided by the city court system are not only inadequate but often work to the women's detriment. Not only are there very few South Asian language interpreters, but those who do such work are men who are neither trained on domestic violence, nor are monitored nor held accountable for their actions . . . we have often witnessed that the interpreters when they do show up, speak the language inadequately; the Courts, then do not have an accurate record of what actually occurred and the woman is left anxious and confused about the critical decisions being made concerning her life and children. . . .
>
> While Sakhi has lodged individual complaints of interpreters with the judges hearing the case, there has been no collective campaign to bring about a change in the current system. We believe that it is crucial that the courts provide an equitable forum in which women can exercise their legal rights and make meaningful decisions. This campaign fits squarely with our mission to support and empower women who are experiencing an abusive relationship. (correspondence, March 13, 1998)

Toward achieving this goal, Sakhi was organizing women, speaking with other organizations, building a coalition, and developing a pool of information and criteria for court interpreters.

As another important strategy, all the organizations provided women with legal assistance regarding their rights, the availability of civil and criminal protection, and current information on various legal procedures. When a woman could not afford the legal costs, SAWOs tried to find lawyers who did pro bono work. SAWOs also contacted hospitals in their area, culturally sensitizing health care providers, acting as interpreters for medical personnel, and most important, encouraging medical staff to inform victims of the existence of South Asians organizations committed to addressing the problem of marital violence. For example, Sakhi's interns visited hospitals to distribute literature and made contacts with social workers, advisors, and medical staff. Apna Ghar spoke on domestic violence to health care professionals. In this and other areas, SAWOs have made a serious attempt to articulate both implicitly and explicitly issues pertinent to South Asian women.

Micro level While there were significant efforts to address the problem of marital violence within the South Asian community at the macro level and within the South Asian community itself, a considerable amount was also achieved by SAWOs at the micro level, in direct interaction with and services for individual women. Between 1985 and 1993 these SAWOs recorded approximately 1,071 abused South Asian women who approached them. Almost one third of these women approached these organizations in 1992.[5] By the mid-1990s the number of women approaching SAWOs increased. By mid-1998 Sakhi had been contacted by approximately 1,500 women. Similarly, since their founding Manavi and Apna Ghar have been contacted by thousands of women. Between July 1, 1997, and June 30, 1998, Apna Ghar handled 1,095 hotline calls, and 163 women and children received a total of 3,426 shelter nights (Apna Ghar 1998, 2–12). In 1996–97 SEWAA received about 70–90 telephone calls each year. Increasing numbers of women are seeking the help of these organizations, which are playing a pivotal role in transforming marital violence from a private personal matter to a social problem in the South Asian immigrant community in the United States.

During the period of this study, the following important organizational strategies at the micro level were observed. Abused South Asian women who sought assistance from these organizations were usually assigned to a volunteer who interacted with them at an interpersonal level. These volunteers provided the women with pertinent information, suggested alternative options available to them, listened to them, counseled, and helped in practical ways such as assisting them with removing their personal belongings if they decided to leave their home. They supported them through the steps necessary to end the cycle of violence perpetrated against them. Reena says:

> When I was alone at my aunt's place [a SAWO member] came to visit me and spoke to me. . . . They try and explain what should be done. They also explain the rules and what action one can take. . . . She is very nice and calls me frequently and

asks me if I need any help. I keep asking her for advice and she
explains things to me . . . they have a free lawyer.

Similarly, Rehana explains how a SAWO helped her:

> A friend of mine gave me the address [of a SAWO]. She is very
> good friend of mine. She said that they will help me to stand
> on my own feet. . . . I stayed here for two months, found an apart-
> ment, fixed school for my children. Then through a lawyer sent
> a letter to my husband and got my children. . . . They [the SAWO]
> told me that they would help me to overcome my problems. They
> helped me to apply for aid. The food and lodging was free. They
> gave money for transportation. I didn't have any monetary wor-
> ries. They supported me, and I regained my confidence. I told
> to myself that I shouldn't lose my confidence. I got an apart-
> ment. Then I went to get my children with the court order.

We have also seen in previous chapters the ways in which Yamuna,
Wahida, and Shahida were all helped by SAWOs. Counseling provided
by SAWOs varied from trained counselors to volunteers who were trained
to counsel on an informal nonlegal basis. Volunteers were trained to in-
formally counsel victims of marital violence and provide group support.
For example, Apna Ghar had a 24–hour emergency hotline, as well as
individual and group counseling. Sakhi and SEWAA had training in individual advocacy sessions for volunteers. Narika had a multilingual
helpline. A few of the organizations also provided support groups where
abused women met, discussed their problems, supported one another,
provided solidarity, and helped one another in the process of ending
the violence perpetrated against them. Manavi, Sakhi, and Apna Ghar
had advocacy support group and victim support group meetings. They
played an important role for some of the women I interviewed. Tara
explains:

> Finally I came one day here [to the SAWO]. First for group coun-
> seling, then I had some individual counseling. The first meet-
> ing I had with everybody here made me think of how much I
> needed this support. How much I needed to talk about it. And
> all the time I had been so ashamed, thinking it was my fault all
> the time. But then I realized that it was not I. It was him that
> was sick and needed help. It wasn't me that wasn't attractive
> enough for him. I was not the one whose cooking wasn't good
> for him. I was not the one who wasn't cleaning. It was he. His
> mental sickness that made him abuse me.

Individual legal assistance was provided for these victims whenever possible. This included providing them with referrals to lawyers, helping them attain a protection order, and finding lawyers who would do pro bono work if the women could not afford the legal costs. Manavi ran a free legal clinic and Sakhi, Maitri, Apna Ghar, and SEWAA provided assistance in obtaining lawyers and legal advice. Volunteers went with abused women to the courts and found South Asian female interpreters for them if they had language problems. They also helped them apply for a green card, child custody, and child support. Zakhia says:

> I just said [to the SAWO] that I am in a very difficult situation. I don't have a place to stay, no food to eat, and my husband is always beating me up. I have nowhere to go. I have no family. . . . They [the SAWO] came and took me to the court. They did a lot of paperwork for me. Then they dropped me back at my friend's place, and gave me some money. And they filed all the papers for me in the court. . . . Yes they really helped me. I felt that they are really nice people, who are willing to help me.

Apna Ghar was the most active SAWO at the micro level. The existence of its shelter with a South Asian focus was important in providing not only a much-needed physical space but also a concrete marker of an alternative to a violent home for South Asian women. According to Ranjana Bhargava, then the director of Apna Ghar, there were various reasons for the creation of a South Asian shelter, including the need for women to have a place where they could do some of the things that were important to them. She says:

> [Prior to the creation of Apna Ghar] I had placed them in various shelters and I would talk to them. I found that the people [who] were reading the *Namaaz* [Islamic prayers] had no place. They would be ridiculed if they did. If they used *tadka* [a method of garnishing a dish by frying spices] in their vegetables, it was clear that it was very different. They had different ways of washing their utensils. All of this made them feel even lower than what they seemed when they came to the services. Their self-esteem never got built up and they left the shelter in two or three days. . . .
>
> The aim of [Apna Ghar] has to be culturally specific, linguistically appropriate counseling as well as a support system. I feel that if you are in trauma, that is what you fall back on. For immigrants and refugees, this is very important. . . . Our role

is to show [abused women] that there are better paths, there are options. There are choices that they can take that would lead them to feel better about themselves. (interview, Sept. 25, 1992)

Some of the other women I interviewed also talked about the difficulties in mainstream shelters, particularly language barriers, cooking constraints, and differences in attitudes and behavior. At Apna Ghar there was an attempt to address some of these issues while at the same time providing an environment where women learned to be more open to individual differences.

Because there were no other shelters focused on South Asian women at that time, most of the other organizations helped women by using various additional strategies. These ranged from referring them to Apna Ghar; to referring them to other shelters which were sensitized to some of the cultural specificities of South Asians; to temporarily housing them with a volunteer; to partially paying rent for a temporary accommodation; or to getting the courts to temporarily remove the husband from the home. These activities continued in the late 1990s among most of the SAWOs. In 1997 SEWAA provided temporary shelter to three women. In 1997 Manavi established a transition home called Ashiana.

Because SAWOs had limited funds, it was frequently hard for them to provide women with substantial financial assistance. Whenever possible, however, some funds were allocated to the women on a needs basis. In certain cases, while cash was not provided, tapping into the resources of volunteers or members of the community provided other material necessities such as food, clothing, and blankets. This work has been ongoing in some of the SAWOs. For example, in a note in 1998, SEWAA informed me of some of its activities:

Last year, SEWAA assisted clients with finances to purchase food, clothing and to handle legal matters. The type of services that the volunteers provide include transportation of clients for food and clothing, shopping, accompany and act as their emotional support while waiting for the court hearing, take the families out to parks etc. Sometimes the volunteers are used as translators in the courts and meeting that involve negotiating custody, child support, therapeutical social services. SEWAA works in close coordination with Women Against Abuse of the Greater Philadelphia, Victim Assistance units of the surrounding counties, Women Organized against Rape, Intercultural Services Center, Women's Center in Universities, Coalition of Right to Live in Peace, and the newly formed Interpersonal Violence in Asian

American Communities (IVAAC) to enhance, share and achieve our common goals in their welfare of our women and children—emphasizing their right to live a life free of violence.

The obstacles encountered by abused women in the South Asian community led SAWOs to develop a number of strategies, including developing contacts with job training centers and checking their accessibility to South Asian women, initiating language-training classes or connecting victims with already existing programs, and assisting in writing resumes, locating jobs, and attaining work permits. This was often done through networking with other organizations or using contacts within the community. For example, Sakhi, SEWAA, Manavi, Maitri, and Apna Ghar established contacts with job training centers, Sakhi initiated its own English as a second language (ESL) classes, and Manavi held career counseling and job search workshops. The strategy was one of resource development and community-grounded action that linked the macro and micro levels in addressing issues of central importance to South Asian women.

Community Education

Since social change for South Asian women cannot be addressed without changes in the perception and structure of the South Asian community, an important organizational goal was that of community education.

As religious institutions play an important role in community identity and moral legitimacy, SAWOs developed an organizational strategy that targeted the inclusion of these institutions in bringing about social change. They met with the leaders, discussed the problem of marital violence, sensitized the laity about gender issues, held informative classes, and initiated programs that increased the South Asian community's social awareness. Some of the South Asian organizations, especially Sakhi, used the strategy of "leafletting" in areas dominated by South Asian populations and were successful in spreading the word within the community regarding the seriousness and consequences of marital violence on women. They distributed literature at temples, *gurdawaras* (Sikh places of worship), and mosques on Long Island and in Queens and had leafletting sessions in Brooklyn and other parts of New York. Sakhi conducted workshops at a mosque in Flushing and at Islamic centers in Westchester and on Long Island. In Chicago the president of the board of Apna Ghar spoke to South Asian Youth at a Hindu temple and spoke at Vishwa Hindu Parishad (a Hindu right-wing organization) about violence against women. Narika has developed partnerships with religious centers for faith-sensitive outreach programs. By sensitizing religious leaders and holding talks in religious areas, some SAWOs took a major initial step in attaining some recognition of the problem and emphasizing the need for community leaders and religious leaders to address the issue.

SEWAA invited speakers on domestic violence among South Asians to various cultural functions, with high turnouts of 150–200 people. Similarly Sakhi held South Asian film festivals, and other SAWOs also held various cultural functions. The strategy of including speakers at such functions ensured that the large audiences, who most likely were drawn to the cultural event, would also be compelled to learn about domestic violence. By participating in the mainstream cultural activities of the South Asian community and holding cultural functions, as well as presenting their topic at schools and universities, SAWOs increased their visibility within the community. They also reached out to victims who may have been unaware of the existence of such organizations. Some of these organizations empowered abused women by writing articles about domestic abuse and publishing them in ethnic newspapers, thereby bringing attention to the problem and publicly shaming the abuser.[6] Most important, by increasing their organizations' visibility through multiple strategies, the SAWOs demonstrated the prevalence of violence against women in the South Asian community in the United States. Although nearly all these SAWOs, especially those whose ideology was value oriented, experienced negative reactions from the community, attitudes have been gradually changing. Though not all are positive, there has been increasing acceptance of these SAWOs and, in some cases, the provision of community support through individual donations and by allowing them to do outreach at religious institutions and cultural functions. SAWOs have also received media coverage in mainstream South Asian magazines.

Central to any community mobilization process is galvanizing and mobilizing a great number of people within the community to perceive the problem as real and its resolution as critical. Mobilization involves a core group of people to articulate the problem, a leadership to organize and mobilize others to participate as well as to systematically formulate strategies to respond to the problem. This is crucial to the success of the mobilization process. The growing awareness of the problem of marital violence, through the articulation of the SAWOs, has resulted in increasing numbers of South Asian abused women approaching them, an increased pool of volunteers, and more funding from within the community and from external funding agencies. Gradually these SAWOs have shifted marital violence from a private problem to a public issue.

It is important to understand that ethnic minority women frequently derive their identification from their ethnicity, gender, and class and hence may seek a space that can address the complex issues that arise from such a position. These SAWOs create and maintain this space for South Asian women. While helping South Asian women at the individual level, they also organize and empower them. By articulating their various problems SAWOs socially reconstruct grievances into demands and seek to change the existing dominant cultural and patriarchal structure that oppresses minority immigrant women. They are of vital relevance as they fulfill the need to intersect gender, ethnicity, and class in addressing the problem of marital violence in the South Asian immigrant context.

Despite limited funds, through predominantly voluntary teamwork, by tapping into the professional qualifications of the members within the community, by networking with other organizations, and by being a valuable information resource, these SAWOs provide abused women with various forms of psychological, social, legal, and economic support. They link the macro and micro levels, while empowering South Asian women by moving them from silence to speech. Most important, they raise community and public awareness of the problem of marital violence within the South Asian community. The visible role that SAWOs have come to play within the community and in the larger society is demonstrated by the media coverage that they have received. Leaders of some of these SAWOs have been interviewed on television and radio and their organizations have had extensive coverage in ethnic newspapers. They have also received attention from the mainstream press.

Gusfield (1979, 298) states, "The impact of movements is not only in their intended and stated goals. It is also what they signify by being." The very existence of SAWOs has a crucial impact in that they defy attempts to deny the existence of violence against South Asian women. By their ideology, structure, goals, and actions they demonstrate the need for the careful consideration of gender, ethnicity, and class. Despite some organizational variance, together they can be defined as a growing social movement. Protecting and empowering, these SAWOs perform a dual function. First, they create a dialogue within their organizations and their community and are an important resource for South Asian women who are victims of marital violence. Second, they address the cause of South Asians as a whole in the United States by breaking down stereotypes of South Asians, especially of South Asian women, and by engaging in issues such as immigrant rights and the cultural sensitivity of law enforcement, medical, and educational institutions. Thus they address issues of both gender and ethnicity at the individual, community and societal level. By engaging in dialogue within the South Asian community and between South Asians and the larger movement in the United States, these organizations contribute to the South Asian community and increase the political efficacy of the larger movement in the struggle to end the violence perpetrated against women (Abraham 1995).

The movement is still quite young and its possibilities, direction, and long-term outcomes are still to be seen. As the organizations routinize, we will have to evaluate their ideology, goals, structure, membership, and activities from time to time. This is vital to refresh members' philosophy, maintain organizational integrity, modify the organization's structure if necessary, and determine the most effective ways to direct future efforts. To address domestic violence, we need to mobilize the different segments that make up the South Asian community and transcend ethnic, national, religious, class, and gender divisions. We must simultaneously shift the community's dependence on the model minority image and stop scapegoating the lower socioeconomic classes for all the community's problems. As long as we are vested in a "model" image, we will not be able to truly respond to any problem, be it domestic violence, AIDS, or poverty, for fear of eroding a community image that is perceived as good and desirable. Mobilizing the community to respond to domestic violence involves shifting the focus to explain the limitations and irrelevance of such images for our community identity and its success.

Although my research focused on SAWOs that addressed marital violence, the last decade in the United States also witnessed mobilization concerning other important issues, including health, poverty, religious fundamentalism, gay and lesbian rights, and domestic worker's rights in the South Asian community (Khandelwal 1997b, 1998; Dasgupta 1998). The South Asian population in the United States doubled, new South Asian organizations proliferated, and many more scholars—including a new generation of South Asian students—began writing on the issues that impact our lives.[7] The 1990s also saw the coming of age of a second generation of South Asians in the United States who are addressing diverse concerns growing out of their perceptions and experiences of American and South Asian culture. Women's and men's different backgrounds, including country of origin, age, class, sexuality, ethnicity, region, education, socioeconomic situation, and personal histories, all play into the dynamics of organizations and how we envision change.

9 | Looking Back, Looking Ahead
Reflections on Our Transformational Politic

Mobilizing the community to address domestic violence and other social problems has forced SAWOs
to grapple with a multiplicity of issues and approaches in organizing.
As we attempt to expand the base of the movement and envision change
through a plurality of organizational forms, we continue to be confronted
by the nature of our transformational politic.[1] Hence, in this chapter I
reflect on some of the issues we need to contend with in organizing to
end violence against women. My thoughts here are informed in important ways by my discussions with members of SAWOs and, particularly,
by my involvement with Sakhi over the years, including its period of
crisis following the 1997 decision by Sakhi's board of directors to separate the domestic workers committee (DWC) into an independent organization.[2] I write this chapter not as a critique but rather in the spirit of
optimism, hoping that such reflections have the potential to stimulate
further discussions.

When I started this research almost a decade ago, I thought I would
complete this book in about two years. After all, once I had collected
the data and analyzed it, I was going to concentrate on the task of writing up and disseminating my findings. I could not have been more wrong.
My entrée may have been as a researcher but, like many other South
Asian women, I soon became an active participant in a small but growing movement to address a spectrum of issues that confront us as South
Asians in the United States. Although my identity as a researcher and
my goal to write about domestic violence were always central, increas-

ingly I found there was no easy way to compartmentalize my multiple roles, especially in the context of my work with Sakhi. The lines between researcher, activist, friend, confidante, volunteer, teacher, partner, and mother all seemed to intersect, on occasion even blur, as I sought to find my way in this climate of social change.

Looking back, I have no doubt that at the forefront of progressive change in the South Asian community were South Asian women's organizations. Their survival and growth are essential in addressing social problems and resituating our community identity in ways that create a space for those who are usually unseen and unheard. Although the achievements of SAWOs are considerable, the implicit and explicit organizational identity politics within some organizations, as I saw them evolve over the years in Sakhi, compel me to reflect on issues we need to address within the movement as we move forward. These issues, which are not unique to Sakhi, have an impact on the nature of our struggles in terms of our definition of the problem, strategies for mobilization, and resolution of the problem. These isues are especially important because organizations are one of the crucial channels through which we bring about change. Our transformational politic must challenge the sociopolitical arrangements that oppress us within our communities while also compelling us to be self-reflective within our organizations about the way we think, the way we act, and why we do the things we do.

The organizational structure should reflect what Wini Breines (1989) terms *prefigurative politics*, where the organization through its structure and practices manifests, to some degree, the movement's vision of the ideal society. I deliberately use the word "degree" here, because I believe that, due to practical constraints, the organizational structure cannot be totally in synchrony with an organization's political philosophy. Rather than see issues as dichotomous or in binary opposition, as is often the case in Western models, our transformational politic must draw upon an additive and interconnected paradigm that allows us to link vision and reality, even when practiced within the context of organizations. Six issues are important to consider in the context of SAWOs: (1) organizational orientation, (2) organizational tactics, (3) voice and representation, (4) accountability, (5) funding, and (6) alliances.

Organizational Orientation: Service and Consciousness Raising

Whether the efforts to address domestic violence should be oriented toward service or consciousness raising continues to be debated. The relative importance of service and consciousness raising for an organization's orientation is not a new one for the battered women's movement. Yet the shape it takes in the immigrant context and with regard to the particular issues that arise in SAWOs are important. Given limited resources and the cultural and structural constraints that abused immigrant women face in this country, the issue of orientation has implications not only for an organization's membership but also for the numerous isolated abused South Asian women who seek its support. The question of whether an organization should or can deal with the practical considerations individual abused women face and, at the same time, be effective in producing fundamental sociopolitical change is a tricky one.

Within SAWOs, members' personal histories and their social, economic, and political backgrounds play a major role in the way they view the relative importance of service and consciousness raising. These factors also shape whether members approach marital violence primarily in terms of the maltreatment of women or from a more structural approach to the issue of subordination and social transformation. Many of the founding members of the initial SAWOs and their early membership came from middle-class or upper-middle-class backgrounds in South Asia and were professionals in the United States.

In the mid- and late 1990s, the second-generation South Asians who joined or started new South Asian organizations tended to be the children of wealthy professionals or immigrant families whose parents, despite their own constraints, were economically vested in their children's education. Many of these second-generation volunteers are young upcoming professionals or college students whose worldview is shaped by the ongoing discourse on the politics of class, race, and sexuality. They often take a more structural view. Age, class, education, ethnic background, and life circumstances appear to influence the relative value allocated to service or consciousness raising as an organizational goal.

In the mid-1990s, as Sakhi expanded both in its number of volunteers and in its activities, issues such as service versus consciousness raising led to increasing conflict among the members about the political philosophy and priorities of the organization. Questions concerning priorities, strategies, and the underlying philosophy of the organization were debated, especially the relative worth of service versus consciousness raising for Sakhi's larger agenda. Some segments within the organization felt that Sakhi's ongoing services were diluting the organization's political philosophy. This period witnessed considerable tensions over ideological issues and a perceived lack of sensitivity of some volunteers to issues such as class, sexuality, and religious fundamentalism.

Sakhi's domestic workers committee, with an active body of volunteers whose focus was to organize for the rights of domestic workers in the South Asian community, increasingly appeared to take on the form of a semi-autonomous organization. This was an outcome of factors such as personal differences within Sakhi; some members' dissatisfaction with the day-to-day functioning of the organization and the perception that Sakhi had lost its radical edge; the belief held by some that Sakhi did not adequately address individual and class politics; and some members' fears that some board members and the program director were assuming too much power in the decision-making process. This dissatisfaction manifested itself in factionalism, lack of trust within the organization, and challenges to the roles of some members within the organization. While there were important questions that could have been addressed, little was achieved as critical political issues were frequently reduced to personal acrimony.

In April of 1997, feeling that the organization was in jeopardy from this internal crisis, Sakhi's board of directors took the decision to dissolve the domestic workers committee, while simultaneously committing to help create a new independent organization that Sakhi would support until it was able to establish itself. This decision was followed by a period of internal and public conflict, with different segments in support or opposition. Over time this organizational and ideological conflict subsided, with both Sakhi and the then newly created Workers Awaaz trying to build their respective organizations. However, this crisis took its toll on the organizations and on the individuals involved.

For me personally this was a very hard time, because I admired many of the women who worked in Sakhi, including some domestic workers committee members. I believe many of them made important contributions. Yet having observed the ideological and practical dilemmas within the organization in 1997, I am convinced that many of these issues could not be reconciled due to increasing differentiation between the different groups in goals and strategies. The increasing factionalism within Sakhi's membership as well as the denigration of some individuals by others led to an environment in which the organization could no longer sustain itself. The immaturity and irresponsibility of certain voices added fuel to this fire, leaving no room for any sustained constructive dialogue. Lack of trust and blatant hostility among some members also contributed to the organizational crisis.

In my interactions with Sakhi members prior to the 1997 break-up, I found that those who perceived themselves as more radical within the organization believed that consciousness raising and collective-oriented action were ultimately the only mechanisms for social transformation, while service was seen as primarily a Band-aid.[3] They tended to view service as "social work," the realm of practitioners, not as a place for advocates seeking radical social transformation.[4] These radicals pointed to the danger of becoming bogged down in service without time for collective critical thinking and action. Yet others, whom I shall label "moderates" only for purposes of differentiation, felt that in any immigrant context where women lack support both within and outside their community, exclusion of service is an unrealistic approach to social transformation, especially for organizations addressing domestic violence. They argued that in a country where abused immigrant women lack knowledge of and access to mainstream support services, there could be no real empowerment without some organizational commitment to addressing the immediate, day-to-day problems that abused women face. These moderates felt that consciousness raising without sensitivity to the practical needs of abused women, especially in recent immigrant communities, hinders women from leaving abusive relationships. Therefore the provision and accessibility of resources was seen as essential in reducing South Asian women's vulnerability to abuse and therefore as an integral component of the empowerment process.

The history of the battered women's movement has shown us that there is no easy resolution to this dilemma. Although the service orientation in itself does not provide many prospects for substantive structural change, those who have a more radical agenda should not lightly dismiss the value of service as one possible avenue of consciousness raising through individual empowerment in the immigrant community. Service can be an effective way of bringing abused women into the organization, recruiting and incorporating volunteers as a part of the larger grass-roots mobilization process.[5] Engaging the mainstream through the provision of services can become a form of radical intervention. It can empower abused women to participate in the organization at some point and not define themselves as passive recipients of support. Service can also be a form of consciousness raising if it publicizes the issue and thus helps bring change in institutional policy and practice.

In the United States, where such dichotomies often prevail, it is relatively easy to assume an organizational model that views service and consciousness raising as mutually exclusive. Framing the issue as services versus consciousness raising, however, belies the reality of the immigrant experience.[6] This is not to say that organizations must not set goals and priorities, but that each organization must also reflect on the challenges it will face in achieving them and take realistic stock of the resources it has. While SAWOs have to be careful not to be spread too thin, they must at the same time allow for some degree of flexibility based on practicality. The cultural and socioeconomic constraints immigrant women encounter in seeking help in the current milieu necessitate that organizations, despite their set goals and strategies, creatively intertwine service and consciousness raising. This is imperative until we develop a solid support network among organizations that allows for both specialization and interdependence. The future success of the movement lies in our present ability within organizations to confront immediate problems while simultaneously addressing the structural causes for these problems.[7]

Tactics toward the Community: Negotiation and Confrontation

Given that the community is diverse and competing loyalties are a part of identity politics, how do we create a consciousness of the need for substantive changes within the community? We know that major segments of the South Asian community continue to be reluctant to acknowledge marital violence as a social problem. For much too long, many in the South Asian community have accepted the model minority image as good and desirable. We ignore the many ways such images oppress us and deny the reality of the problems we need to address both within our community and in our relations with other ethnic minorities.

Some mainstream South Asians think that to challenge the oppressive elements of our culture means discarding our entire South Asian identity. All too often the wealthy male members and religious leaders of the community manage both external and internal impressions of its identity. They become gatekeepers, controlling the image of the South Asian community. Frequently the interests of the gatekeepers are not truly representative of the community's needs, yet these individuals attain legitimacy through the power they derive on the basis of their socioeconomic status, either within the community or in the larger American society. Many South Asian women too collude in maintaining these specific identity constructions. Tensions therefore inevitably exist among the diverse segments of the community as members struggle with competing forces that shape community identity and the actualities of the lives we live.

While there is no doubt among SAWOs that pressure must be applied by organizations to bring about social change within the community, there is contention over tactics. Within the movement, radical sections see the method of confrontation as most effective and more likely to bring longer-lasting gains. Moderates feel that the tactic of negotiating, or persuading the community that it is in its best interest to address issues such as marital violence, is more likely to gain popular appeal and help achieve transformation from within.

I believe that while persuasion may have greater appeal, the danger exists that such a tactic will lead to limited issue-based change without challenging the essential core of dominant and subordinate relations within the community. While persuasion has its merits, those who focus on that tactic alone must be careful not to compromise the larger agenda for small gains within the community. Persuasion can also imply that the onus of bringing about change lies primarily with the organization and as such minimizes the responsibility of the community for its own actions. At the same time those who choose a confrontational approach must carefully weigh whether such a tactic really allows us a base to maintain control of the issues important to us or whether the act of confrontation becomes a limited end in itself.

Given the social construction of South Asian identity and the arenas where it is symbolically articulated, those of us addressing marital violence cannot afford exclusion from mainstream cultural activities. Rather than exclude ourselves or be excluded, we should use these arenas as sites for challenging the status quo in multiple ways. Sometimes this may entail persuasive tactics and participatory activities that creatively challenge the existing normative order while strategically claiming a space that is otherwise denied to us. At other times such an approach may not be appropriate and confrontation may be essential so that we do not blunt the challenge or shield the very people and acts that we fight against. Participatory activities can run the risk of compromise and collusion if there is no serious commitment to the agenda of progressive change. Similarly continuous confrontation can thwart the chances for change if it pushes further away those whom we want to include in our struggles.

Part of the mobilization process must be continuously to bring varying degrees of pressure through all means possible rather than assuming there is only one definitive way. It is important for those of us involved in SAWOs to understand that immigrants do not always fit into an either/or category as defined by the dominant culture. Therefore, the mobilization process must also not limit itself to an either/or approach. Instead an additive approach aids us in achieving our shared values and common concerns. Immigrants frequently draw upon certain cultural values on the basis of their histories and look at future possibilities to create imagined communities in a foreign country.[8] This is an important part of the transnational experience and the process of renegotiating ties and bonds in a foreign land. Rather than totally dismissing the cultures of these imagined communities, organizations should strategically use both tactics to redefine our communities. We should make clear that our community is best served when all segments of community consciously discard those elements that oppress some of us. This belief can be articulated by strategically using both confrontation and persuasion through multiple forums where these issues are raised. The community must be sensitized to problems even as strategies for resolution are continuously addressed. We also need to convey the idea that addressing problems, both within the community and in mainstream American society, may be perceived not as detrimental to the community image but rather as an important part of progressive change.

While the community should be given no opportunity to deny the existence of social problems or attitudes and acts of discrimination, it also behooves organizations to systematically think of their tactics when dealing with our communities. In the existing political climate of anti-immigrant and racist sentiment that our communities confront, SAWOs must be consistently conscious of the meaningfulness and relevance of our tactics for the work we do. There will always be some tensions between the issues we seek to address and the tactics we choose. However the movement is best served when our tactics carefully link vision with pragmatism as we work within, at the margin, and from outside the communities we seek to transform.

Voice: Language and Representation

A transformational politic involves organizations that consciously reflect on the nature of voice within the movement. The more I looked at SAWOs and spoke to individuals within them, I found myself reflecting on the complexity of voice and representation. We criticize segments of the South Asian population, particularly the elite, for their false representation of the community and for appropriating a voice that silences. We also need to address how language is used within SAWOs. Who become the voices within the organization, in the work we do with other organizations and in our interactions with the larger communities we seek to change? We need to understand what space these voices claim and to what end.

When SAWOs initially began addressing the problem of domestic violence in the community, they became an important alternative, albeit marginalized, voice that challenged the existing community construction of South Asian homes as harmonious and violence free. In the early stages of organizational development, it was the voices of committed individuals in SAWOs, particularly the founding members, that determined strategy rather than voices from the organizational base. This was not much of an issue within most SAWOs, as the membership was still in the incipient stage. Founders implicitly and explicitly claimed and attained the legitimacy of voice from their involvement in the creation of these organizations, their vision, and their commitment. Despite differences among organizations in membership, all the early organizations had a large degree of homogeneity in the profile of their membership in terms of age, class, and professional background. Ethnicity and gender, however, were the more manifest expressions of organizational identity formation within these organizations and frequently were the implicit criteria used by new volunteers entering the organization. Yet as these SAWOs grew and membership increased beyond the initial burst of energy by a few of volunteers, particularly in organizations such as Sakhi, the membership profile changed. I found Sakhi throughout the 1990s to be an organization struggling to work through organizational goals, organizational processes, and volunteers' subjective notions of transformation. Here the issue of voice and representation became crucial.

As Sakhi grew, an organizational dilemma developed. Despite a serious attempt at using voice to retain the spirit of collective decision making, organizational decisions were frequently based on the ability of a select few voices to influence emotions. Some of these women did play an important role in building the organization, of course, yet the danger lay when one or two women used voice to control ownership of the organization's agenda or to assume to speak for all. As the organization expanded, friction increasingly arose over the priority of competing projects and strategies. Rather than a strict collective adherence to a particular political philosophy or organizational goal, decisions increasingly depended on a specific individual's ability to use her voice to sway the collective on the particular agenda at hand. Thus the disparities in the power of voices within the organization took on more significance in terms of priorities, strategies, and the realization of goals. Those women who were not as articulate or were relatively quiet tended to get lost in the decision-making process.

One such example was the important idea of bringing the domestic workers project into Sakhi's larger framework, as previously discussed. This idea stemmed from the belief of some members of the organization that doing so would truly challenge and redefine the way domestic violence was constructed and create an alternative paradigm. It would also incorporate class issues more systematically into the organization and make it a stronger grass-roots organization in which the power structure developed from the bottom. Sakhi would be an organization where members of the immigrant working class, particularly those that were exploited, could find a space to voice a range of issues that they confronted at home, at work, and in the community. As a result, workers' empowerment and agency would be increased. Yet what was a brilliant vision and an important addition to the organization was slowly corroded. This corrosion occurred when a segment of the organization tried to make the domestic workers issue the major priority of Sakhi rather than one important but connected aspect of Sakhi's commitment to end all forms of violence against women. While the rhetoric within the organization still expressed a commitment to address all aspects of violence against women, increasingly some members with considerable influence within the domestic workers committee began strategically shifting the focus to the issue of domestic workers' rights. Simultaneously relations among Sakhi's members became acrimonious, and various allegations were made about volunteers' relations with domestic workers or ties with employers of domestic workers.

Although working with serious commitment, some members of this more radicalized faction of the domestic workers committee increasingly began using voice in ways that denigrated the work of other segments of the organization, particularly that of the program director and some members of the board. Time and again ideological and personal conflicts between members working on different committees were expressed by using voice to socially construct some members (particularly some board members) as oppressors and others as victims challenging this oppression. Most of the latter part of 1996 was spent on internal organizational efforts trying to retain the spirit of collectivity, working at restructuring the decision-making process. However, most general meetings broke down as voices were raised in personal conflict and in conflict over agendas, strategies, or the types of decisions, including the power and role of the board. In this atmosphere, voice and representation took on a very different meaning. For some, the new divisiveness of voices was seen as a necessary process of political engagement, even hailed as a victory depending on who won the issue. Yet for others who were the target of many of the oppositional labels, the use of voice was experienced as an act of oppression. Real differences somehow became personal, and perhaps some individuals exploited the situation for personal power. Clearly internal politics diverted our attention from Sakhi's important issues in the world outside the organization.

Some of this conflict is essentially a part of organizational growth and the ongoing struggle to link the cultural and structural aspects of organizations that are part of a movement. Oppositional voices should be raised to challenge oppressors within organizations or to raise the consciousness of those whose own life circumstances may not have provided an understanding of all facets of oppression. This was the original goal of the voices on behalf of the domestic workers. Oppositional voices can also take on an agenda of personal power, however, seeking to silence those who oppose them. This is what I believe happened in

Sakhi in 1996. On both sides issues were blurred by personal power politics. Having observed and participated in what went on, I am not convinced that there is great value in using voice in ways that allow for a façade of dialogue within organizations but in reality become an arena for some to abuse others indiscriminately without any sense of accountability. I was amazed, for example, at how often certain members of the domestic workers committee strategically used the rhetoric of political correctness, arbitrarily labeling others within the organization as "homophobic," "bourgeois corporate wives," "religious fundamentalists," or "racists," without devoting any time to verifying the authenticity of such labels. Women so labeled were either silenced or forced in self-defense to prove that these allegations and labels were untrue and unfair. Such labels do not allow room for change or negotiation.

There were mistakes and pain caused on both sides. Thus I strongly believe that reflecting on the use and misuse of voice within organizations should be a crucial part of our transformational politic. Surely there is room to use voice to challenge while also building a strong and supportive community where women can be helped to reflect upon the complexity of competing loyalties and their ramifications for the work we do.

Despite claims of diversity as some SAWOs have grown, the language and activities within the organizations often contain an implicit assumption that individuals who seek a space within the organization must think, speak, and behave like the core membership. This can result in the type of homogeneity that silences those individuals who cannot speak "in the same way" and has frequently led, often unconsciously, to the exclusion of members on the basis of age and class difference. This forced homogeneity can then finally and explosively break down, as happened in Sakhi in 1996 and early 1997. Without a practice and a structure of dialogue to explore real differences, when differences do break through the façade of agreement, they tend to become grounds for division. They are experienced as divisive and generate power struggles rather than organizational growth. Organizations in their transformational politic must reflect on how they can increase inclusiveness without jeopardizing the goals of the organizations. Each individual's point of entrée into the organization is different, based on her personal life experience and level of political awareness of the various facets of oppression and the underlying causes. It is up to older members to use their voices to recruit and socialize newer members to the organization's ideology and strategies. But it is also important for these older members to be open to new ways of thinking rather than using their entrenched powerful voices to drown out others' ideas. The type of entry new members have within an organization can affect how they use their voice and how they experience this opportunity for empowerment. Therefore it is crucial for SAWOs to reflect on the role of language and voice and their impact on volunteers seeking to participate in our transformational politic.

Voice is also an important issue in terms of the organization's interaction with the public. Members within an organization may be critical of the fact that certain individuals constantly serve as the organization's front-stage voice, enhancing their own personal status in the public arena while claiming collective representation. Despite the increased membership base of these organizations and a commitment to the work by many individuals within them, I found that the SAWOs' public voice was usually that of those committed individuals who could clearly navigate the rhetoric of political correctness as defined either by liberal mainstream institutions or by radical groups. In addition to Sakhi, concerns of voice and representation were also issues for other SAWOs such as SEWAA and Apna Ghar as they expanded and became established.

It must become an organizational goal of SAWOs to make their organizational voice more inclusive, so that their public voice better represents all the women who seek a space within the organization (as well as the women it represents). Of course this means not just adding blindly to the representative voices but a commitment by those who have already attained such a space to make room for other voices to be heard both within the organization and in the public arena. This entails a genuine belief on the part of prominent and more experienced leaders within the organizations in the principle that we can best mobilize and build when we have allowed for the heterogeneity of voices without compromising the movement.[9]

Finally, voice plays an important role in the process of acknowledgment. As human beings we all need reinforcement of the value of the work we do. In most cultures, women's work is taken for granted and important individual achievements go unacknowledged. Therefore using voice to acknowledge one another's work, especially the work that often remains unseen, should be an important part of our transformational politic. As part of the ongoing movement our collective voice should acknowledge the important individual efforts of those whose vision and commitment put issues such as domestic violence in the South Asian community in the United States on the map. Using our voices to celebrate such individuals should be a part of our transformational politic. At the same time prominent individuals who receive such recognition and have gained legitimacy in various important arenas must acknowledge the work of unseen others. These individuals must generously use the power of their voice to highlight the work of others and not misuse their voice to devour smaller voices within their organization. When voice is wielded without attention to critical self-reflection and accountability, whether by individuals or by a collective, in service or in consciousness raising, within the organization or out in the public, we run the risk of jeopardizing the movement.

Accountability: Individual and Collective

To reflect on voice is also to reflect on accountability. Accountability is a constant challenge that individuals and collectives have to address within organizations and in the work that they do. An important part of our transformational politic should be to be accountable to ourselves and to the women we work with as we try to build an active, broadly based, grass-roots movement to end domestic violence. If we want to create a base from which abused women can challenge their position of oppression, we need to systematically think of how we organize to support these individuals through our collective action. To engage in such action we need to build a sense of individual and collective accountability as we mobilize, organize, reach out, and protest.

One important arena of accountability lies in our organizational strategies in supporting abused women. For example, we know that individual recourse to the legal system is an important avenue through which a woman can challenge her abuser and seek redress in this legally oriented society. For immigrants such as Syeda Sufian, however, we saw that social pressure from Sakhi through public protest can be an extremely effective alternative strategy in the South Asian community, where "honor and shame" are an integral part of the value system.[10] The same notions of honor and shame that are used to keep women silent about their abuse in the South Asian community were strategically used by Sakhi to publicly shame the abuser and seek redress for the victim. Taking this step can demonstrate to the abuser and other potential abusers that the woman has alternative sources of power and support. Not only did Sakhi publicly demonstrate but it also continued with important follow-up support for Syeda. Such actions should be a part of the larger political strategy of organizations, but they also entail a high degree of accountability on the part of members in organizations.

In a society such as the United States, where some acts of public protest may lead to legal suits against the organization, it is important that members assume collective responsibility for all potential legal action. Members of an organization and those who partake in public protest should be individually and collectively accountable for their actions. They should not presume that a legal suit is a nonissue or abrogate their legal responsibility once the protest is over so that the burden falls on the organization, especially in cases where the organization does not have the resources to handle such suits. Within the organization there should be a coordinated effort to address the problems, mobilize people in support of the issue, and seek effective strategies to achieve the desired goal.

Similarly, when organizations use public strategies of resistance such as supporting a victim by collectively demonstrating outside her abuser's home so as to shame him, organizational accountability to the abused woman should include careful attention to ongoing support for her. An abused woman, who may have felt empowered by the public support, may end up feeling betrayed and isolated in its aftermath if there is no adequate follow-up. In the immigrant context, for organizations to encourage women to take action toward ending their own abuse without providing an appropriate support system is problematic. While public support can be an effective strategy, especially for undocumented women, these women also fear that public visibility, by drawing attention to their abuse, may also draw attention to their illegal status. Therefore without organizational follow-up such a strategy may have limited success for the individual.

SAWOs often find it hard to manage the fragile balance between the needs of an individual case and an organization's larger political strategy in addressing the case. Organizations must be careful about how they use public strategies of resistance in individual cases. Time and again they need to critically evaluate the connection between a woman's choice of action and the organization's choice of response. Identifying the oppressor alone is not enough if this is not followed with same level of commitment to support the victim so that she is truly empowered. For example, I was amazed at the handful of South Asian women who came to support Syeda Sufian when her case came up in the criminal courts in May 1999. While there were a few members from Sakhi and there could have been more, what struck me most was the absence of all those (many members of Workers Awaaz) who had been there for the public protest outside the abuser's house a few years earlier. I believe it was as important for these protesters to have been there in court, supporting Syeda Sufian and letting the perpetrator, the community, and the courts know that the SAWOs will not tolerate violence against women. Personal and organizational conflict should have been put aside as we made an individual's fight for justice a part of our collective struggle.

Public protest can become a means of organizational aggrandizement rather than an important mechanism of empowerment and change if there is no follow-up. When organizations lose the momentum after a public protest and don't follow through in their continued support of the victim, they have lulled the abused woman into a false sense of security and

shown a lack of organizational accountability in their strategy of resistance. Besides public protest and legal recourse, we must also find alternative strategies of protest and resistance.

Accountability of individuals to the organization to which they belong is also important. We all have time constraints and juggle multiple
aspects of our lives, yet the very nature of volunteer work in SAWOs
requires a high degree of individual and collective accountability if the
movement is to be successful. Individuals need to feel a strong sense of
commitment to the goals of the organization and a commitment to partake in its activities. Individuals need to reflect on the ways that they
can commit to the organization and not make promises they cannot follow through on, especially as others depend on their ability to come
through. This is often the hardest struggle, yet it must be a part of the
reality of our transformational politic. It is even more important within
organizations that are collectively oriented in structure for individuals
to be accountable for their actions. In such organizations, there is a danger
that the collective can become the mantle that allows a lack of individual
accountability in the collective work process. Organizations have to develop mechanisms to evaluate individual and collective accountability
and connect the two for a more effective movement.

Funding: Public and Private

To many the issue of funding may seem inconsequen-
tial to the larger mobilizing process. However, given that SAWOs are crucial to the movement, funding of these organizations is an important issue.
Funding is needed for community building and for the kind of sustained
consciousness-raising activities involved in transforming our thinking
about sociopolitical issues such as domestic violence, worker's rights,
gay and lesbian rights, and health care. Often the issue of funding is seen
by organizations, particularly those that work within a radical framework, as an administrative liability and as peripheral to the larger issue
of transformation. Yet funding must not be dismissed as mere organizational maintenance; rather, it should be integrated into our transformational politic.

The issue of fund-raising, especially for organizations addressing
domestic violence, is a complex one. Funding sources include state funding, grants from corporations, grants from foundations, individual contributions, fund-raising activities, and membership fees. A part of the
transformational politic entails devoting attention to reconciling the demands of funding sources and the organization's own philosophical position on issues. The question to be asked is how to acquire funding
without compromising the values that are at the heart of the organiza-

tion. Obtaining state funds helped an organization such as Apna Ghar run a shelter and expand its services. Although there were some state limitations and restrictions within which Apna Ghar had to work, the organization did not perceive obtaining state funds as conflicting philosophically with its ideology. But what happens if the structure of such funding does conflict with the very principles that an organization collectively holds?

Sakhi provides a useful context for discussion. From its inception until 1997, Sakhi was unwilling to obtain state funding. This position was based on the conviction of some members, especially those involved in the organization prior to spring 1997, that such funding would run the danger of compromising Sakhi's more radical agenda. Wary of the mainstreaming of previous radical organizations in the larger battered women's movement through their adherence to state-defined parameters for the use of funds, Sakhi avoided such aid so as to maintain its autonomy. However, Sakhi also needed funds for outreach activities, organizational building, and organizational maintenance that would enhance the efficacy of the work it did. Where should the money come from?

As the organization grew, some Sakhi members used corporate sponsorships for certain forms of outreach events, viewing these corporations as a legitimate alternative source for funds. Within the organization, however, radical members saw acceptance of such monies as indirectly collaborating with those very corporations that are a part of the systemic oppression individuals face in the capitalist economy. They saw this as even more problematic than taking money from the state. This led to important and crucial discussions as to which corporations were relatively acceptable on the basis of their corporate policies. But here too there were differences. Some members assumed that all funding should be restricted to appropriate liberal or radically oriented granting agencies or drawn from individual donors and the community. These sources too, however, have their own limitations, both politically and pragmatically.

Prior to the recent allocation of state funds under VAWA, many members within SAWOs, especially those that saw themselves as radical, tended to be dismissive of state and private corporations as possible avenues of funding and preferred to rely on grants from progressively oriented organizations. This was extremely limiting. With the exception of a few, the majority of foundations that supported SAWOs tended to give to those organizations that had already gained some visibility in order to publicly profile their own foundations as multicultural or progressively oriented. Sometimes these foundations will stop funding if they sense an ongoing power struggle within the organization they fund and if they have concerns about organizational goals and procedures. Losing funding, needless to say, is a major setback for organizations that depend on such funds for their survival. For example, a funder that had financially supported Sakhi abstained from continued support during the 1997 upheaval, leaving Sakhi scrambling for an alternative source or risking the sudden death of the organization. In Sakhi's case the generosity of some individuals who were committed to Sakhi's goals kept the organization financially afloat in this period of conflict. However, obtaining sufficient funds from individual donors in the long run is unlikely. To do so also implies a reliance either on those who often already have very limited resources or on an elite whose politics may be totally antithetical to the SAWO's ideology. In the context of domestic violence, there is also no guarantee that some of the potential individual donors may themselves not be perpetrators of marital abuse or other forms of class- or religion-based oppression.

If funding sources are so restricted, how do we obtain funds so that organizations can actually do the work that enhances the goals of the movement and not devote large portions of their time to obtaining the funds vital to survival? My own observations lead me to say that since most SAWOs inevitably do need some form of funding to support their work, funding in the future will have to become an integral part of the processes of organization building and political change. I believe the choice of funding must be guided both by ideology and by pragmatism. Focus on ideology alone without some understanding of the value of a pragmatic feminism, especially as it pertains to the issue of domestic violence, can ultimately be our own undoing in our struggle to end violence. By being organizationally too self-limiting about funding in the short run, we may lose more in the long run when unrealistic boundaries result in the dissolution of the organization. Lack of funding over a long period jeopardizes the survival of the very organizations crucial to the movement. I don't mean that we should subvert our ideological positions by taking funds indiscriminately. Organizations need to critically reflect on their funding sources, and carefully draw lines so that they don't subvert their vision in their search for funding. I am convinced there is room to increase our avenues of financial support so that we can maximize the efficacy of our organizations and of the movement.

As part of our long-term vision, we need to be practical and strategically tap those very sources that use institutional criteria as a form of gatekeeping, particularly to exclude the funding of radically oriented organizations. While being careful not to be coopted, utilizing mainstream funding in the short run is one means of appropriating that which is frequently denied to us for achieving more long-term gains. Similarly, connecting with funding organizations can become an entrée for some individuals from SAWOs into the decision-making process whereby they can influence the direction of future fund allocation in more radical ways. Ultimately, reclaiming what is kept away from us through strategic maneuvering but without losing sight of our main political agenda may have to be part of the long-term strategy to challenge existing paradigms of state and corporate funding and to create new ones.

It is imperative that as we work within our communities to address domestic violence we also try and draw resources from the community. The larger community should be encouraged to support organizations that address domestic violence in whatever ways possible, including the funding of organizations addressing domestic violence. We know that members of the larger South Asian community participate in $1,000-a-plate dinners for political parties and other galas and contribute large funds to build temples, mosques, and churches. Often this is done to enhance their status within the community, to further political connections, or to articulate the importance of our rich cultural heritage. SAWOs need to continue to attempt to strategically shift South Asian community interests and funding toward issues such as domestic violence that do indeed affect all segments of our community. In a capitalist culture where money is valued so highly, we need to challenge our community to invest in the social well-being of our community in all its diversity.

Organizations seeking funds must focus on consciousness-raising activities in community fund-raising, politicizing social events. They must systematically inculcate a belief, particularly among the elite, that such financial support cannot derive from a mentality oriented toward "charity to the poor" but rather must come from an understanding that issues such as domestic violence are social problems that cut across ethnic, class, and national boundaries. Only then can funding from the community be integral to our transformational politic.

Alliances: Conviction and Pragmatism

Alliances with other oppressed groups in the United States are an important mechanism for gaining equal rights and for struggling against discrimination on the basis of the color of our skin, accent, class, gender, country of origin, or legal status. Coalitions are based on common interests and do not necessarily entail ideological conformity among the different organizations participating in the coalition (Ferree and Miller 1985). In the larger battered women's movement, the formation of coalitions has been an important mechanism for organizations of different ideological perspectives to link up with one another to pursue a common concrete goal (Bunch 1987; Arnold 1995). Yet coalition-based work is very difficult among diverse groups due to both external and internal pressures for balancing the needs of the coalition with those of each organization's membership (Staggenborg 1986). Gretchen Arnold, in an article entitled "Dilemmas of Feminist Coalitions," argues that the problem in sustaining coalitions arises primarily from the "contradiction between the structural features of coalitions and the organizational requirements of some feminist ideologies" (1995, 277). Given the diversity of issues to be addressed and the differences in organizational ideologies among SAWOs, it is important to reflect on the nature of our coalition or on what I will refer to here as alliances. As we move forward we need to explore the possibilities and limitations of alliances. How do we avoid letting issues related to the alliance undermine or threaten the very existence of some of the organizations that are part of the alliance? How do we resolve differences based on members' latent or manifest allegiance to basic propositions of class, sexual orientation, ethnicity, and nationality as they pertain to the nature of our alliances?

From 1991 onward, Sakhi had managed to have the FIA (Federation of Indians in America), the official organizers of the India Day parade, include it as a participant in the parade. Sakhi saw this as an important public site to show that domestic violence was a problem and that organizations such as Sakhi existed as a sisterhood of women committed to support and bring about social change in their community. As Madhulika Khandelwal (1997b, 28) puts it, "The Indian organizations sponsoring these events showed displeasure at the radical politics of the new South Asian Organizations but they did not bar them from participating as they were considered insignificant." In 1994, when the FIA banned the South Asian Lesbian and Gay Association (SALGA) members from marching as a contingent, Sakhi took the important decision of inviting members of SALGA to march in Sakhi's contingent. This was an important type of alliance.

Such an alliance in this mainstream activity thus becomes a site to challenge the status quo. It resulted in FIA's displeasure with Sakhi. This was indicated in 1995 when the FIA did not allow Sakhi, SALGA, or SAAA (South Asian AIDS Action) to participate in the parade. They claimed that this was an "India Day" parade and that organizations with "South Asian" in their name represented a constituency larger than India and therefore did not fit into the official rubric of the parade. An important outcome of this exclusion was an alliance in the form of a task force among these organizations to protest against FIA's discriminatory policies and its stand on issues such as women's rights, homosexuality, and AIDS. Attempts were made to put pressure on the FIA, but the latter held to its original position. The alliance sought broader support through the mainstream media, but ultimately the organizations remained excluded from the official parade. However, the alliance, with the support of other organizations, publicly confronted the FIA by shouting slogans, raising banners, and voicing their objection to the FIA exclusionary tactics, especially in an event that culturally symbolized a form of ethnic pride. Such alliances are crucial.

Some of the struggles within Sakhi in 1996 exemplify the complexity of alliance. At times it becomes important to weigh the relative worth of an alliance in a particular event and the types of competing pressures it places on an organization and its responsibilities to its members. In 1996 Sakhi was not able to participate in the India Day parade because it did not get a sponsor (a requirement for inclusion) that would take on the liability for its participation, nor was SALGA allowed to particpate. The same year, however, the Pakistan Day parade was willing to include Sakhi but not SALGA. SALGA was told by one of the organizers "not to show their gay and lesbian faces at the parade." For Sakhi this situation was extremely difficult. The group was trying to make inroads into the Pakistani community, where it itself had little legitimacy, and also wanted to use this mainstream event as an arena to publicly demonstrate that domestic violence existed within the Pakistani community. The question that now lay before Sakhi was whether to march alone and/or protest with SALGA. According to Sakhi's August 1996 notice to its members, the following positions were put forth at the initial meeting on the subject that seventeen volunteers attended:

> Some volunteers who felt that without showing our support for SALGA, we are not staying true to our mission statement which includes our commitment to fighting oppression based on sexuality. Some other volunteers felt that despite Sakhi considering itself to being a "South Asian" group, Sakhi is not yet visible in the Pakistani community and that Sakhi itself has very few Pakistani volunteers. Keeping in mind our long-term commitment to making inroads into the Pakistani community, we should thus march in the parade and assert our presence. These volunteers also felt that marching in the parade does not mean that we are compromising our commitment to fighting all form of oppression against women" (Sakhi, Aug. 1996 notice to members)

At this meeting it appeared that the group could not reach a consensus. On the basis of Sakhi's written policy of November 1995, approved at a general body meeting, it was decided that if a consensus was not reached, then the Sakhi board and staff would make the final decision. This decision was to take into consideration the diverse opinions of its volunteers and the larger interests of Sakhi as a South Asian group (Sakhi letter, Aug. 1996). Thus the board, "respecting the views of all volunteers, including those in the minority and keeping in mind that one minority group in Sakhi are Pakistanis," took the following decision:

> Sakhi will officially march in the Pakistan day parade on Sunday, August 25th 1996 with Sakhi banners and flyers. This year, we will also include specific material about our opposition to welfare and immigration reform. Sakhi will also distribute a one-page flyer stating Sakhi's commitment to fighting oppression based on sexuality and our support of SALGA's right to march in the parade. At the point of passing the SALGA demonstration on the parade en route, we will show our respect and solidarity with them by hold[ing] hands and turning towards the protesters. We will request that the SALGA protestors be respectful of our marching in the parade. (Sakhi volunteer information, Aug. 20, 1996)

At a general meeting, however, immediately after this announcement, there were some members who were outraged by the board members' decision and insisted that they rescind it. Others felt that while the SALGA alliance was important, it should not force Sakhi to ignore an ethnic minority within the community. Ultimately, after considerable discussion for which I was the facilitator, it was decided that we would vote on whether we had confidence in the board's decision. Confidence in the board decision was demonstrated by a narrow 15–14 vote. Members who had wanted the board to rescind the decision then claimed that the vote was too close a call, and ultimately they were able to pressure the organization not to participate in the Pakistan Day parade. In reality such an outcome was not helpful substantively either for our alliance or for the organization. In a way the organizers of the parade had won, for they no longer had to contend publicly with gays and lesbians or domestic violence. So in demonstrating the strength of our alliance, we had in fact silenced an important minority, those Pakistani women who wanted to march in the parade and show their community that domestic violence existed and that individually and collectively we could fight it. There may be no one right answer or easy solution. We need to think seriously about the nature of our alliances and their impact and what types of compromises (if any) we will make on the basis of the multiple competing needs of both the alliance and the members of our respective organizations.

Finally, while they are difficult, alliances should be an important part of our transformative politic. They allow us to forge those links and connections that usually provide us with a strong base when we fight for issues. At the same time, we need to delineate our goals and the basis of our alliances for mobilizing to respond to the various problems that face our community. Responding to a diverse community with diverse needs involves multiple approaches and important alliances to bring about a social transformation.

My reflections here stem from a strong conviction that our transformational politic must link vision with pragmatism, voice with action. This is easier said than done, of course, and it is easier to write about than to act out. We don't need homogeneity, but an acknowledged heterogeneity. We need those individuals who have a vision who can challenge our ways of thinking. At the same time, we need those individuals who do the important practical, organizational maintenance work essential for the movement.

Let us be careful that in the process of our social transformation we do not demonize those who share our goals but who use different strategies. To do so only allows the dominant groups to take advantage of our divisiveness for their own gain.

There are no simple solutions as we work at our uphill task of social transformation. We must work together while acknowledging difference so that we increase the momentum of the movement rather than fracture it. To mobilize the community, South Asian women's organizations that address domestic violence need to work together and tap into one another's communication networks and resources. The leadership and the larger membership have to be willing to invest considerable time and to hold out against cooptation. Because there will be ideological differences and varied organizational approaches to address the problems within the community, we need to engage in productive dialogue rather than succumbing to issue-based separateness. When we get embroiled in one approach as definitive, we exclude the possibility of uniting the multiple segments of our community in addressing a problem such as domestic violence.

Mobilization is a sociopolitical process, and therefore we have to help members in the community, especially those who are relatively disempowered, understand that they have the potential to participate in the process of social change. We must show that while as individuals it is often difficult to fight oppressive forces, as a collective working within organizations we become empowered and can effectively contribute to the movement to end violence against women.

Since the larger community is often watching the activities of

SAWOs, it becomes increasingly important to avoid explicit conflict between members of organizations that can potentially threaten the legitimacy of our work and our ability to achieve social transformation. What organizations do, why we make the choices we make, and what effects these choices have for members within the organization, the community, and the larger society must be taken into account in our transformational politic. It is not only what we do, but how we do it that is important. As a relatively young immigrant community, South Asian women and men involved in organizations seeking social transformation will have to survive organizational growing pains as they struggle for change. It is also important to understand that we are not all at the same point in our political awareness. Part of the movement involves linking individuals with different levels of awareness into the collective learning process as we envision change. We will have to make difficult but important choices about goals and strategies, and work to bridge the gap between what we say and the actualities of our lives.

As we expand the base of the movement we will have to deal with a plurality of organizational forms. While we may disagree and confront one another on our strategies, we must self-consciously avoid letting symbolic dissension within and between organizations paralyze the movement. Rather than seeing the diversity of organizational forms and approaches as a deterrent to the movement, we should see it as a mechanism of expansion, as long as it allows the inclusion of a plurality of approaches without losing sight of the key goals of the movement. A transformative politic must entail a space for both individual and collective empowerment. Ultimately it is only by linking vision with pragmatism in our individual and collective efforts that we can effectively seek to end all forms of violence against women. We are our communities . . . our communities are ourselves.

Profile of Respondents at Time of Interview (Self-Report)

NO.	PSEUDONYM	AGE	IMMIG. STATUS	MARITAL STATUS	TYPE OF MARRIAGE	RELIGION	EDUC. STATUS	OCCUP. STATUS	ANNUAL INCOME
1.	Reena	30	GC*	Legally separated	Arranged	Hindu	10th gr.	Clerical	$12,000
2.	Yamuna	30	GC	Divorced*	Arranged	Hindu	B.A.	Clerical	18,000
3.	Mandeep	32	GC	Divorced	Arranged	Sikh	B.A.	Bank assistant	30,000
4.	Zarina	47	GC	Married	Love	Muslim	B.A.	Unemployed	4,800
5.	Jayathi	41	GC	Divorced*	Arranged	Hindu	B.A.	Hospital assistant	6,000
6.	Malti	47	GC	Divorced	Love	Hindu	B.S.	Systems engineer	48,000
7.	Shahida	34	GC	Divorced*	Arranged	Muslim	M.S.	Chemist	22,000
8.	Nalini	34	No GC	Separated	Arranged	Hindu	B.A.	Self-employed	600
9.	Deepa	30s	Citizen	Divorced	Arranged	Hindu	B.A.	Gas station	N.A.
10.	Mary	32	Citizen	Married	Arranged	Christian	Medical	Dentist	60,000
11.	Sheetal	44	Citizen	Divorced	Arranged	Hindu	B.S.	Nurse	17,000
12.	Tara	37	GC	Separated	Arranged	Christian	B.A.	Secretary	24,000
13.	Mala	32	No GC	Divorced*	Arranged	Hindu	Ph.D.*	Graduate	12,000
14.	Geeta	29	GC	Legally separated	Arranged	Hindu	Medical	Student	Pub. aid
15.	Rehana	26	GC	Divorced*	Arranged	Muslim	9th gr.	Unemployed	Pub. aid
16.	Tahira	35	GC	Divorced*	Arranged	Muslim	M.A.	Unemployed	13,000
17.	Nadira	30s	GC	Divorced	Love	Muslim	M.A.	Unemployed	18,000
18.	Seema	26	GC	Divorced	Arranged	Hindu	1-yr. coll	Packer	17,000
19.	Shehanaz	22	GC	Divorced	Love	Muslim	2-yr. coll	Teacher	18,000
20.	Prema	49	GC	Divorced	Arranged	Hindu	3-yr. coll	Programmer	30,000
21.	Mumtaz	31	Citizen	Married	Arranged	Muslim	2-yr. coll	Unemployed	28,000
22.	Wahida	28	Citizen	Separated	Arranged	Muslim	H.S.	Travel agent	18,000
23.	Usha	32	Citizen	Divorced*	Arranged	Hindu	B.S.	Insurance agent	32,000
24.	Zakhia	33	GC	Divorced*	Arranged	Muslim	6th gr.	Seamstress	7,800
25.	Kamla	30s	GC	Divorced	Arranged	Hindu	B.A.	Teacher	30,000

Note: GC = green card; N.A. = not available; * = pending.

Notes on the
Research Process

The research for this book was conducted over a three-year period (1991–1994). Because research in the area of domestic violence, when compared with most other types of research, has its limitations in terms of ethical and practical barriers, sources for data collection were extremely difficult and limited (Strube 1988). To maximize data collection, the data for this study were drawn from diverse sources. Data sources included unstructured taped interviews I conducted with twenty-five South Asian women who were victims of marital violence, questionnaires sent to South Asian organizations, participant observation of some of these organizations, and gathering of secondary sources such as newspaper articles, monthly bulletins, and pamphlets.

The privatization of the problem of marital violence, especially in the immigrant community, made access to interviews with abused South Asian women a long, arduous process.[1] I began by contacting a South Asian activist who played an important role in one of the South Asian women's organizations and told her about my research project. I asked her if she would mention my name and the nature of my project to her organization and see if it could assist me in contacting some of the abused women it worked with so I could ask them whether they were interested in participating in my research. At the time, I was told by her to attend the group's general meetings and that she would bring up the issue of my research at one of these meetings. The question of my research was to come up only several meetings later. At that time I was informed that the organization had an unwritten policy that its members would not broach such issues with the abused women who contacted their organization. I could understand their need to protect the interests of their clients.

The process by which the question of my research was presented and the subsequent discussion was interesting. The contribution of academics in such work was thought to be limited, since such scholarship was published in academic journals written in language rarely accessible to the public. I did try to set forth my position, emphasizing the need for such research to be incorporated into the discourse. I said that I hoped my work would be accessible to the public and bridge some of the gap between activists and scholars. However, I did not achieve much success in persuading them that the only way I could gain access to these women was through their organization. After further discussion, I was told that they would assist by mentioning my work in their newsletter and listing my phone number for women interested in contacting me. From my understanding of the dynamics of the South Asian community, I knew that this was not going to work for multiple reasons. First, not everyone read the newsletter, which was published in English. Second, I had an anglicized name, which I knew could be a potential barrier to many South Asians. Third, advertising in a newsletter seemed to be too superficial a technique for something that is often considered a private and painful subject. I had failed to communicate that my work was an attempt not only to incorporate marital violence among South Asians into the discourse but also to write in a way that was accessible to a wide spectrum of readers and be an agent of change through my work. I could understand to some degree the activists' skepticism toward academics and their responsibilities to the women who contacted them, yet it was painful to hear these questions concerning the validity and value of research project itself. It is important to note here that this group did support my research by responding to the questionnaires I mailed to the organizations. But meanwhile, dejected and disillusioned, I hoped that I would have better luck with other organizations. Fortunately, I did.

Three other organizations that I approached to assist me in contacting potential participants for this research were extremely helpful. These were Sakhi for South Asian women in New York, SEWAA in Philadelphia, and Apna Ghar in Chicago. In all these organizations, specific individuals who knew abused South Asian women or were case workers talked about my work to some of the women and told them that if they were interested in knowing more about the project or in participating in it, they could either contact me or have me contact them. When we made contact I spoke in greater detail about my research. The women then decided whether or not they wanted to talk with me. I also informed them that at any point in the interview they could decide not to answer a question or stop the interview. Of the twenty-eight people who were contacted, twenty-five agreed to participate. The women I interviewed were Indian, Pakistani, and Bangladeshi, ranged in age from their early twenties to their late forties, were from different socioeconomic backgrounds and different religions (Hindu, Muslim, Christian, and Sikh), and were all first-generation immigrant women to the United States (see appendix A). The primary data collection technique was unstructured taped interviews ranging in length from one to three hours. Interviews were conducted in English, Hindi, Malayalam and Bengali.[2]

Questions that guided the interview included profiles of the subject and her abuser, factors leading to their marriage, the nature of the abuse, its frequency, the parties involved, whether help was sought, the type of help sought and responses, modes of intervention, perceptions, and strategies for change. The attempt was to elicit the type of detail that approximated the actual lives and marital violence as experienced by these women. I worked to instill a sense of safety, trust, intimacy, and a sense of cultural bonding, hoping to encourage the women to speak about issues that are perceived as private and normatively unspeakable. At the time some of the interviews were conducted, I myself was pregnant, and this became a bond between some of my respondents and me. They were able to tell me of some of the abuse that they had experienced when they were pregnant and the strategies of resistance that they took against their abuser.

The interviews were transcribed and analyzed. Based on patterns that emerged from the analysis of the coded categories and the researcher's interpretation, typologies were developed for the causation of violence, results of violence, manifestations of violence, responses of organizations, and suggested strategies to assist abused immigrant women. Pseudonyms have been given to the subjects to protect their identity. The attempt is not to make generalizations but to demonstrate how alienation occurs for immigrant women within the family, community, and the larger social institutions of society.

Many of these women felt that such research was important in bringing about social change. It was important in that it let others know that marital violence is a pervasive problem and cannot be seen as an isolated incident. Most of them felt that the more we write on such issues and the more people read, the greater will be the awareness of the problem and the realization that women too have the right to live a life free of violence. Many saw the research as a way of reaching a larger audience and challenging the existing monolithic image of South Asian families in the United States:

> I think it's good that you are doing this. Lots of Indians still don't believe that these kinds of things should come out. It should be kept inside the four walls. But I think it's getting worse and worse. It is not going to get any better. That's my personal experience. So bringing this out in the public, and people are more aware of this kind of thing happening. I read several articles about battered women before I came out, so I knew the psychology of men who abused women. So I think the more you can print, more things published and more women read this . . . I think it will help to give them the courage to get out, and do something and stand up for their rights. People should read. Hopefully they would then realize that it is not their fault, and it is not right. (*Tara*)

> It is great, because if you have statistics you can back it up. At least you would come to know of the different situations, and know why people do what they do. I think people take it [domestic violence] very lightly. (*Jayathi*)

> It should be there, so people know about these problems and how to face them. It would help others in the same situation, as there would be a record. (*Malti*)

> I think it is a very good job because we need it. At least if you do research you will find out what battered women need more— emotionally, financially, and their placement specially. . . . Just that they do not live in a shelter their whole life, but have to be educated and get a job and be independent. Also for the child, because the child needs education and an outside world from the shelter and social life too. Women need to be independent to take care of her child and own self too. (*Sheetal*)

> I think it is excellent. I think it is a very good idea and we need a lot of data on the subject. We need to educate ourselves. This kind of research is probably the first step in educating ourselves and then educating other people if you have statistics and if you have first-hand information from people. Right now people think that the percentage of women who are physically and emotionally abused is not high as it is. I say that you can be an ostrich

and close your eyes and pretend there is no danger but that doesn't avert the danger. The more you close your eyes the worse it gets. This is probably a way of opening your eyes and telling our people to see and let us not live in an imaginary world and dream. Ideally that is the way we would like to be but that is not the way it is. How do we learn about it? If you have done scientific research and have come up with figures that is one way of telling people that this is not something that is just created. It lends more authenticity. Let us put it this way research I think is always good. (*Nadira*)

Besides unstructured interviews, a secondary component of the research was an analysis of some of the South Asian women's organizations that addressed the problem of violence against women. Analysis of organizations for this book is drawn from data gathered from six South Asian women's organizations (SAWOs): Apna Ghar in Chicago, Maitri in California, Manavi in New Jersey, Sakhi in New York, SEWAA in Philadelphia, and Sneha in Connecticut. In the absence of any systematic list of South Asian organizations that addressed the issue of marital violence at the time this research was initiated, I developed a list of such South Asian organizations and contacted them to cross-check and seek out names of organizations that might have been excluded. A list of fifteen organizations was the result. The first stage was an open-ended questionnaire sent to all fifteen. Nine of these organizations replied; three did not reply despite three follow-ups. Three questionnaires were returned unopened.[3] The questionnaire included questions on organizational profile, aims and goals, organizational strengths and weaknesses, contacts with other organizations, nature of assistance and resources, causal factors for marital violence, areas for improvement in organizational support, and areas for legislative change.

Replies were coded into categories. On the basis of an analysis of the first questionnaire, additional questions were formulated and a second questionnaire with two sections (close-ended and open-ended questions) was sent to each of the nine responding organizations in 1993. Six of the nine organizations replied. Guiding the research were questions on topics such as organizational profile, goals, strengths, weaknesses, ideology, causal factors, and strategies for the resolution of marital violence. In addition, I observed four of the organizations at their meetings or functions and had informal conversations with a few of the founding members.

Data were analyzed using the grounded theory method.[4] Data analysis included the organizations' strategies, structure, ideologies, and relevance. Central to the analysis were questions such as: Why were these organizations created? How do they differ from other mainstream organizations? What roles do they play in shifting domestic violence from a private problem to a public social issue? Drawing on the patterns that emerged, this book discusses the relevance of these organizations and their contribution in both the South Asian community and the larger movement against domestic violence.

Notes

CHAPTER ONE: INTRODUCTION

1. Sakhi for South Asian Women is a New York City–based organization founded in 1989 that is committed to ending violence against South Asian women.
2. Most South Asian organizations have names in South Asian languages. For example, Sakhi means "woman friend," Narika means "woman," ASHA means "hope," and SEWAA means "to help." SEWAA and ASHA are also acronyms for Service and Education for Women Against Abuse and Asian [Women's] Self-Help Association.
3. By recent immigration I mean the fourth wave of migration, primarily from Latin America and Asia, that began in 1965 and continues to this day. See Pedraza (1996).
4. Terms such as domestic violence, marital violence, spouse abuse, wife abuse, and intimate violence are all used, and there is much discussion among writers regarding which is preferred. I use "marital violence" for a number of reasons. I believe that "domestic violence" incorporates a wider spectrum of abuse within which wife abuse is but one form, some of the others being child abuse, sibling abuse, and elderly abuse within the family. Should "wife abuse" be used? Feminist writers have used the term "wife abuse" to emphasize the gendered nature of the violence. This term specifies that the cause of a woman's abuse lies largely in male domination and the institutional support for a man's position as the husband in the social construction of the family. I believe this is a strong argument in support of using the term. However, I prefer to use the term "marital violence," as I draw upon the cultural understanding of marriage among South Asians, which is based on the cultural construction of gender inequality in the South Asian marital arrangement. The differentiation between a marriage based on an alliance between families and that based on a relationship between two

individuals is important; it plays a central role in understanding the power dynamics within the South Asian family.

5. Pseudonyms have been used to protect the identity and confidentiality of the abused women I interviewed. All interviews were conducted in English or Hindi or a combination of both unless otherwise specified in the text. Names of spouses and places have been changed, and specific organizations' names have been replaced with the acronym SAWO (South Asian women's organization).

CHAPTER TWO: MARRIAGE AND FAMILY

1. Over the last few years this negative attitude toward divorce has been gradually changing both in South Asia and among South Asians living in the United States.
2. Kumkum Sangari and Sudesh Vaid (1989, 7) point out that both tradition and modernity are vehicles of patriarchal ideology. They also aptly stress that "the relationship between classes and patriarchies is complex and variable. Not only are patriarchal systems class differentiated, open to constant and constant reformulation, but defining gender seems to be crucial to the formation of classes and dominant ideologies."
3. Among some Hindu groups in South India, however, the preferred marriage is between niece and maternal uncle or between cousins.
4. Statistics for India were unavailable.
5. For an important discussion on dowry and bride price, see Tambiah (1973).
6. This death is falsely presented by the in-laws as a suicide or an accident while cooking. In most cases, the method of murder is burning the woman to death. In registered cases with the police between 1976 and 1977, 5,587 women died of burns in India, but these were not recorded as dowry deaths. In 1987 alone, the police recorded 1,786 dowry deaths in all of India. Women's action groups believe this figure to be a gross underrepresentation and estimate that in a state such as Gujarat alone, the deaths from burns were approximately 1,000.
7. A green card is a permit given to immigrants by the United States Immigration and Naturalization Service to permanently reside and legally work in the United States.
8. U.S. citizens and green card holders who marry non-U.S. citizens or non-green card holders have to file for resident status in order for their spouses to legally enter the United States, which can take up to two years.

CHAPTER THREE: IMMIGRATION STATUS AND MARITAL VIOLENCE

1. For immigration patterns from India and Pakistan to U.S, see table 2.1 in Barringer, Gardener, and Levin (1993), 24–26. Also note that the 1990 census undercounted the total South Asian population in the United States.
2. The doctrine of coverture has its roots in English common law. For a more detailed discussion of the legacy of coverture in immigration law and its negative consequences for immigrant women, see an excellent article by Janet M. Calvo (1991). I have primarily drawn upon her work for the legal aspects of the immigration history recounted in this chapter.
3. For a discussion of "chastisement," see Calvo (1991).

4. According to Edna Bonacich, "Each Asian group came to face hostile reactions of multiple kinds from the surrounding population, including riots, anti-immigration legislation, and ultimately, exclusion laws or efforts to prohibit further immigration. These came in sequence, with each group arriving and then facing mounting hostility and, finally exclusion" (Bonacich 1984, 173–174).

5. Act of May 29, 1921, Pub. L. No. 5 section 2(a), (d), 42 Stat. 4.

6. The term "alien" is an Immigration and Naturalization Service (INS) designation for noncitizens residing in the United States.

7. Act of May 26, 1924, pub. L. No. 139, section 6(a) (2) page 155 as cited in Calvo, footnote 57 & 60.

8. According to the 1924 law, an alien wife whose nationality was different from that of her citizen husband could enter the United States under the quota allocated for her husband's nationality, if her own nationality quota was full. However, this privilege did not apply to an alien husband of a citizen wife.

9. Letter from Bonnie Derwinski, Acting Director for Congressional and Public Affairs, Oct. 19, 1989, reproduced in 66 Interpreter Releases 1428–29, APP III (Dec. 18, 1989) and cited in Calvo (1991).

10. Under the 1990 immigration law, immediate kin, including spouses of citizens, could become LPRs and were not subject to numerical quota restrictions. Preference was also given to spouses of LPRs within quotas.

11. Although the burden of proof is on the conditional resident to demonstrate the legitimacy of the beginning and end of the marriage, she does not have to be the one initiating the divorce. Once proceedings have begun, the conditional resident can also apply for the waiver and get an extension of her conditional resident status.

12. Conditional Basis of Lawful Permanent Residence for Certain Alien Spouses and Sons and Daughters; Battered and Abused Conditional Residents, 56 Fed. Reg. 22,635 (1991) codified at 8 C.F. R. 216.5(E)(3)(i) (1992).

13. 8 U.S. C. #1186a (c) (4) (C) (1991).

14. 8 C. F. R. 216.5(E)(3) (iii).

15. See Pressman (1994).

16. H.R. 1133, 103d Cong., 1st sess. (1993).

17. Title IV of the Crime Bill, 201 (b) (2) (A) (I) or 203 (a) (2) (A) of Section 40701 of "The Violence Against Women Act of 1994."

18. Violent Crime Control and Law Enforcement Act, "the Crime Bill" (Pub. L. No. 103–3222, 108 Stat. 1796 (1994)—Title IV, Subtitle G, section 40701 Alien Petitioning Rights for Immediate Relatives or Second Preference status.

19. Section 40701 of the Crime Bill directs the INS not to revoke the approval of a self-petition only on the basis that the marriage has been legally terminated.

20. For greater detail, see Stubbs (1997).

CHAPTER FOUR: ISOLATION

1. Similar levels have been described by Stets (1991) and Lin (1986) in identifying layers of integration to indicate the degree of belonging, bonding, and binding that individuals experience at the formal, informal, and interpersonal levels.

2. It is also true, however, that the sexism and cultural prescriptions in South Asia in general allow men considerable latitude and power in their relationships with women. Often a woman's family and friends, while sympathetic to the woman's situation, may suggest that the woman stay with her abusive husband due to various cultural factors.

CHAPTER FIVE: SEXUAL ABUSE

1. By notions of sexuality, I mean those norms and values that define the nature of female and male sexuality, including notions of sexual propriety and deviance, notions of male and female sexual disposition, and cultural expectations about desirable and undesirable sexual behavior in a given society.

2. The difficulty of doing research in the area of sexual abuse and sexuality is addressed in Krishnan et al. (1998).

3. See observations on this issue by Shamita Das Dasgupta in Mazumdar (1998), 37.

4. For an excellent collection on issues of sexuality in India, see Uberoi (1996).

5. This is also discussed by Vivien Ng (1994) with reference to Qing China.

6. Nancy Cook (1998) points out the ways in which the public and state discourse in Pakistan construct women's identity primarily as mothers and wives who are vulnerable and need the protection of men. Women's main goal is to nurture, socialize, and sacrifice for the good of the nation.

7. Today in South Asia, the women's movement challenges existing notions of gender relations and attempts to reconceptualize sexuality in ways that empower South Asian women.

8. Many years ago while watching Hindi films on TV, I remember nearly all the films as having a hero, heroine, and villain, with at least one segment of the film dealing with the villain's intent to rape the heroine or supporting actress. This was followed by the woman's mother or father finding out and saying, "*Osne mery beti ki izzat loot lia! Hamari khandan ki izzat mitti me miladi*" (He has robbed my daughter's honor and ground our family honor into mud.) This was how sexual abuse was conceptualized—not as violence against a woman, but as a violation of patriarchal family honor. Although these images have partially changed in South Asia, immigrants, depending on their period of migration, still hold on to some of these images.

9. I believe this is also applicable to other religions as practiced in South Asia, particularly in India, where other religions have been strongly influenced by Hinduism.

10. For details on laws on domestic violence in India, see Lawyers' Collective (1992).

11. See Patricia Uberoi (1996, 319–346) for a discussion of legal interpretation and judicial discourse around sexuality and marriage in Hindu marriage in India.

12. Billie Wright Dziech and Linda Weiner, in the context of the lecherous professor, point to forms of sexual harassment that are relevant to the immigrant woman's predicament vis-à-vis her significant other. For some of these characteristics, see Dziech and Weiner (1994).

CHAPTER SIX: INTERNAL AND EXTERNAL BARRIERS

1. Mary Mathew is not to be confused with Mary, the woman I interviewed and who is discussed in chapter 7 under "Personal Strategies."
2. Since this chapter was written, Mary's husband has been convicted of the murder and is serving a 17^1/$_2$-year sentence.
3. In 1990, 85 percent of the Asian American self-employed population were immigrants and included both highly educated and relatively uneducated people. See Ong and Hee (1994).
4. It is important to note here that job insecurity is very high in South Asia as well, but it is tempered by the assumption there will be some form of familial support. Obviously this varies based on class differences.
5. Even here, some religious centers emphasize what is termed the improvement of women's well-being rather than marital violence per se. In some cases this has been used by women as a strategic move in a male-dominated environment. For example, at the Islamic Center of Long Island, New York.
6. See Ferraro for an excellent discussion of the role of the police, criminal courts, and civil courts in addressing domestic violence.
7. For a discussion of these issues, see Schornstein (1997, 70–116).

CHAPTER SEVEN: FIGHTING BACK

1. In a survey conducted by Mildred Pagelow, approximately 50 percent of the abused women in her sample contemplated suicide and 23 percent attempted suicide at least one time. See Pagelow (1981).
2. This is Mary, the woman I interviewed, and not Mary Mathew who was battered to death by her husband. One of the women who sought the help of family was Shehanaz, the young Muslim woman. When her husband and mother-in-law abused her, she called her father, who was visiting Canada, and told him of her situation.
3. It is important to note here that my research was only conducted after the formation of these South Asian women's organizations and that my contact with many of the women I interviewed was through these organizations. Therefore a large number of the women I interviewed were women who had contacted these organizations as a source of support.

CHAPTER EIGHT: MAKING A DIFFERENCE

1. One might question whether organizations with a range of activities should be called a movement. In this case, organizations are vital to the mobilization process. They challenge the status quo and through their activities struggle to bring about social change.
2. The other four founding members are Annanya Bhatacharjee, Tula Goenka, Geeta Misra, and Romita Shetty.
3. It is important to note that since this research was undertaken, many of these organizations have undergone considerable evolution both in ideology and in organizational structure as changes have occurred in the body of volunteers and the leadership over time. Addressing all these changes is beyond the scope of this book. However, I have tried to incorporate more recent information that was kindly provided by members of some of the organizations I contacted. I also discuss in chapter 9 some of the issues

that I saw arise in Sakhi, an organization with which I was personally involved.

4. Also see Purkayastha, Raman, and Bhide (1997).

5. This number is based on adding the numbers reported in the second questionnaire by 6 organizations. It is indicative of these organizations' growing visibility. See Appendix B.

6. See Goenka (1993).

7. These organizations include SALGA (South Asian Lesbian and Gay Association), SAAA (South Asian AIDS Action), YAR (Youth Against Racism), SAN (South Asian Network) in Los Angeles, SAWA (South Asian Women for Action) in Boston, Rakhsha in Atlanta, Sawera in Portland, Chaya in Seattle, Saheli in Austin, and Daya in Texas.

CHAPTER NINE: LOOKING BACK, LOOKING AHEAD

1. I have taken the term "transformational politic" from bell hooks's (1995) article entitled "Feminism: A Transformational Politic." While I have not precisely adhered to her usage of the term I am grateful here for the important insights that I have gained from my reading of her article. She states that "it becomes necessary for us to speak continually about the convictions that inform our continued advocacy of feminist struggle" (p. 492). In this chapter, in the spirit of exploration, I have tried to state some of my convictions on issues that I think we need to address in our struggle against oppression.

2. In April of 1997 Sakhi's board of directors decided to separate Sakhi's domestic workers committee into an independent organization. This decision was met with serious opposition from the domestic workers committee, and a bitter struggle soon ensued between factions within Sakhi both about the decision and about the process. On December 8, 1997, after several months of silence on the part of Sakhi's board, its program coordinators, and those that remained within Sakhi, a letter was sent out to Sakhi supporters explaining the decision and answering some of the statements put forth by the newly created organization Worker Awaaz (members of the previous DWC). The newsletter states, "In April 1997, Sakhi made the difficult but necessary decision to spin-off the domestic workers committee (DWC) into an independent organization. This decision made by the Sakhi Board, which is responsible for the organization's overall health, came as a result of the increasing autonomy exacted by the volunteers in the DWC and after more than a year of dialogue and internal struggle, which threatened to paralyze Sakhi's work. Volunteers in the DWC performed such unprecedented acts as direct supervision of the program coordinator, seeking independent funding, voting at a committee meeting to open a separate account and withholding critical information from the rest of the staff, Board, volunteers and survivors of violence in the organization. The decision to separate the DWC was made to ensure the survival and health of Sakhi and each and every one of its projects" (Sakhi 1997).

3. The term "radical" is used to define those segments that perceived themselves or are perceived as fundamentally challenging the system of power relations and using corresponding tactics in achieving this goal. It is also used to define those individuals who perceived themselves as more attuned

to the complexity of class as the basis for oppression. The term "moderate" is used here for those who also challenge the system of power relations, but in more indirect ways. It is also used for those individuals who believed class issues were important but not the root of all other problems. It is also important to note here that while some members of the organization have used these terms, not all identified themselves as such. Many moderates saw themselves as radical. I am using the terms primarily to differentiate two positions for purposes of analytical clarity but knowing that they are an oversimplification. The use of these terms does not imply that members in the organizations perceive themselves or identify themselves as such. The term "leftist" was also used by a few, particularly those who emphasized class as the dominant axis.

4. In my own work with Sakhi, I found that time and again members struggled with the organization's orientation toward service. This dissension frequently shaped their activities, outreach, friendships, and the politics within the organization.

5. Jennifer Gordon (1995) addresses this issue. She explains that while the provision of legal services is not a long-term solution, the legal clinic of the workplace project provides important functions both in terms of individual support and in terms of recruiting workers into the workplace project. Through the services of the legal clinic the workplace project demonstrates to its recipients (and others) "that the organization is willing to fight with them and on their behalf and that challenges to employers can succeed" (p. 442).

6. Scholars of the Asian experience such as Yen Le Espiritu (1997), Elaine Kim (1993) and Gary Okihiro (1994) have discussed the complexity stemming from the third position that Asians occupy in a dichotomous society.

7. See Gordon (1995).

8. See Anderson (1991) and Bacon (1996).

9. In some cases the choice of a few individuals to represent the membership was based in part on the assumption that they could best articulate the vision and practices of the organization. However the choice also stemmed in part from the leadership's dilemma; it wanted collective representation but feared the inability of some of its members to be its public spokesperson(s), especially in the organization's early stages.

10. See chapter 1 for a discussion of Syeda Sufian's case. On August 26, 1999, Mohammed Mohsin was sentenced to nine to eighteen years for attempted murder and three to six years for two counts of assault against his wife, Syeda Sufian. The sentences are to be served concurrently. The sentencing followed the criminal court conviction that occurred in May 1999 (Sakhi weekly email, Aug. 27, 1999).

APPENDIX B: NOTES ON THE RESEARCH PROCESS

1. It was only in the 1980s, with the creation of South Asian women's organizations, that South Asian women were able to gradually contact these organizations as an alternative power resource.

2. Most of the interviews were either in English or Hindi. One interview was conducted in Malayalam. Another was conducted in Bengali with the help of a translator.

3. These questionnaires were returned unopened by the U.S. Post Office because the addresses were no longer valid and there were no forwarding addresses. An active member of another South Asian organization later informed me that these organizations were no longer active.

4. See Strauss (1987).

References

Abraham, M. 1989. "Ethnic and Identity and Marginality: A Study of the Jews of India." Ph.D. dissertation, Syracuse University.

———. 1995. "Ethnicity, Gender, and Marital Violence: South Asian Women's Organizations in the United States." *Gender and Society* 9 (4): 450–468.

———. 1998a. "Alienation and Marital Violence among South Asian Immigrant Women in the United States." In Devorah Kalekin-Fishman, ed., *Designs for Alienation*, 175–196. Finland: SoPhi.

———. 1998b. "Speaking the Unspeakable: Marital Violence against South Asian Immigrant Women in the United States." *Indian Journal of Gender Studies* 5 (2): 215–241.

———. 1999. "Sexual Abuse in South Asian Immigrant Marriages." *Violence against Women* 5 (6): 587–590.

———. 2000. "Isloation as a Form of Marital Violence." *Journal of Social Distress and the Homeless.*

Adams, D. C., and A. J. McCormick. 1982. "Men Unlearning Violence: A Group Approach Based on the Collective Model." In Maria Roy, ed., *The Abusive Partner: An Analysis of Domestic Battering.* New York: Van Nostrand Reinhold.

Andersen, M. 1993. *Thinking about Women: Sociological Perspectives on Sex and Gender.* New York: Macmillan.

Anderson, B. 1991. *Imagined Communities: Reflections on the Origin and Spread of Nationalism.* London: Verso.

Apna Ghar. 1998. "Our Home." Vol. 2, no. 1 (fall): 1–16.

Arnold, G. 1995. "Dilemmas of Feminist Coalitions: Collective Identity and Strategic Effectiveness in the Battered Women's Movement." In Myra Marx Ferree and Patricia Yancey Martin, eds., *Feminist Organizations: Harvest of the New Women's Movement*, 276–290. Philadelphia: Temple University Press.

Bacchetta, P. 1994. "Communal Property/Sexual Property: On Representations of Muslim Women in a Hindu Nationalist Discourse." In Zoya Hasan, ed., *Forg-*

ing Identities: Gender, Communities, and the State, 188–225. New Delhi: Kali for Women.

Bacon, J. 1996. *Life Lines: Community, Family, and Assimilation among Asian Indian Immigrants.* New York: Oxford University Press.

Baig-Amin, M., Nabila El-Bassel, Louisa Gilbert, Anne B. Waters, and Marianne Yoshioka. 1997. "The Relevance of Feminist, Ecological, and Symbolic Inter-action Frameworks to Understanding Violence against South Asian Immigrant Women." Unpublished.

Barai, S. B. 1998. "Negotiating the Intersection: How and Why Provisions for Bat-tered Immigrant Women Have Become a Part of U.S. Immigration Policy." Princeton University. Unpublished.

Barnett, O. W., and A. D. LaViolette. 1993. *It Could Happen to Anyone: Why Bat-tered Women Stay.* Newbury Park, Calif.: Sage Publications.

Barringer, H., R. Gardener, and M. Levin. 1993. *Asians and Pacific Islanders in the United States.* New York: Russell Sage Foundation.

Bart, P. 1979. "Rape as a Paradigm of Sexism in Society—Victimization and Its Discontents." *Women's Studies International Quarterly* 2: 347–357.

Ben-Rafael, E. 1982. *The Emergence of Ethnicity: Cultural Groups and Social Con-flict in Israel.* Westport, Conn.: Greenwood.

Bhattacharjee, A. 1992. "The Habit of Ex-Nomination: Nation, Woman, and the Indian Immigrant Bourgeoisie." *Public Culture* 5 (1): 19–44.

Bonacich, E. 1994. "Asian Labor in the Development of California and Hawaii." In L. Cheng and E. Bonacich, eds., *Labor Immigration Under Capitalism: Asian Workers in the United States before World War II.* Berkeley: University of Cali-fornia Press.

Bowker, L. H. 1983. *Beating Wife-Beating.* Lexington, Mass.: Lexington Books.

Breines, W. 1989. *Community and Organization in the New Left: The Great Re-fusal.* Rev. ed. New Brunswick, N.J.: Rutgers University Press.

Brislin, R. 1981. *Cross Cultural Encounters.* New York: Pergamon.

Bunch, C. 1987. *Passionate Politics: Feminist Theory in Action.* New York: St. Martin's Press.

Bush, D. M. 1992. "Women's Movements and State Policy Reform Aimed at Do-mestic Violence against Women: A Comparison of the Consequences of Move-ment Mobilization in the U.S. and India." *Gender and Society* 6 (4): 587–608.

Calvo, J. M. 1991. "Spouse-Based Immigration Laws: The Legacies of Coverture." *San Diego Law Review* 28: 593–644.

Campbell, D. W., B. Masaki, and S. Torres. 1997. "'Water on Rock': Changing Do-mestic Violence Perceptions in the African American, Asian American, and Latino Communities." In E. Klein, J. C. Campbell, E. Soler, M. Ghez, eds., *End-ing Domestic Violence: Changing Public Perceptions / Halting the Epidemic*, 64–87. Thousand Oaks, Calif.: Sage.

Campbell, J. C. 1992. "Wife Battering: Cultural Contexts versus Western Social Sciences." In D. A. Counts, J. K. Brown, and J. C. Campbell, eds., *Sanctions and Sanctuary: Cultural Perspectives on the Beating of Wives,* 229–249. San Francisco: Westview Press.

Caputo, R. 1988. "Police Response to Domestic Violence." *Social Casework* 69: 81–87.

Chin, K. 1994. "Out of Town Brides: International Marriage and Wife Abuse Among Chinese Immigrants." *Journal of Comparative Family Studies* 35 (1): 53–69.

Clark, H. 1987. *The Law of Domestic Relations in the U.S.* 2nd ed. Hornbook Series Practitioners edition. St. Paul, Minn.: West Publishing Co.

Collins, P. H. 1990. *Black Feminist Thought: Knowledge, Consciousness, and the Politics of Empowerment.* New York: Routledge.

Cook, N. 1998. "Women as Pawn: Gender Identity Construction in Pakistan." Paper presented at the 14th World Congress of Sociology, Montreal.

Dasgupta, S. D. 1994. "Feminist Consciousness in Women-Centered Hindi Films." In Women of South Asian Descent Collective, eds., *Our Feet Walk the Sky: Women of the South Asian Diaspora*, 56–63. San Francisco: Aunt Lute.

———, ed. 1998. *A Patchwork Shawl: Chronicles of South Asian Women in America.* New Brunswick, N.J.: Rutgers University Press.

Dasgupta. S. D., and S. DasGupta. 1994. "Journeys: Reclaiming South Asian Feminism." In Women of South Asian Descent Collective, eds., *Our Feet Walk the Sky: Women of the South Asian Diaspora.* 123–130. San Francisco: Aunt Lute.

Dasgupta, S. D., and S. Warrier. 1996. "In the Footsteps of 'Arundhati': Asian American Women's Experience of Domestic Violence in the United States." *Violence against Women* 2 (3): 238–259.

Dasgupta, T. 1986. "Looking under the Mosaic: South Asian Immigrant Women." *Polyphony: Women and Ethnicity* 8: 67–69.

Davis, L.V. 1987. "Battered Women: The Transformation of a Social Problem." *Social Work* July-August: 306–311.

Dhaliwal, A. K. 1994. "Reading Diaspora: Self-Representational Practices and the Politics of Reception." *Socialist Review* 24 (4): 18–19.

Dobash, R. E., and R. P. Dobash. 1979. *Violence against Wives: A Case against the Patriarchy.* New York: Free Press.

———. 1981. "Community Response to Violence against Wives: Charivari, Abstract Justice, and Patriarchy." *Social Problems* 28: 563–581

———. 1992. *Women, Violence, and Social Change.* London: Routledge.

Dyal, J., and R. Dyal.1981. "Acculturation, Stress, and Coping." *International Journal of Intercultural Relations* 5: 301–328.

Dziech, B. W., and Linda Weiner. 1994. "The Lecherous Professor: A Portrait of the Artist." In L. Richardson and Verta Taylor, eds., *Feminist Frontiers II: Rethinking Sex, Gender, and Society*, 43–58. New York: McGraw-Hill.

Emmison, M., and M. Western. 1990. "Social Class and Social Identity: A Comment on Marshall et al." *Sociology* 24: 241–253.

Espiritu, Y. L. 1997. *Asian American Women and Men.* Thousand Oaks, Calif.: Sage Publications.

Everett, J. M. 1979. *Women and Social Change in India.* New York: St. Martin's Press.

Fagen, J. A., and A. Browne. 1994. "Violence against Spouses and Intimates: Physical Aggression between Women and Men in Intimate Relationships." In A. J. Reiss, Jr., and J. A. Roths, eds., *Understanding and Preventing Violence.* Vol. 3, 115–292. Washington, D.C.: National Academy Press.

Fernandez, M. 1997. "Domestic Violence by Extended Family in India: Interplay of Gender and Generation." *Journal of Interpersonal Violence* 12 (3): 433–455.

Ferraro, K. J. 1989. "Policing Woman Battering." *Social Problems* 36 (1): 61–72.

———. 1993. "Cops, Courts, and Woman Battering." In Pauline B. Bart and Eileen Geil Moran, eds., *Violence against Women: The Bloody Footprints*, 165–176. Newbury Park, Calif.: Sage Publications.

Ferraro, K. J., and Boychuk, T. 1992. "The Court's Response to Interpersonal Violence: A Comparison of Intimate and Non-intimate Assault." In E. Buzawa, ed., *Domestic Violence: The Changing Criminal Justice Response*, 209–225. Westport, Conn.: Greenwood.

Ferraro, K. J., and J. M. Johnson. 1983. "How Women Experience Battering: The Process of Victimization." *Social Problems* 30 (3): 325–339.

Ferree, M. M., and F. D. Miller. 1985. "Mobilization and Meaning: Toward an Integration of Social Psychological and Resource Perspectives on Social Movements." *Sociological Inquiry* 55: 38–61.

Field, M., and H. Field. 1973. "Marital Violence and the Criminal Process: Neither Justice nor Peace." *Social Service Review* 47: 221–240.

Gaines, J. 1990. "White Privilege and Looking Relations: Race and Gender in Feminist Film Theory." In P. Erens, ed., *Issues in Feminist Film Criticism*, 197–214. Bloomington: Indiana University Press.

Geertz, C. 1963. *Old Societies and New Societies.* Chicago: Free Press.

Gelles, R. J. 1997. *Intimate Violence in Families.* London: Sage Publications, Inc.

Gelles, R. J., and M. A. Straus. 1988. *Intimate Violence: The Causes and Consequences of Abuse in the American Family.* New York: Simon & Schuster.

Glazer, N. 1976. Foreword. In Parmatama Saran and E. Eames, eds. *The New Ethnics: Asian Indians in the United States*, vi–viii. New York: Praeger.

Goenka, T. 1993. "Battered Kiran Kumari Speaks Out." *New India*, June 18: 4.

Gordon, J. 1995. "We Make the Road by Walking: Immigrant Workers, the Workplace Project, and the Struggle for Social Change." *Harvard Civil Rights–Civil Liberties Law Review* 30 (2): 407–450.

Gordon, L. 1989. *Heroes of Their Own Lives: The Politics and History of Family Violence.* London: Virago Press.

Graetz, B. 1986. "Social Structure and Class Consciousness." *Australian and New Zealand Journal of Sociology* 22: 46–64.

———. 1992. "Inequality and Political Activism in Australia." *Research in Inequality and Social Conflict* 2: 57–77.

Grewal, I., and C. Kaplan. 1994. "Introduction." In I. Grewal and C. Kaplan, eds., *Scattered Hegemonies: Post-modernity and Transnational Feminist Practices.* Minneapolis: University of Minnesota Press.

Gusfield, J. 1979. "The Modernity of Social Movements: Public Roles and Private Parts." In Amos H. Hawley, ed., *Societal Growth*, 290–316. New York: Free Press.

Hamlin II, E. R. 1991. "Community-Based Spouse Abuse Protections and Family Preservation Team." *Social Work* 36 (5): 402–406.

Harding, S. 1991. *Whose Science? Whose Knowledge?* Ithaca, N.Y.: Cornell University Press.

Healey, J. F. 1995. *Race, Ethnicity, Gender, and Class: The Sociology of Group Conflict and Change*, 421–430. Thousand Oaks, Calif.: Pine Forge Press.

Hecter, M. 1975. *Internal Colonialism: The Celtic Fringe in British National Development.* Berkeley: University of California Press.

Ho, C. K. 1990. "An Analysis of Domestic Violence in Asian American Communities: A Multicultural Approach to Counseling." *Women and Therapy* 9 (1–2): 129–150.

Hochschild, A. 1989. *The Second Shift: Working Parents and the Revolution at Home.* New York: Viking Penguin.

hooks, b. 1995. "Feminism: A Transformational Politic." In P. S. Rothenberg, ed.,

Race, Class, and Gender in the United States, 491–498. New York: St. Martin's Press.

Hornung, C., B. McCullough, and T. Sugimoto. 1981. "Status Relationships in Marriage: Risk Factors in Spouse Abuse." *Journal of Marriage and the Family* 43: 679–692.

Hossfeld, K. J. 1994. "Hiring Immigrant Women: Silicon Valley's 'Simple Formula.'" In M. Baca Zinn and B. T. Dill, eds., *Women of Color in U.S. Society,* 65–93. Philadelphia: Temple University Press.

House, J. S., and R. L. Kahn. 1985. "Measures and Concepts of Social Support." In Sheldon Cohen and S Leonard Syme, eds., *Social Support and Health,* 83–108. New York: Academic Press.

Hughes, M., and W. R. Gove. 1981. "Living Alone, Social Integration, and Mental Health." *American Journal of Sociology* 14: 293–318.

India Abroad. 1998. Jan. 30: 52–54.

India in New York. 1997. July 18.

India Today. 1998. Jan. 12: 24e.

Islam, N. 1994. "In the Belly of the Multicultural Beast I am Named South Asian." In Women of South Asian Descent Collective, ed., *Our Feet Walk the Sky: Women of the South Asian Diaspora,* 242–245. San Francisco: Aunt Lute.

Kang, T. S., and G. E. Kang. 1983. "Adjustment Patterns of the Korean-American Elderly: Case Studies of Ideal Types." *Journal of Minority Aging* 8: 47–55.

Kanuha, V. 1994. "Women of Color in Battering Relationships." In L. Comas-Diaz and B. Greene, eds., *Women of Color,* 428–454. New York: Guilford.

Kelly, L. 1988. "How Women Define Their Experiences of Violence." In K. Yllo and M. Bograd, eds., *Feminist Perspectives on Wife Abuse,* 114–133. Newbury Park, Calif.: Sage Publications.

Khandelwal, M. 1995. "Indian Immigrants in Queens, New York City: Patterns of Spatial Concentration and Distribution, 1965–1990." In Peter Van Der Veer, ed., *Nation and Migration: The Politics of Space in South Asian Diaspora,* 179–196. Philadelphia, PA: University of Pennsylvania Press.

———. 1996. "Indian Networks in the United States: Class and Transnational Identities." In H. Duleep and P. Wunnava, eds., *Immigrants and Immigration Policy: Individual Skills, Family Ties and Group Identities,* 115–130. Greenwich: Conn.: JAI Press.

———. 1997a. "Defining Community and Feminism: Indian Women in New York City." *Race, Gender, Class* 4 (3): 95–111.

———. 1997b. "Community Organizing in an Asian Group: Asian Indians in New York City." *Another Side* 5 (1): 23–32.

———. 1998. "Reflections on Diversity and Inclusion: South Asians and Asian American Studies." In Lane Ryo Hirabayashi, ed., *Teaching Asian America: Diversity and the Problem of Community.* New York: Rowman & Littlefield.

Kibria, N. 1994. "Household Structure and Family Ideologies: The Dynamics of Immigrant Economic Adaptation among Vietnamese Refugees." *Social Problems* 41 (1): 81–96.

Kim, E. 1990. "Such Opposite Creatures: Men and Women in Asian American Literature." *Michigan Quarterly Review* 29: 58–93.

———. 1993. Preface. In J. Hagedorn, ed., *Charlie Chan Is Dead: An Anthology of Contemporary Asian American Fiction,* vii–xiv. New York: Penguin.

Kinder, D. R. 1986. "The Continuing American Dilemma: White Resistance to Racial Change: 40 Years after Myrdal." *Journal of Social Issues* 42: 189–194.

Kishwar, M., and R. Vanita, eds. 1986. *In Search of Answers: Indian Women's Voices from Manushi.* London: Zed Books.

Kitano, H.H.L., and R. Daniels. 1995. *Asian Americans: Emerging Minorities*, 105–111. Englewood Cliffs, N.J.: Prentice Hall Press.

Klandermans, Bert. 1993. "A Theoretical Framework for Comparisons on Social Movement Participation." *Sociological Forum* 8: 383–402.

Klein, E., J. C. Campbell, E. Soler, and M. Ghez. 1997. *Ending Domestic Violence: Changing Public Perceptions / Halting the Epidemic.* Thousand Oaks, Calif.: Sage.

Krishnan, S. P., B.A. Malahat, L. Gilbert, N. El Bassel, and A. Waters. 1998. "Lifting The Veil of Secrecy: Domestic Violence among South Asian Women in the U.S." In Shamita Das Dasgupta, ed., *A Patchwork Shawl: Chronicles of South Asian Women in America.* New Brunswick, N.J.: Rutgers University Press.

Kurz, D. 1987. "Emergency Department Responses to Battered Women: Resistance to Medicalization." *Social Problems* 34 (1): 69–81.

———. 1989. "Social Perspectives on Wife Abuse: Current Debates and Future Direction." *Gender & Society* 3: 489–505.

Kwong, P. 1992. "The First Multicultural Riots: Los Angeles after the Fire." *Village Voice.* June 9.

Laslett, B. 1978. "The Family as a Public and Private Institution: A Historical Perspective." *Journal of Marriage and the Family* 35: 480–492.

Lauer, R. H., and J. C. Lauer. 1997. *Marriage and Family: The Quest for Intimacy.* Madison, Wisc.: Brown and Benchmark.

Launius, M., and C. U. Lindquist. 1988. "Learned Helplessness, External Locus of Control and Passivity in Battered Women." *Journal of Interpersonal Violence* 3: 307–316.

Lawyers' Collective. 1992. *Legal Handbook 1.* New Delhi: Kali for Women.

Lempert, L. B. 1996. "Women's Strategies for Survival: Developing Agency in Abusive Relationships." *Journal of Family Violence* 11: 269–289.

Liddle, J., and R. Joshi. 1986. *Daughters of Independence: Gender, Caste, and Class in India.* London: Zed Books.

Lin, N. 1986. "Conceptualizing Social Support." In N. Lin, A. Dean, and W. Ensel, eds., *Social Support, Life Events, and Depression*, 17–30. New York: Academic Press.

Lorde, Audre. 1984. *Sister/Outsider.* Thomansburg, N.Y.: The Crossing Press.

Lum, J. L. 1998. "Family Violence." In L. C. Lee and N.W.S. Lane, eds., *Handbook of Asian American Psychology*, 505–525. Thousand Oaks, Calif.: Sage.

Luthra, R. 1989. "Matchmaking in the Classifieds of the Immigrant Indian Press." In Asian Women United of California., ed., *Making Waves: An Anthology of Writings by and about Asian American Women.* Boston: Beacon.

Luu, V. 1989. "The Hardships of Escape for Vietnamese Women." In Asian Women United of California, ed., *Making Waves: An Anthology of Writings by and about Asian American Women.* 60–72. Boston: Beacon.

Maynard, M. 1993. "Violence against Women." In Diane Richardson and Victoria Robinson, eds., *Introducing Women's Studies: Feminist Theory and Practice.* London: Macmillan.

Mazumdar, R. 1998. "Marital Rape: Some Ethical and Cultural Considerations." In Shamita Das Dasgupta, ed., *A Patchwork Shawl: Chronicles of South Asian Women in America*, 129–144. New Brunswick, N.J.: Rutgers University Press.

Mazumdar, S. 1989a. "General Introduction: A Woman-Centered Perspective on Asian American History." In Asian Women United of California, ed., *Making Waves: An Anthology of Writings by and about Asian American Women*, 1–22. Boston: Beacon.

Mazumdar, S. 1989b. "Race and Racism among South Asians." In G. M. Nomura, S. H. Sumida, R. C. Leong, eds., *Frontiers of Asian American Studies: Writing, Research, and Commentary*, 25–28. Pullman, Wash.: Washington State University Press.

Mazumdar, S. 1991. "Asian American Studies and Asian Studies: Rethinking Roots." In S. Hume, H. C. Kim, S. S. Fugita, and A. Ling, eds., *Asian Americans: Comparative and Global Perspectives*, 29–44. Pullman, Wash.: Washington State University Press.

McAdam, D., John McCarthy, and Mayer N. Zald. 1988. "Social Movements." In Neil J. Smelser, ed., *Handbook of Sociology*. Beverly Hills, Calif.: Sage.

McWilliams, M., and J. McKiernan. 1993. *Bringing It Out in the Open: Domestic Violence in Northern Ireland*. Belfast: HMSO.

Mehrotra, M. 1999. "The Social Construction of Wife Abuse: Experiences of Asian Indian Women in the United States." *Violence against Women* 5 (6): 619–640.

Mernissi, F. 1987. *Beyond the Veil*. 2nd ed. Indiana: Indiana University Press.

Mies, M. 1980. *Indian Women and Patriarchy*. New Delhi: Concept.

———. 1986. *Patriarchy and Accumulation on a World Scale: Women in the International Division of Labour*. London: Zed.

Min, P. G. 1992. "Korean Immigrant Wives' Overwork." *Korea Journal of Population and Development* 21: 23–36.

Moane, G. 1996. "Some Feminist Concerns about Pornography." In Ailbhe Smyth, ed., *Feminism, Politics, Community*, 76–85. Dublin: Women's Education Research and Resource Centre, University College Dublin Ireland.

Mohanty, C. T. 1991. "Cartographies of Struggle: Third World Women and the Politics of Feminism." In C. T. Mohanty, A. Russo and L.Torres, eds., *Third World Women and the Politics of Feminism*, 1–47. Bloomington: Indiana University Press.

Moon, J., and J. H. Pearl. 1991. "Alienation of Elderly Korean American Immigrants as Related to Place of Residence, Gender, Age, Years of Education, Time in the U.S., Living With or Without Children, and With or Without a Spouse." *International Journal of Aging and Human Development* 32 (2): 115–124.

Narayan, U. 1995. "'Male-Order' Brides: Immigrant Women, Domestic Violence and Immigration Law." *Hypatia* 10 (1): 104–119.

Ng, V. 1994. "Sexual Abuse of Daughters-in-Law in Qing China: Cases from the Xing'An Huilan." *Feminist Studies* 20 (2): 373–391.

Ngan-Ling Chow, E. 1993. "The Feminist Movement: Where Are All the Asian American Women?" In Alison M. Jagger and Paula S. Rothenberg, eds., *Feminist Frameworks*. New York: McGraw-Hill.

NiCarthy G., K. Merriam, and S. Coffman. 1984. *Talking It Out: A Guide to Groups for Abused Women*. Seattle: Seal Press.

Okihiro, G. Y. 1991. "African and Asian American Studies: A Comparative Analysis and Commentary." In Shirley Hune, Hyung-chan Kim, Stephen S. Fugita, and Amy Ling, eds., *Asian Americans: Comparative and Global Perspectives*, 17–28. Pullman: Washington State University Press.

———. 1994. *Margins and Mainstreams: Asians in American History and Culture*. Seattle: University of Washington Press.

Omi, M. 1988. "It Just Ain't the Sixties No More: The Contemporary Dilemmas of Asian American Studies." In G. Y. Okihiro, S. Hume, A. A. Hansen, and J. M. Liu, eds., *Asian Americans: Comparative and Global Perspectives*. Pullman, Wash.: Washington State University Press.

———. 1992. "Elegant Chaos: Postmodern Asian American Identity." In L. C. Lee, ed., *Asian American: Collages of Identities*, 143–154. Ithaca, N.Y.: Cornell University Press.

Ong, P., and S. Hee. 1994. "Economic Diversity." In P. Ong, ed., *The State of Asian Pacific America: Economic Diversity, Issues, and Policies*, 31–56. Los Angeles: LEAP, Asian Pacific American Public Policy Institute and University of California at Los Angeles, Asian American Studies Center.

Orloff, L. E., D. Jang, and C. F. Klein. 1995. "With No Place to Turn." *Family Law Quarterly* 29 (2): 313–329.

Ortner, S. 1978. "The Virgin and the State." *Feminist Studies* 4: 19–37.

Pagelow. M. D. 1981. "Secondary Battering and Alternatives of Female Victims to Spouse Abuse." In Lee H. Bowker, ed., *Women and Crime in America*, 277–300. New York: Macmillan.

———. 1984. *Family Violence*. New York: Praeger Publishers.

———. 1992. "Adult Victims of Domestic Violence: Battered Women." *Journal of Interpersonal Violence* 7 (1): 87–120.

Pedraza, S. 1996. "Origins and Destinies: Immigration, Race, and Ethnicity in American History." In S. Pedraza and G. E. Rumbaut, eds. *Origins and Destinies: Immigration, Race, and Ethnicity in America*. Belmont, Calif.: Wadsworth Pubishing Co.

Pillai, S. 1997. "Domestic Violence: Issues in the South Asian Community," 1–22. School of International and Public Affairs, Columbia University. Unpublished.

Pirog-Good, M., and J. Stets. 1986. "Programs for Abusers: Who Drops Out and What Can Be Done?" *Response* 9: 17–19.

Pleck, E. 1983. "Feminist Responses to 'Crimes Against Women,' 1868–1896." *Signs* 8 (3): 451–469.

Pressman, S. 1994. "The Legal Issues Confronting Conditional Resident Aliens Who Are Victims of Domestic Violence: Past, Present, and Future Perspectives" *Maryland Journal of Contemporary Legal Issues* 6 (1): 129–154.

Purkayastha, B., S. Raman, and K. Bhide. 1997. "Empowering Women: SNEHA's Multifaceted Activism." In Sonia Shah, ed., *Dragon Ladies: Asian American Feminists Breathe Fire*, 100–107. Boston: South End Press.

Rayaprol, A. 1992. "Gender Dynamics in Cultural Practices among South Indian Immigrants." Paper presented at the annual meeting of the Association for Asian Studies.

Richardson, L. 1988. *The Dynamics of Sex and Gender: A Sociological Perspective*. New York: Harper Collins.

Richie, B. E., and V. Kanuha. 1993. "Battered Women of Color in Public Care Systems: Racism, Sexism, and Violence." In B. Blair and S. E. Cayleff, eds., *Wings of Gauze: Women of Color and the Experience of Health and Illness*, 228–299. Detroit: Wayne State University Press.

Russell, D. 1993. *Making Violence Sexy: Feminist Views on Pornography*. Buckingham: Open University Press.

Sakhi Collective. 1992. "Break the Silence." *Committee on South Asian Women Bulletin* 7: 17–19.

Sakhi. 1997. "Breaking the Silence: Facts about Sakhi and Worker's Awaaz." *Sakhi Newsletter.*

Sangari, K. K., and S. Vaid. 1989. *Recasting Women: Essays in Colonial History* New Delhi: Kali for Women.

Saran, P. 1983. *The Asian Indian Experience in the United States.* Cambridge, Mass.: Schenkman.

Saunders, D. G., and P. Size. 1986. "Attitudes about Women Abuse among Police Officers, Victims, and Victim Advocates." *Journal of Interpersonal Violence* 1 (1): 25–42.

Schechter, S. 1982. *Women and Male Violence: The Visions and Struggles of the Battered Women's Movement.* Boston: South End Press.

Schornstein, S. 1997. *Domestic Violence and Health Care: What Every Professional Needs to Know.* Thousand Oaks, Calif.: Sage Publication.

Scully, D., and J. Marolla. 1985. "Riding the Bull at Gilley's: Convicted Rapists Describe the Rewards of Rape." *Social Problems* 32 (3): 251–263.

Seeman, M. 1959. "On the Meaning of Alienation." *American Sociological Review* 24: 783–790.

———. 1972. "Alienation and Engagement in the Human Meaning of Social Change." In A. Campbell and P. Converse, eds., *The Human Meaning of Social Change* 467–527. New York: Russell Sage.

Shah, S. 1994. "Presenting the Blue Goddess: Toward a National, Pan-Asian Feminist Agenda." In K. Aguilar-San Juan, ed., *The State of Asian America: Activism and Resistance in the 1990's,* 147–158. Boston: South End.

Sharma, U. 1984. "Dowry in North India: Its Consequences for Women." In R. Hirschron, ed., *Women in Property,* 62–73. New York: St. Martin's Press.

Shokied, M., and S. Deshen. 1982. *Distant Relations: Ethnicity and Politics among Arabs and North African Jews in Israel.* New York: Praeger Publishers.

Shon, S. P., and D. Y. Ja. 1982. "Asian Families." In Mona McGoldrick, John K. Pearce, and Joseph Giordano, eds., *Ethnicity and Family Therapy,* 208–229. New York: Guilford Press.

Sluzki, C. E. 1979. "Migration and Family Conflict." *Family Process* 18: 379–390.

Smith, D. 1987. *The Everyday World as Problematic.* Boston: Northeastern University Press.

Snell, J. E., R. J. Rosenwald, and A. Robey. 1964. "The Wifebeater's Wife." *Archives of General Psychiatry* 11: 107–112.

Sorenson, S. B. 1996. "Violence against Women: Examining Ethnic Differences and Commonalities." *Evaluation Review* 20 (2): 123–145.

Stacey, J., and B. Thorne. 1985. "The Missing Feminist Revolution in Sociology." *Social Problems* 32: 301–316.

Stacey, W., and S. Shupe. 1983. *The Family Secret: Domestic Violence in America.* Boston: Beacon Press.

Staggenborg, S. 1986. "Coalition Work in the Pro-Choice Movement: Organizational and Environmental Opportunities and Obstacles." *Social Problems* 33 (5): 374–390.

———. 1989a. "Organizational and Environmental Influences on the Development of the Pro-Choice Movement." *Social Forces* 68 (1): 204–240.

———. 1989b. "Stability and Innovation in the Women's Movement: A Comparison of Two Movement Organizations." *Social Problems* 36 (1): 75–92.

Stanko, E. 1985. *Intimate Intrusions.* London: Routledge & Kegan Paul.

Steinberg, S. 1991. *The Ethnic Myth: Race, Class, and Ethnicity in America.* Boston: Beacon Press.

Stets, J. E. 1991. "Cohabiting and Marital Aggression: The Role of Social Isolation." *Journal of Marriage and the Family* 53: 669–680.

Stordeur, R. A., and R. Stille. 1989. *Ending Men's Violence against Their Partners.* Newbury Park, Calif.: Sage.

Straus, M. A., R. J. Gelles, and S. K. Steinmetz. 1980. *Behind Closed Doors: Violence in the American Family.* Garden City, N.Y.: Anchor Book.

Strauss, A. 1987. *Qualitative Analysis for Social Scientists.* Cambridgeshire: Cambridge University Press.

Strube, M. J. 1988. "The Decision to Leave an Abusive Relationship: Empirical Evidence and Theoretical Issues." *Psychological Bulletin* 104 (2): 236–250.

Strube, M. J. and L. S. Barbour. 1983. "The Decision to Leave an Abusive Relationship: Economic Dependence and Psychological Commitment." *Journal of Marriage and the Family* 45: 785–793.

Stubbs, E. 1997. "Welfare and Immigration Reform: Refusing Aid to Immigrants." *Berkeley Women's Law Journal.* 12: 154–156.

Tambiah, S. J. 1973. "Dowry and Bride Wealth and the Property Rights of Women in South Asia." In J. Goody and S. J. Tambiah, *Bride Wealth and Dowry*, 59–169. Cambridge: Cambridge University Press.

Thapan, M. 1996. "Image of the Body and Sexuality in Women's Narratives on Oppression in the Home." *Economic and Political Weekly*, 30, WS-72.

Uberoi, P. 1996. *Social Reform, Sexuality, and the State.* New Delhi: Sage Publications.

Vaid, J. 1989. "Seeking a Voice: South Asian Women's Groups in North America." In Asian Women United of California, ed., *Making Waves: An Anthology of Writing by and about Asian American Women*, 395–405. Boston: Beacon Press.

Vohra, P. 1995. "About Welfare Reform: How It Traps Battered Women." *New York Newsday*, June 26: A22.

Wadley, S. S. 1994. *Struggling with Destiny in Karimpur, 1925–1984.* Berkeley and Los Angeles: University of California Press.

Walker, L. E. 1979. *The Battered Woman.* New York: Harper and Row.

———. 1983. "Victimology and the Psychological Perspective of the Battered Woman." *Victimology: An International Journal* 2: 525–534.

Warshaw, C. 1993. "Limitations of the Medical Model in the Care of Battered Women." In P. B. Bart and E. G. Moran, eds., *Violence against Women: The Bloody Footprints*, 134–146. Newbury Park, Calif.: Sage.

Waters, M. 1994. "Succession in the Stratification System: A Contribution to the 'Death of Class' Debate." *International Sociology* 9 (3): 295–312.

Wei, W. 1993. *The Asian American Movement*, 49. Philadelphia: Temple University Press.

Weinstein, M. 1997. "The Violence against Women Act after United States v Lopez: Defending the Act from Constitutional Challenge." *Berkeley Women's Law Journal* 12: 119–131.

West, C., and Don H. Zimmerman. 1987. "Doing Gender." *Gender and Society* 1: 125–51.

Willigen, J. V., and V. C. Channa. 1991. "Law, Custom, and Crimes against Women: The Problem of Dowry Death in India." *Human Organization* 50 (4): 369–377.

Wilson, A. (1978). *Finding a Voice: Asian Women in Britain.* London: Virago Press.

Wolfe, D. A., C. Wekerle, and K. Scott. 1997. *Alternatives to Violence: Empower-*

ing Youth to Develop Healthy Relationships. Thousand Oaks, Calif.: Sage Publications.

Wong, C. 1993. *Reading Asian American Literature: From Necessity to Extravagance.* Princeton, N.J.: Princeton University Press.

Yalman, N. 1963. "On the Purity of Women in the Cases of Ceylon and the Malabar. *Journal of the Royal Anthropological Institute of Great Britain and Ireland* 93 (1): 25–58.

Young, K. 1993. "The Imperishable Virginity of Saint Maria Goretti." In P. Bart and E. G. Moran, eds., *Violence against Women*, 105–113. Newbury Park, Calif.: Sage Publications.

Zin, M. B., and D. S. Eitzen. 1990. *Diversity in Families.* New York: Harper and Row.

Index

abortions, forced, 97–98
absolutism, 156
abuse: forms of, 15; nondisclosure of, 43; trivialization of, 82–83
abused women: contacting, 199, 200; and court system, 125, 127; help sought by, 142; lack of support for, 118, 157; "learned hopefulness" of, 144; and legal system, 186; mothers-in-law and, 109; numbers of, 166; obstacles encountered by, 170; suicide contemplated by, 139
abusers, fiscal control used by, 137–138
abusive relationships, culture and, 105
accountability, lack of, of abuser's family, 109
activism: holistic model of, 160; of South Asian women's organizations, 4 (see also South Asian women's organizations)
advertisement, matrimonial, 24, 25, 45; examples of, 28; in South Asian women's narrative, 27–28, 33
advocacy, of SAWOs, 164
aggression, male, acceptance of, 155
AIDS, 192
"alien," designation as, 207n. 6
alien registered card, 62

alien spouse: conditional status of, 55, 56–57; "extreme hardship" faced by, 65, 364; immigration status of, 52, 53, 54; options for, 60; and "self-petition" provision, 65
"Americanization," fear of, 69
American society: addressing problems of, 181; color consciousness of, 27; and control of minorities, 10–11
androcentrism, 156
anti-immigrant climate, 2, 66
anti-immigration legislation, 207n. 4
Apna Ghar (Chicago), x, 157, 166, 169, 200, 203; community education of, 170; emergency hotline of, 167; ideology of, 158; interpreters provided by, 164– 165; legal assistance provided by, 168; public voice of, 185; shelter run by, 160, 168; state funds for, 189
Arnold, Gretchen, 192
ASHA (Washington, D.C.), 1, 157, 205n. 2
Ashiana, 169
Asian American movement, xii
Asian Americans, xii; as model minority, 9; self-employed population among, 209n. 3
Asian Indian Women in America (AIWA), 163

Biography

Margaret Abraham is an associate professor in the department of sociology and anthropology at Hofstra University. Her areas of specialization are ethnicity and gender, and she has presented and published papers in these areas. She has been a recipient of a Rockefeller fellowship. Margaret is a board member of the Asian and Pacific Islander Coalition on HIV/AIDS (APICHA) and a national advisory board member for the National Evaluation of the Arrest Policies Program under the Violence Against Women Act Project of the National Institute for Law and Justice. She has been involved in research and activism in the field of domestic violence in the South Asian immigrant community for a decade. In 1999 the organization Sakhi for South Asian Women honored her for this work.